D1533689

Graphic Classics:
JACK LONDON

Graphic Classics Volume Five
Second Edition
2006

Edited by Tom Pomplun

EUREKA PRODUCTIONS
8778 Oak Grove Road, Mount Horeb, Wisconsin 53572
www.graphicclassics.com

ILLUSTRATION ©2003 ROGER LANGRIDGE

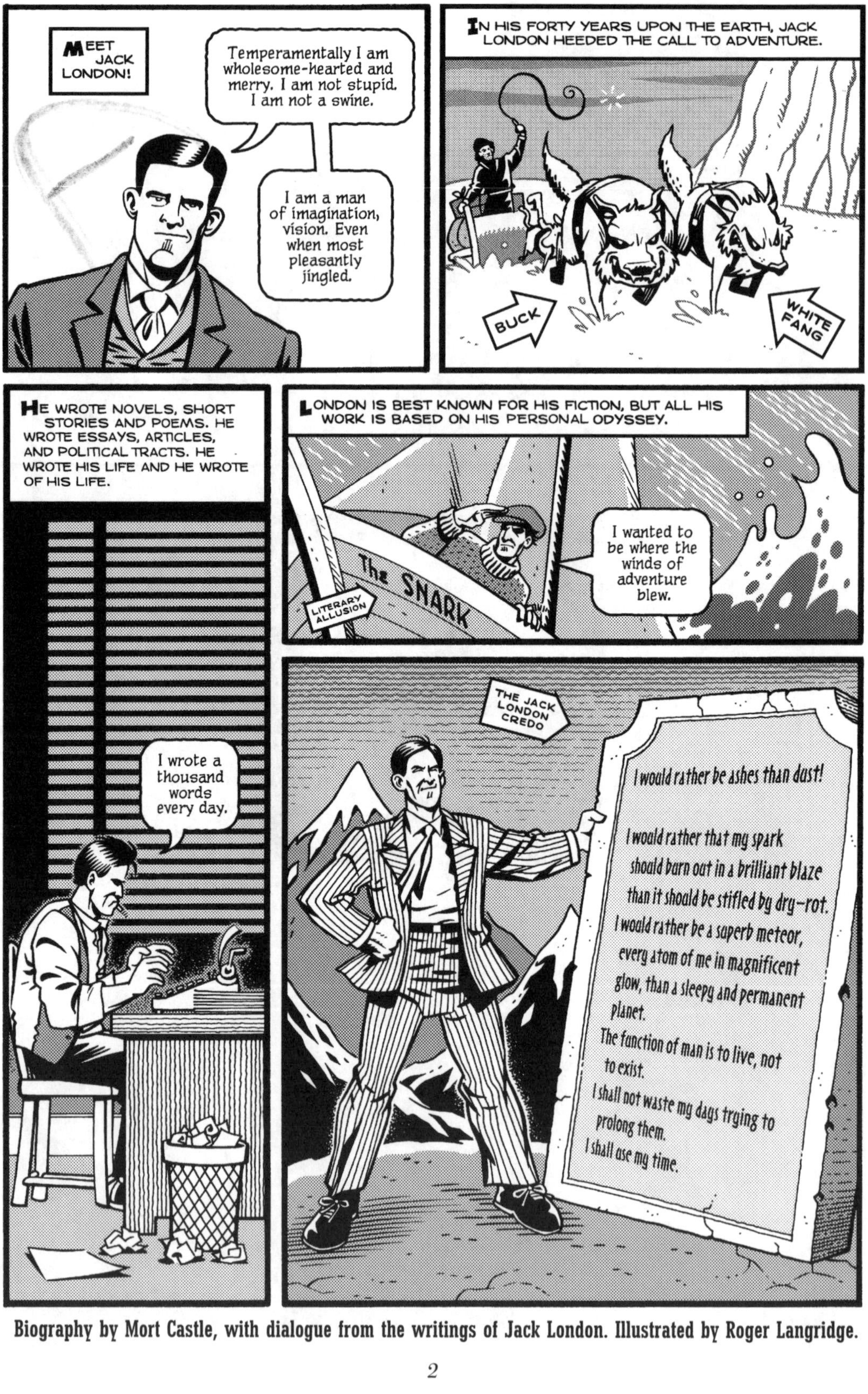
MEET JACK LONDON!
Temperamentally I am wholesome-hearted and merry. I am not stupid. I am not a swine.
I am a man of imagination, vision. Even when most pleasantly jingled.
IN HIS FORTY YEARS UPON THE EARTH, JACK LONDON HEEDED THE CALL TO ADVENTURE.
BUCK
WHITE FANG
HE WROTE NOVELS, SHORT STORIES AND POEMS. HE WROTE ESSAYS, ARTICLES, AND POLITICAL TRACTS. HE WROTE HIS LIFE AND HE WROTE OF HIS LIFE.
I wrote a thousand words every day.
LONDON IS BEST KNOWN FOR HIS FICTION, BUT ALL HIS WORK IS BASED ON HIS PERSONAL ODYSSEY.
The SNARK
LITERARY ALLUSION
I wanted to be where the winds of adventure blew.
THE JACK LONDON CREDO
I would rather be ashes than dust!
I would rather that my spark should burn out in a brilliant blaze than it should be stifled by dry-rot.
I would rather be a superb meteor, every atom of me in magnificent glow, than a sleepy and permanent planet.
The function of man is to live, not to exist.
I shall not waste my days trying to prolong them.
I shall use my time.

Biography by Mort Castle, with dialogue from the writings of Jack London. Illustrated by Roger Langridge.

Graphic Classics:
JACK LONDON

©2006 ARNOLD ARRE

Cover illustration by Jim Nelson / Back cover illustration by Nick Miller

Graphic Classics: Jack London is published by Eureka Productions. ISBN:13 #978-0-9746648-8-0 / ISBN:10 #0-9746648-8-X. Second edition, 2006. Price US $11.95, CAN $14.50. Available from Eureka Productions, 8778 Oak Grove Road, Mount Horeb, WI 53572. Tom Pomplun, designer and publisher, tom@graphicclassics.com. Eileen Fitzgerald, editorial assistant. Compilation and all original works ©2006 Eureka Productions. All rights revert to creators after publication. Graphic Classics is a trademark of Eureka Productions. For ordering information and previews of upcoming volumes visit the Graphic Classics website at http://www.graphicclassics.com. Printed in Canada.

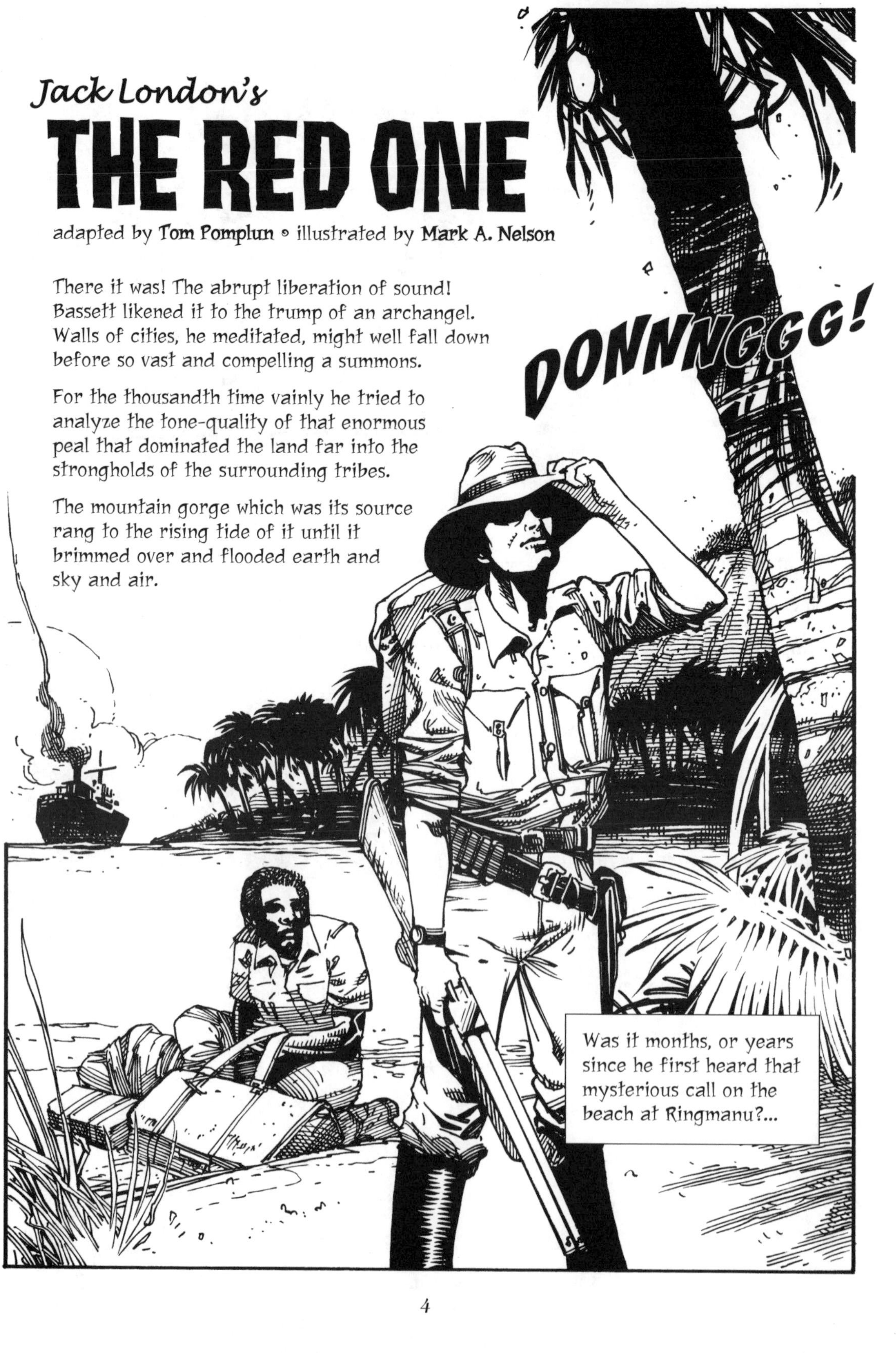
Jack London's
THE RED ONE
adapted by Tom Pomplun ∘ illustrated by Mark A. Nelson
There it was! The abrupt liberation of sound! Bassett likened it to the trump of an archangel. Walls of cities, he meditated, might well fall down before so vast and compelling a summons.
For the thousandth time vainly he tried to analyze the tone-quality of that enormous peal that dominated the land far into the strongholds of the surrounding tribes.
The mountain gorge which was its source rang to the rising tide of it until it brimmed over and flooded earth and sky and air.
DONNNGGG!
Was it months, or years since he first heard that mysterious call on the beach at Ringmanu?...

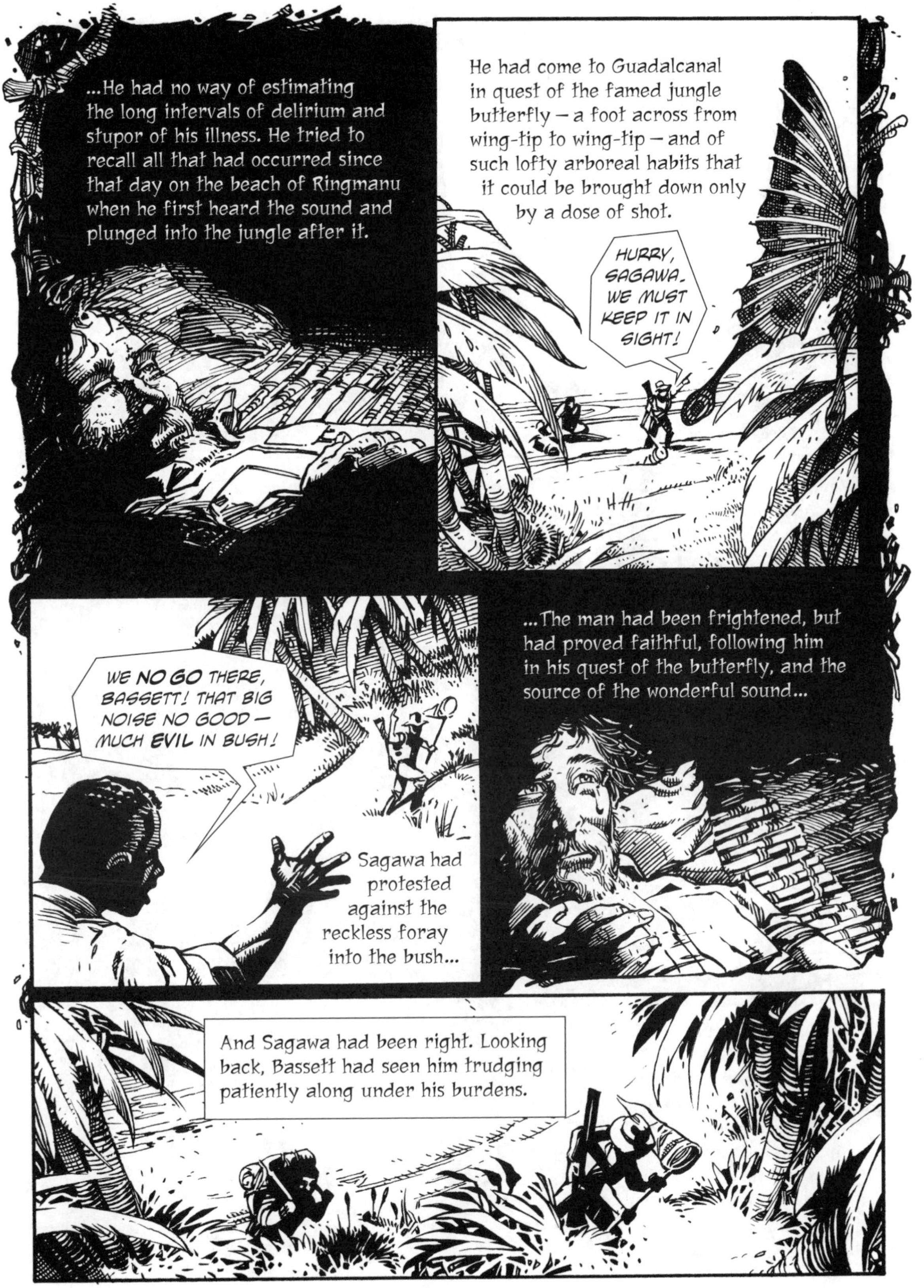
...He had no way of estimating the long intervals of delirium and stupor of his illness. He tried to recall all that had occurred since that day on the beach of Ringmanu when he first heard the sound and plunged into the jungle after it.
He had come to Guadalcanal in quest of the famed jungle butterfly – a foot across from wing-tip to wing-tip – and of such lofty arboreal habits that it could be brought down only by a dose of shot.
HURRY, SAGAWA. WE MUST KEEP IT IN SIGHT!
WE NO GO THERE, BASSETT! THAT BIG NOISE NO GOOD – MUCH EVIL IN BUSH!
Sagawa had protested against the reckless foray into the bush...
...The man had been frightened, but had proved faithful, following him in his quest of the butterfly, and the source of the wonderful sound...
And Sagawa had been right. Looking back, Bassett had seen him trudging patiently along under his burdens.

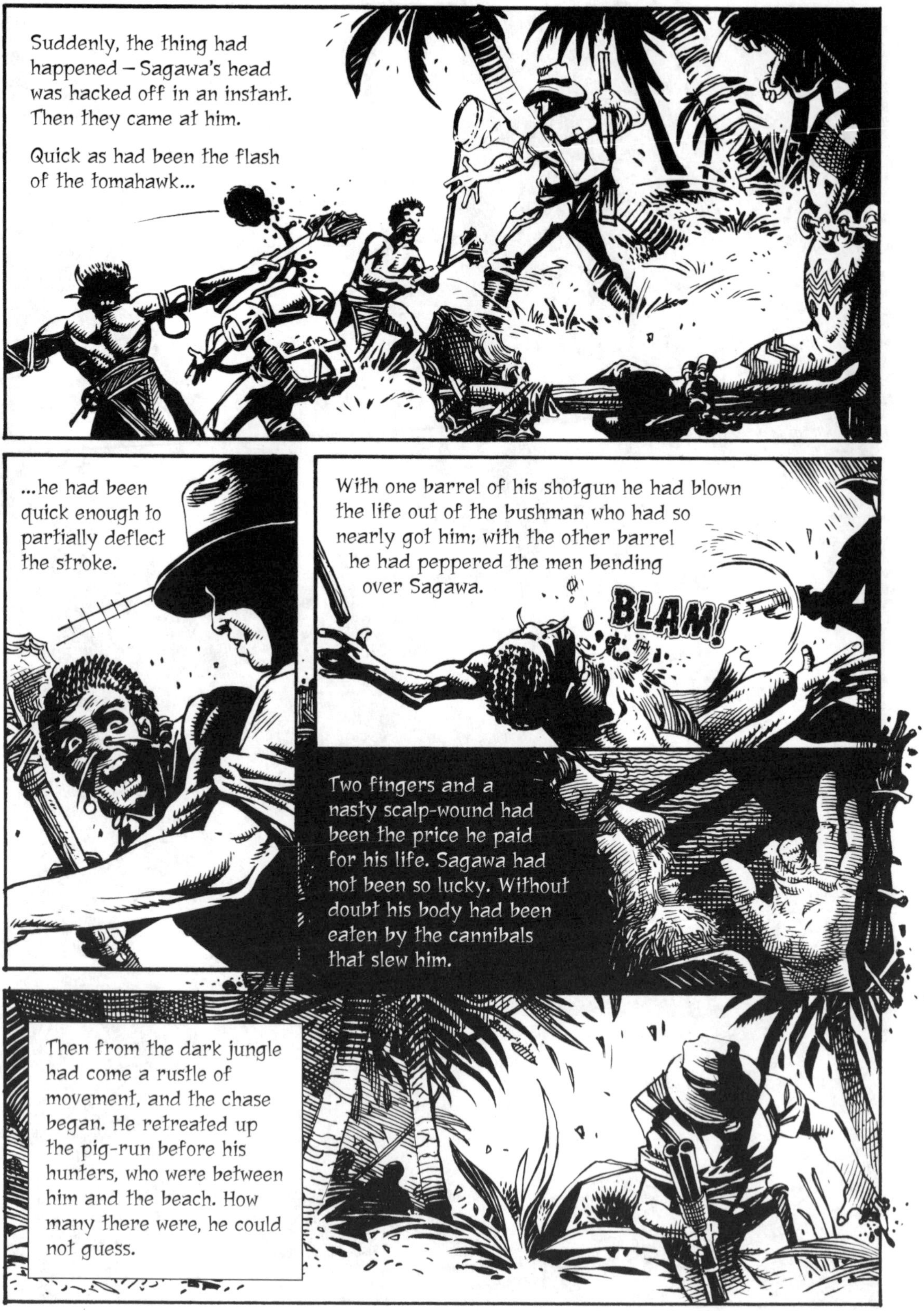
Suddenly, the thing had happened – Sagawa's head was hacked off in an instant. Then they came at him.
Quick as had been the flash of the tomahawk...
...he had been quick enough to partially deflect the stroke.
With one barrel of his shotgun he had blown the life out of the bushman who had so nearly got him; with the other barrel he had peppered the men bending over Sagawa.
BLAM!
Two fingers and a nasty scalp-wound had been the price he paid for his life. Sagawa had not been so lucky. Without doubt his body had been eaten by the cannibals that slew him.
Then from the dark jungle had come a rustle of movement, and the chase began. He retreated up the pig-run before his hunters, who were between him and the beach. How many there were, he could not guess.

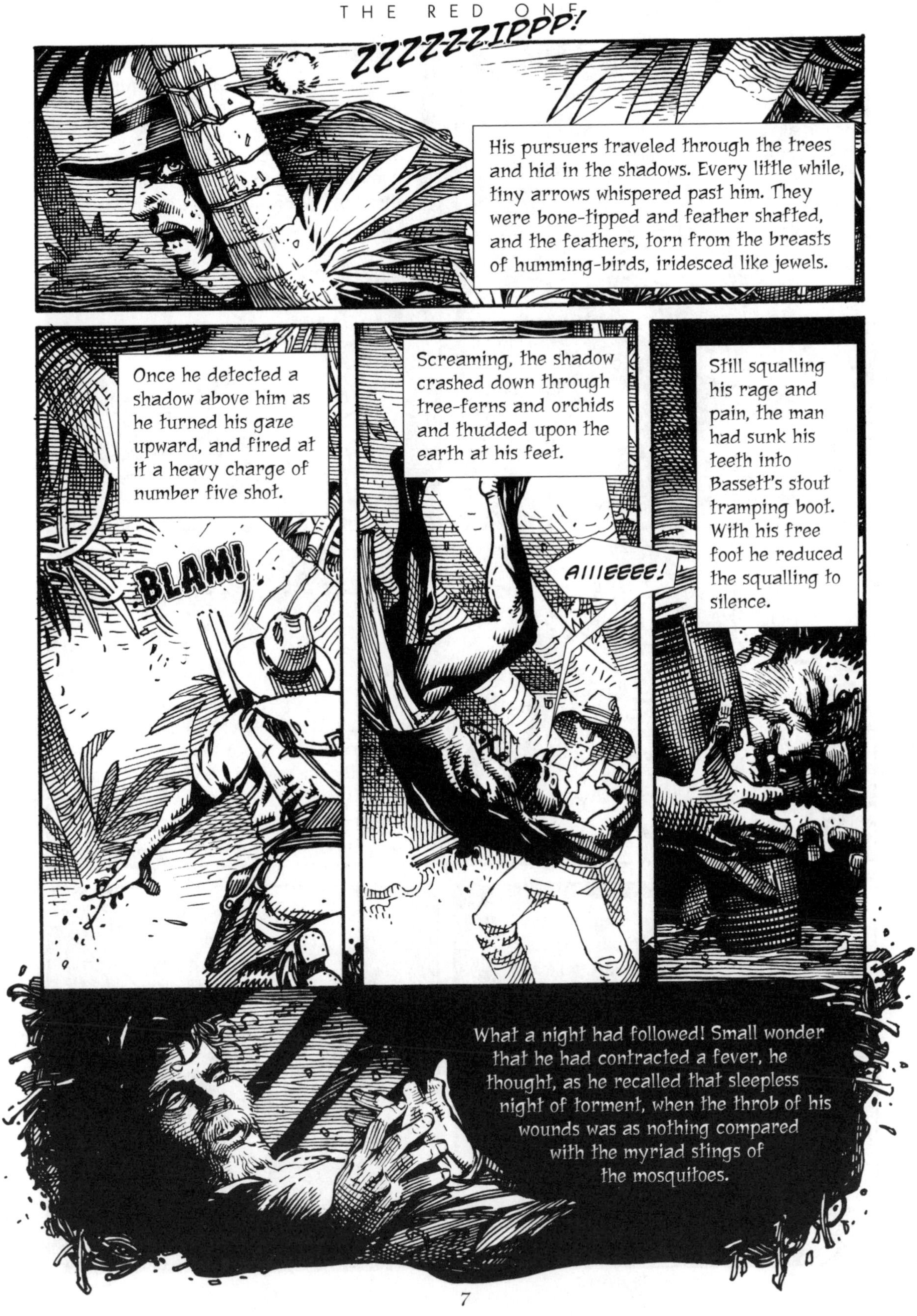
ZZZZZZIPPP!
His pursuers traveled through the trees and hid in the shadows. Every little while, tiny arrows whispered past him. They were bone-tipped and feather shafted, and the feathers, torn from the breasts of humming-birds, iridesced like jewels.
Once he detected a shadow above him as he turned his gaze upward, and fired at it a heavy charge of number five shot.
BLAM!
Screaming, the shadow crashed down through tree-ferns and orchids and thudded upon the earth at his feet.
AIIIEEEE!
Still squalling his rage and pain, the man had sunk his teeth into Bassett's stout tramping boot. With his free foot he reduced the squalling to silence.
What a night had followed! Small wonder that he had contracted a fever, he thought, as he recalled that sleepless night of torment, when the throb of his wounds was as nothing compared with the myriad stings of the mosquitoes.

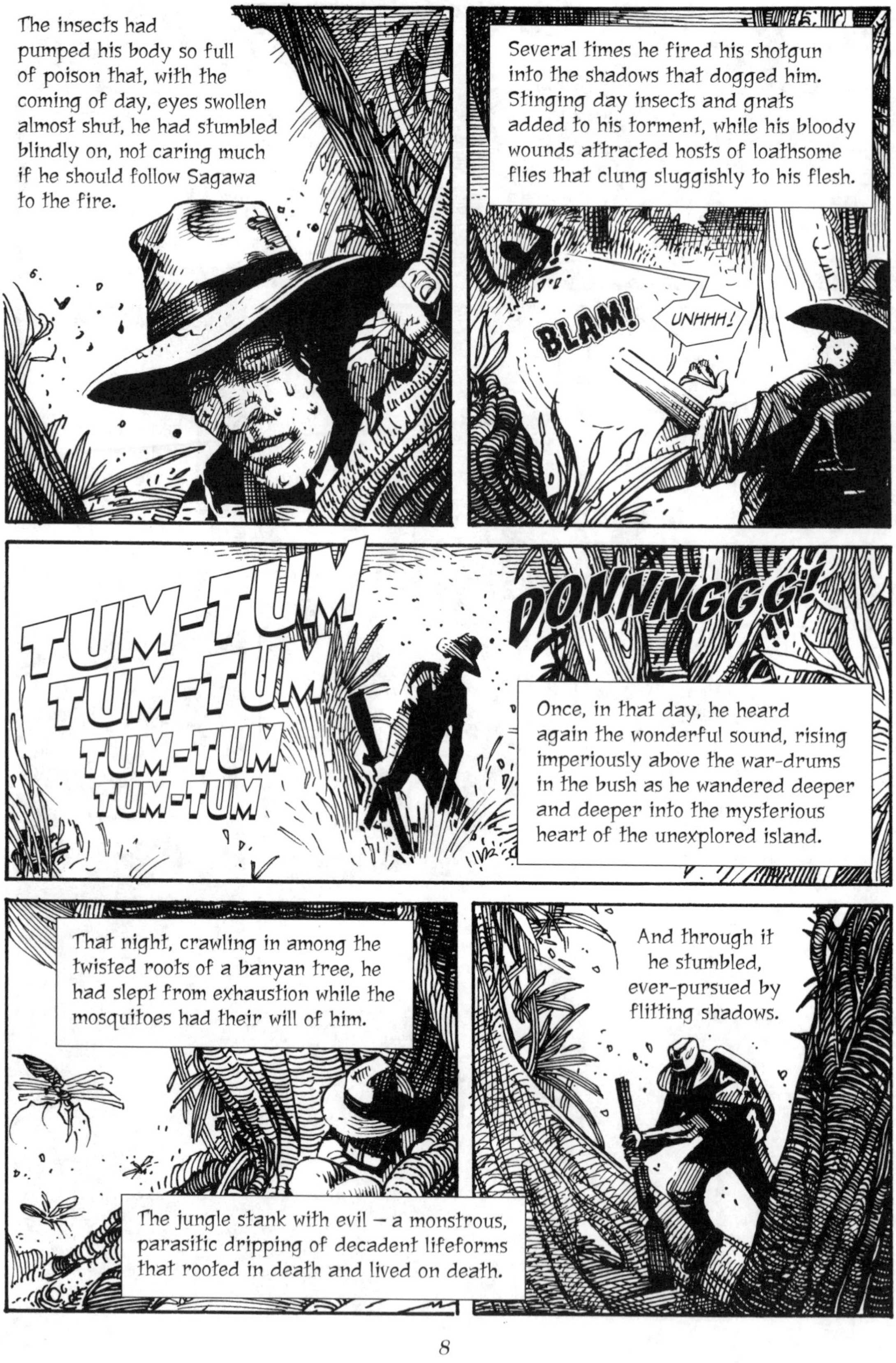

The insects had pumped his body so full of poison that, with the coming of day, eyes swollen almost shut, he had stumbled blindly on, not caring much if he should follow Sagawa to the fire.
Several times he fired his shotgun into the shadows that dogged him. Stinging day insects and gnats added to his torment, while his bloody wounds attracted hosts of loathsome flies that clung sluggishly to his flesh.
BLAM!
UNHHH!
TUM-TUM
TUM-TUM
TUM-TUM
TUM-TUM
DONNNGGG!
Once, in that day, he heard again the wonderful sound, rising imperiously above the war-drums in the bush as he wandered deeper and deeper into the mysterious heart of the unexplored island.
That night, crawling in among the twisted roots of a banyan tree, he had slept from exhaustion while the mosquitoes had their will of him.
The jungle stank with evil – a monstrous, parasitic dripping of decadent lifeforms that rooted in death and lived on death.
And through it he stumbled, ever-pursued by flitting shadows.

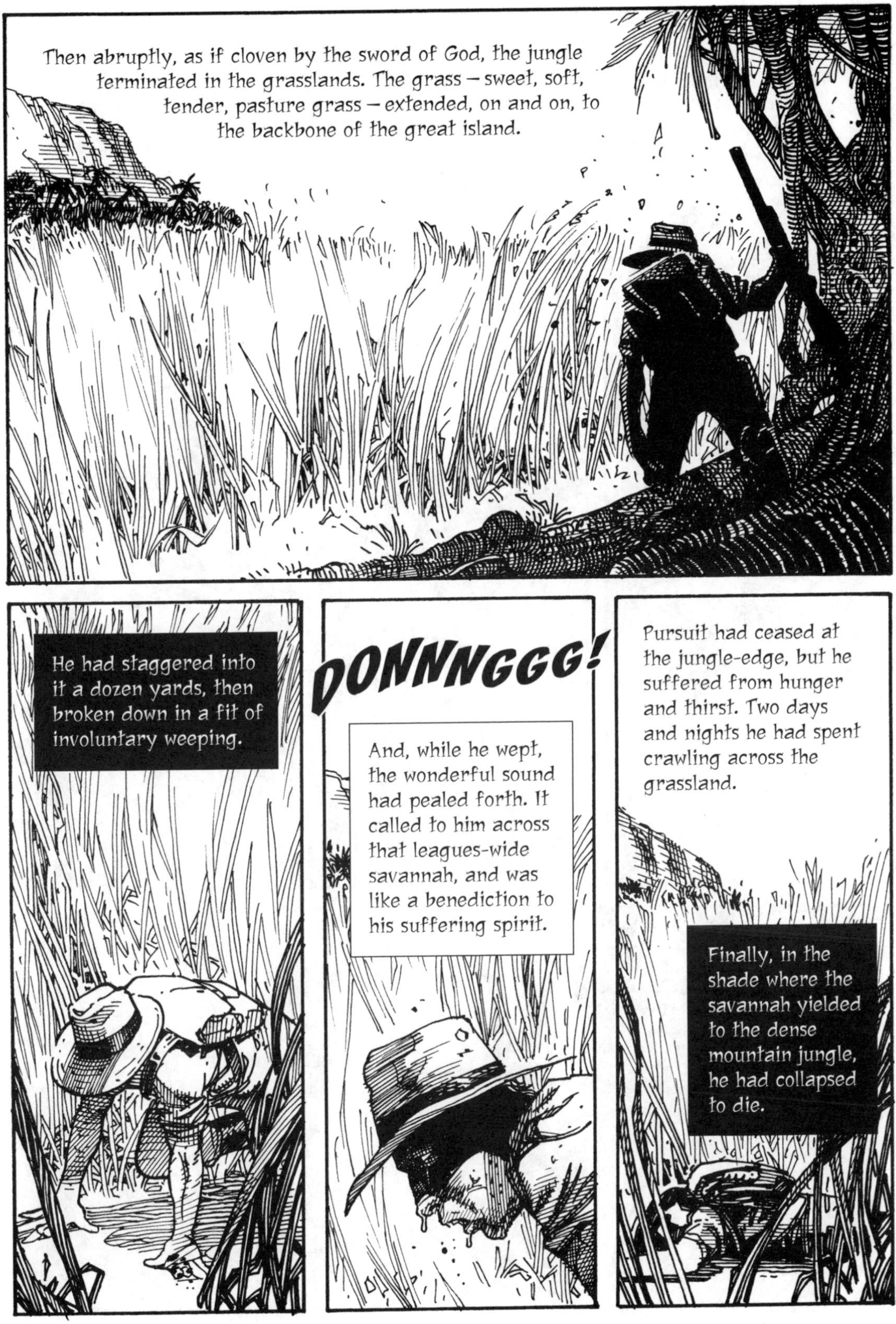
Then abruptly, as if cloven by the sword of God, the jungle terminated in the grasslands. The grass – sweet, soft, tender, pasture grass – extended, on and on, to the backbone of the great island.
He had staggered into it a dozen yards, then broken down in a fit of involuntary weeping.
DONNNGGG!
And, while he wept, the wonderful sound had pealed forth. It called to him across that leagues-wide savannah, and was like a benediction to his suffering spirit.
Pursuit had ceased at the jungle-edge, but he suffered from hunger and thirst. Two days and nights he had spent crawling across the grassland.
Finally, in the shade where the savannah yielded to the dense mountain jungle, he had collapsed to die.

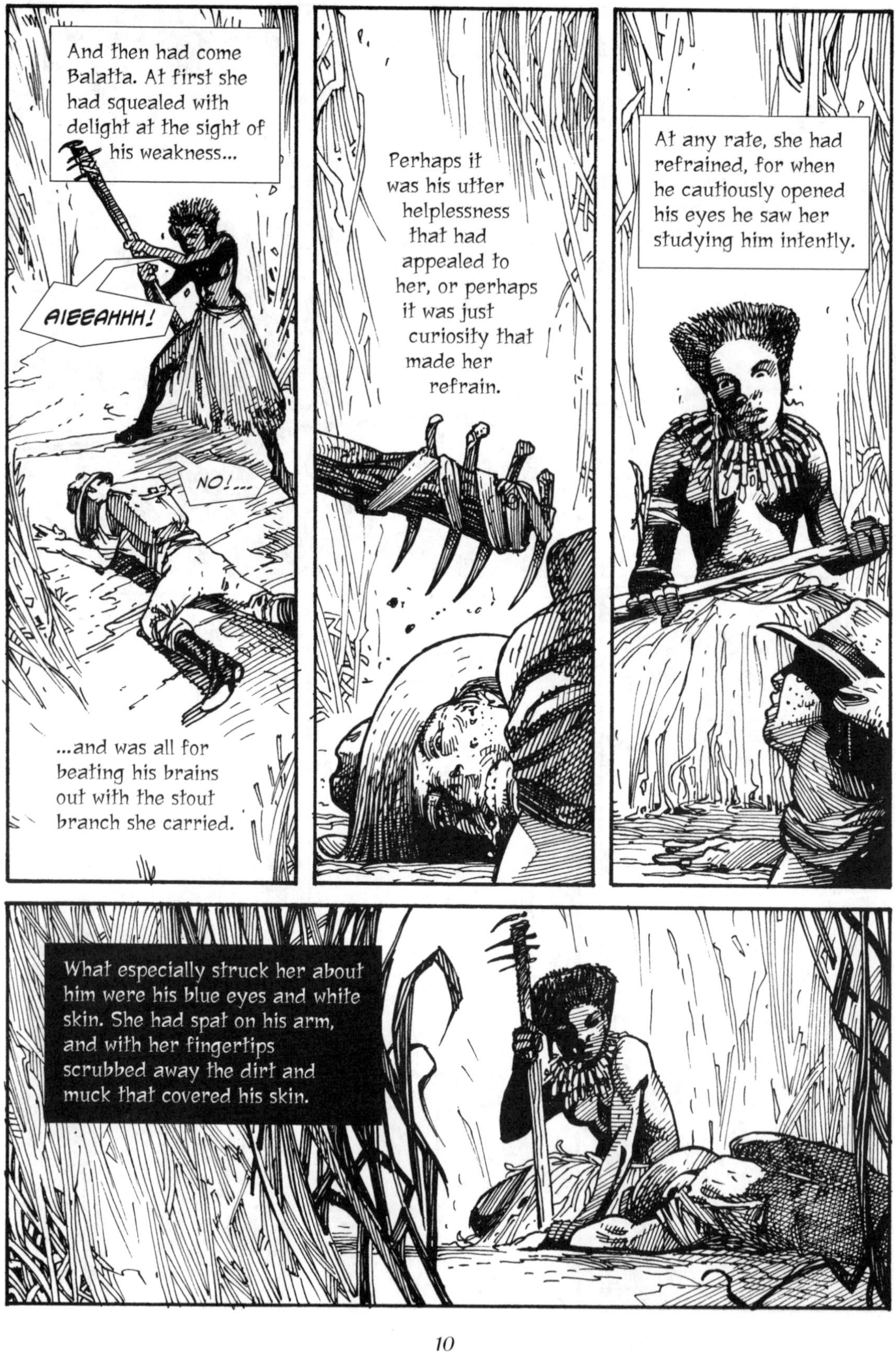
And then had come Balatta. At first she had squealed with delight at the sight of his weakness...
AIEEAHHH!
NO!...
...and was all for beating his brains out with the stout branch she carried.
Perhaps it was his utter helplessness that had appealed to her, or perhaps it was just curiosity that made her refrain.
At any rate, she had refrained, for when he cautiously opened his eyes he saw her studying him intently.
What especially struck her about him were his blue eyes and white skin. She had spat on his arm, and with her fingertips scrubbed away the dirt and muck that covered his skin.

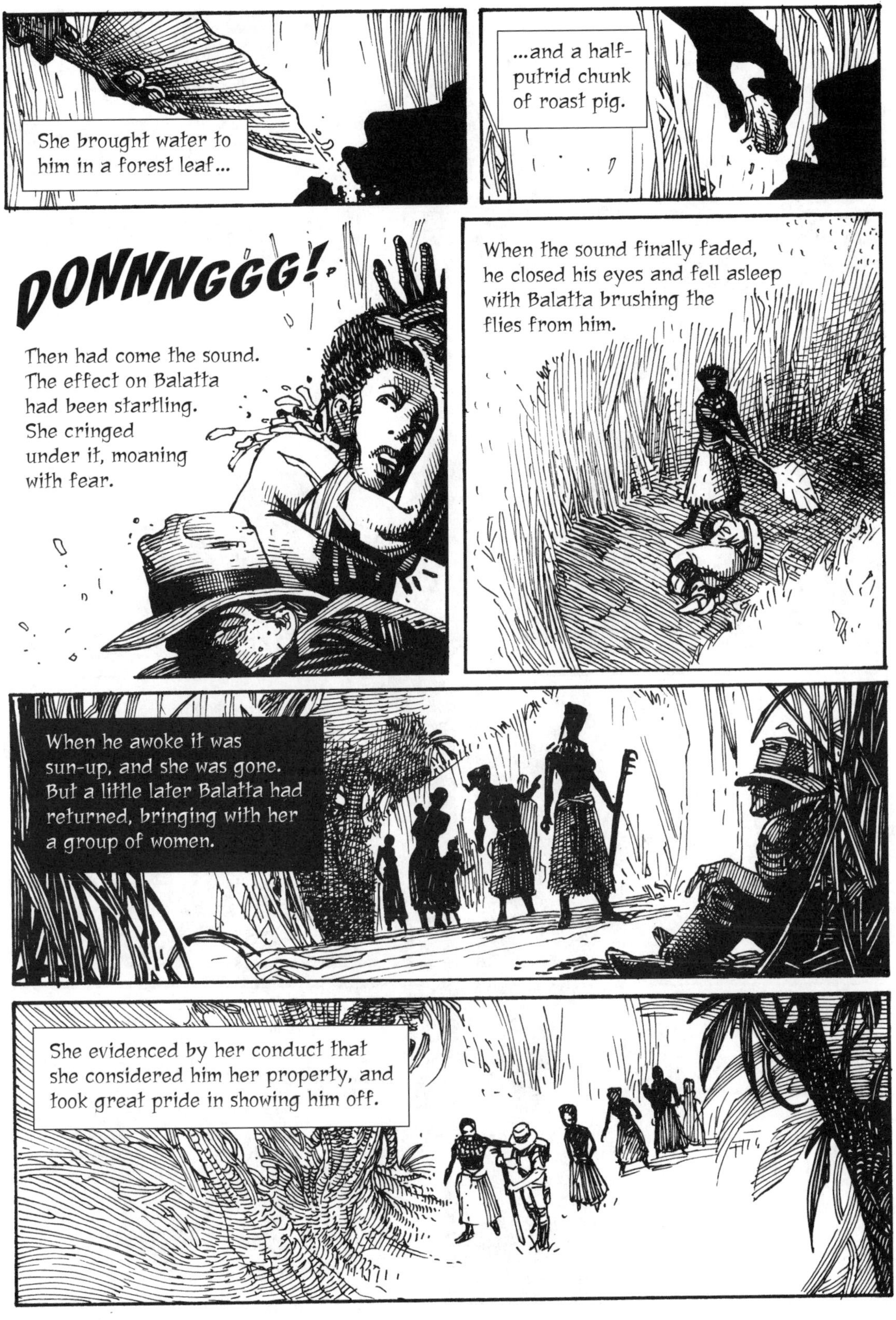
She brought water to him in a forest leaf...
...and a half-putrid chunk of roast pig.
DONNNGGG!
Then had come the sound. The effect on Balatta had been startling. She cringed under it, moaning with fear.
When the sound finally faded, he closed his eyes and fell asleep with Balatta brushing the flies from him.
When he awoke it was sun-up, and she was gone. But a little later Balatta had returned, bringing with her a group of women.
She evidenced by her conduct that she considered him her property, and took great pride in showing him off.

Upon finally reaching the native village, Bassett had collapsed in the shadow of a breadfruit tree. Balatta showed very lively ideas on the matter of retaining possession of him.

Ngurn, the medicine man of the village, had wanted his head, while others had wanted his body for the roasting oven.

Balatta had been losing the debate rapidly, when the accident happened.

BLAM!

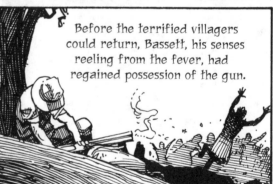

Before the terrified villagers could return, Bassett, his senses reeling from the fever, had regained possession of the gun.

STAND BACK! YOU'VE SEEN WHAT THIS CAN DO! I'LL SHOW YOU MORE!

He had slain one of their domesticated pigs as an example.

BLAM!

SQUEEEEE!

YOU'LL NOT HAVE ME IN YOUR DINNER POT!

Now, following the many months of his suffering, Bassett was shockingly emaciated. He dragged himself slowly to his feet, fearing that he could not much longer endure the pernicious fevers.

But he would not be content to die until he had solved the secret of the sound. He staggered the few steps to the devil-devil house. In the intervals of convalescence from his long sickness, Bassett had mastered the language of the tribe, and Ngurn had become his favorite crony and gossip.

WILL THE RED ONE SPEAK TODAY?

IT WILL BE TEN DAYS MORE UNTIL THIS IS FINISHED. NEVER HAS ANY MAN FIXED HEADS LIKE THESE.

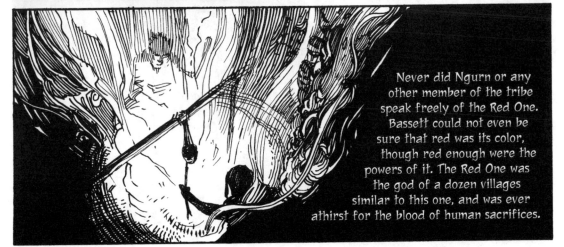

Never did Ngurn or any other member of the tribe speak freely of the Red One. Bassett could not even be sure that red was its color, though red enough were the powers of it. The Red One was the god of a dozen villages similar to this one, and was ever athirst for the blood of human sacrifices.

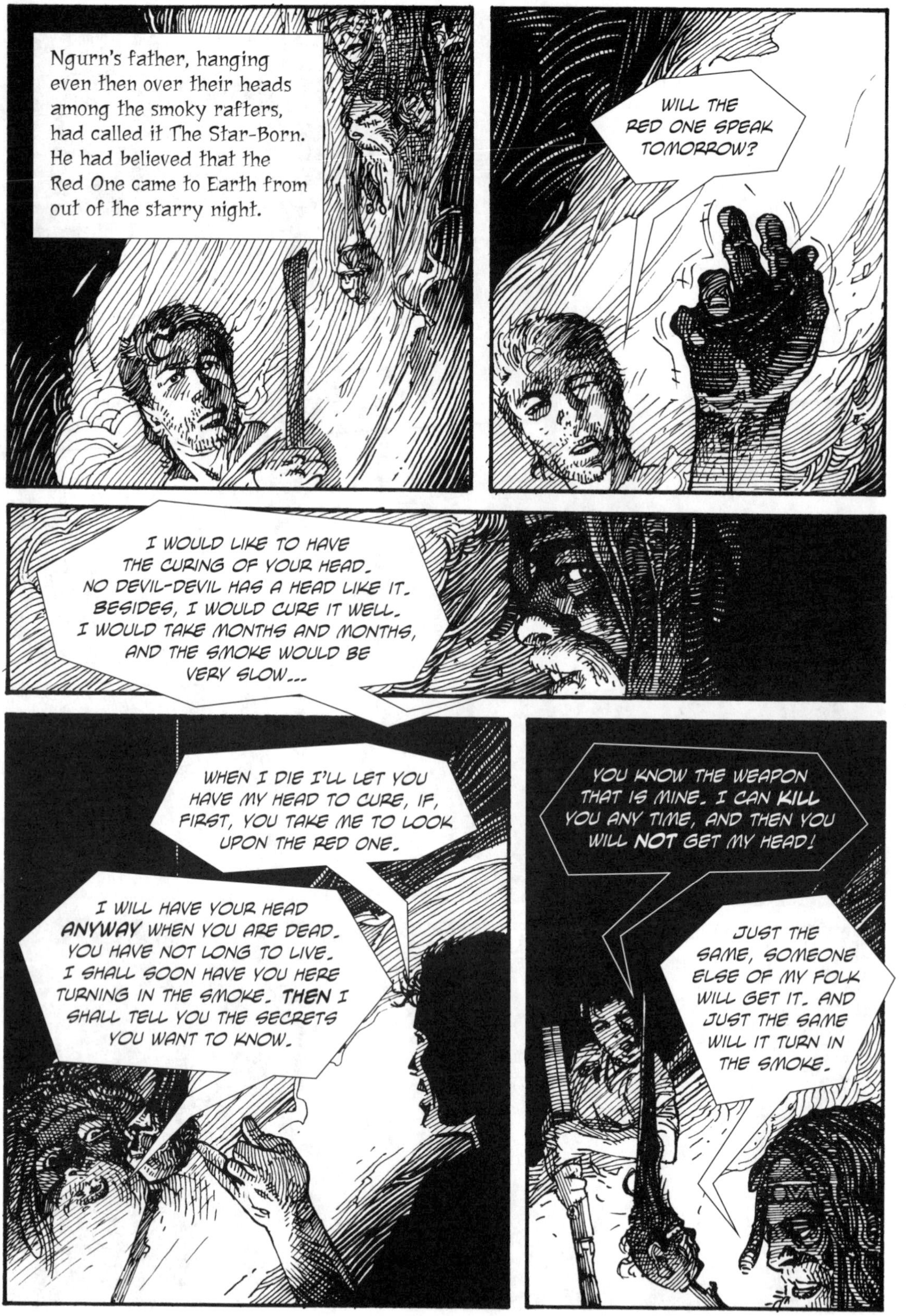
Ngurn's father, hanging even then over their heads among the smoky rafters, had called it The Star-Born. He had believed that the Red One came to Earth from out of the starry night.
WILL THE RED ONE SPEAK TOMORROW?
I WOULD LIKE TO HAVE THE CURING OF YOUR HEAD. NO DEVIL-DEVIL HAS A HEAD LIKE IT. BESIDES, I WOULD CURE IT WELL. I WOULD TAKE MONTHS AND MONTHS, AND THE SMOKE WOULD BE VERY SLOW...
WHEN I DIE I'LL LET YOU HAVE MY HEAD TO CURE, IF, FIRST, YOU TAKE ME TO LOOK UPON THE RED ONE.
I WILL HAVE YOUR HEAD **ANYWAY** WHEN YOU ARE DEAD. YOU HAVE NOT LONG TO LIVE. I SHALL SOON HAVE YOU HERE TURNING IN THE SMOKE. **THEN** I SHALL TELL YOU THE SECRETS YOU WANT TO KNOW.
YOU KNOW THE WEAPON THAT IS MINE. I CAN **KILL** YOU ANY TIME, AND THEN YOU WILL **NOT** GET MY HEAD!
JUST THE SAME, SOMEONE ELSE OF MY FOLK WILL GET IT. AND JUST THE SAME WILL IT TURN IN THE SMOKE.

Bassett knew he was beaten in the discussion. Still he was determined to find the source of the wonderful sound he had heard at the taboo distance for so long.

He had failed to bribe Ngurn, but Balatta continued his adorer. Bassett knew that the way to win the forbidden knowledge was through her heart.

From then on he devoted himself to her like a true swain. But marriage, which she ardently suggested, he balked at. He had no intention of staying with the tribe any longer than necessary for the recovery of his fragile health.

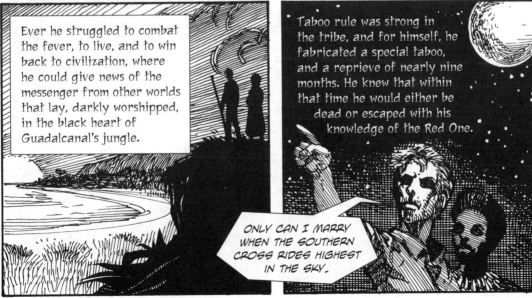

Ever he struggled to combat the fever, to live, and to win back to civilization, where he could give news of the messenger from other worlds that lay, darkly worshipped, in the black heart of Guadalcanal's jungle.

Taboo rule was strong in the tribe, and for himself, he fabricated a special taboo, and a reprieve of nearly nine months. He knew that within that time he would either be dead or escaped with his knowledge of the Red One.

ONLY CAN I MARRY WHEN THE SOUTHERN CROSS RIDES HIGHEST IN THE SKY.

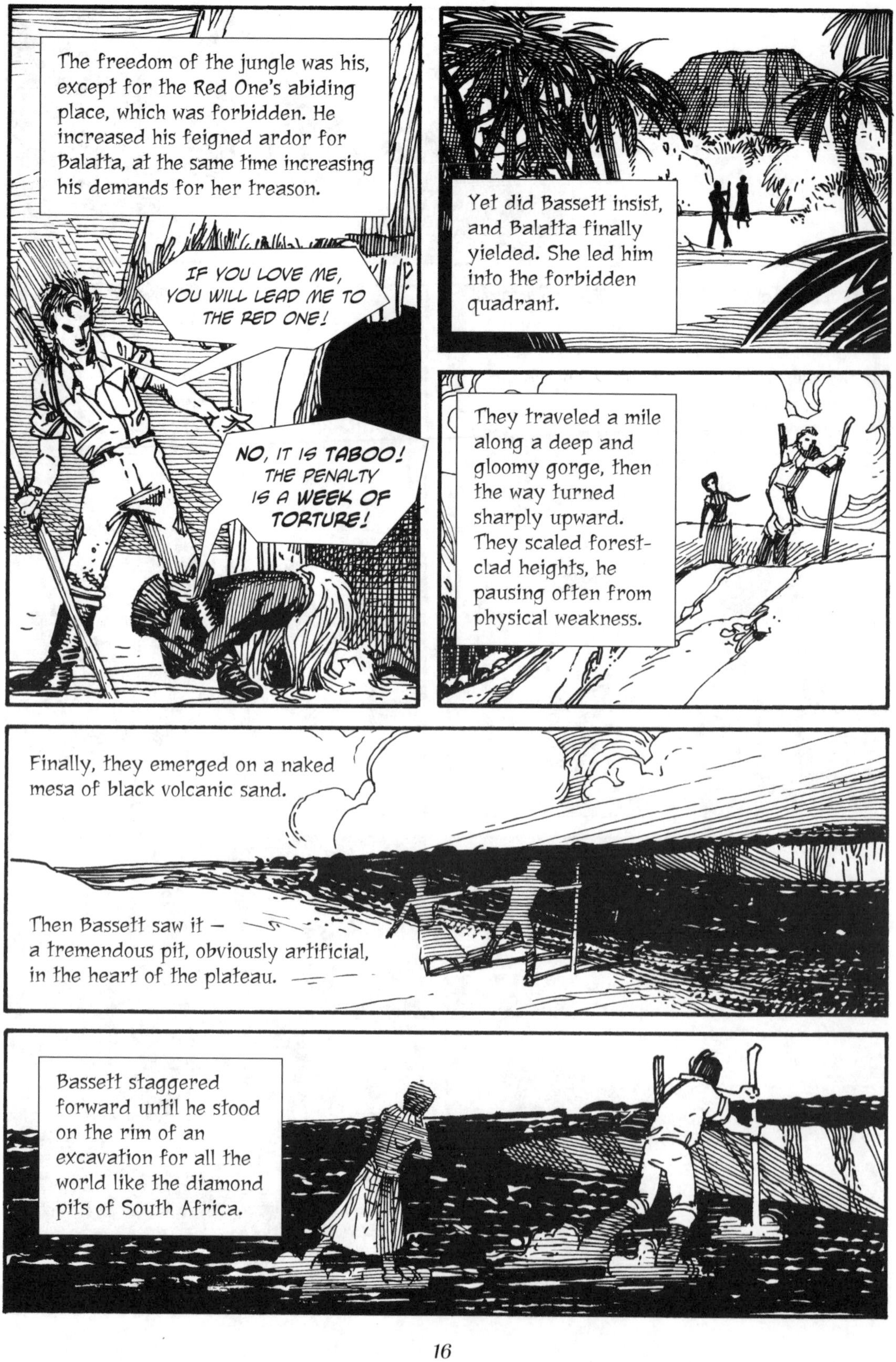
The freedom of the jungle was his, except for the Red One's abiding place, which was forbidden. He increased his feigned ardor for Balatta, at the same time increasing his demands for her treason.
IF YOU LOVE ME, YOU WILL LEAD ME TO THE RED ONE!
NO, IT IS TABOO! THE PENALTY IS A WEEK OF TORTURE!
Yet did Bassett insist, and Balatta finally yielded. She led him into the forbidden quadrant.
They traveled a mile along a deep and gloomy gorge, then the way turned sharply upward. They scaled forest-clad heights, he pausing often from physical weakness.
Finally, they emerged on a naked mesa of black volcanic sand.
Then Bassett saw it — a tremendous pit, obviously artificial, in the heart of the plateau.
Bassett staggered forward until he stood on the rim of an excavation for all the world like the diamond pits of South Africa.

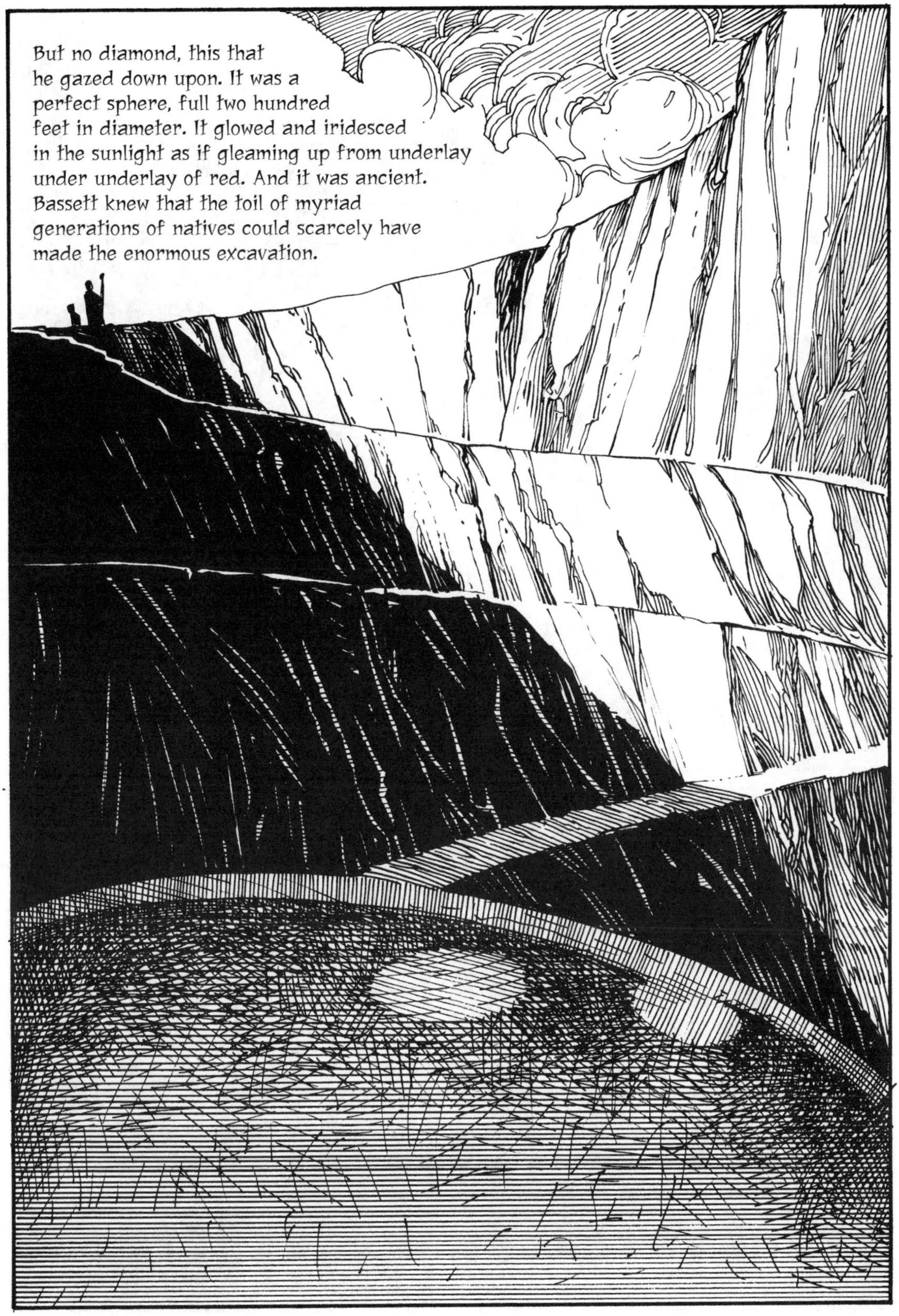
But no diamond, this that he gazed down upon. It was a perfect sphere, full two hundred feet in diameter. It glowed and iridesced in the sunlight as if gleaming up from underlay under underlay of red. And it was ancient. Bassett knew that the toil of myriad generations of natives could scarcely have made the enormous excavation.

In vain Balatta strove to dissuade him from descending. But when he continued she followed, whimpering in terror.

He found the pit bottom carpeted with human bones and gods of wood and stone, covered with obscene totemic designs.

The substance of it was metal, though unlike any metal he had ever known. Its surface was corrugated and pitted, with signs of heat and fusing.

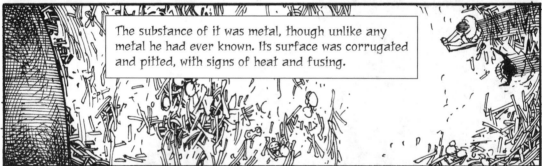

As he touched the surface, he felt the gigantic sphere quiver in rhythmic vibrations that became whisperings of sound, elusively thin; like a peal from some bell of the gods reaching earthward from across space.

IT RESPONDS TO MY TOUCH! INCREDIBLE!

The object was right-named as the Star-Born. Only from the stars could it have come, and no thing of chance was it. Such perfection of form was a creation of artifice and mind.

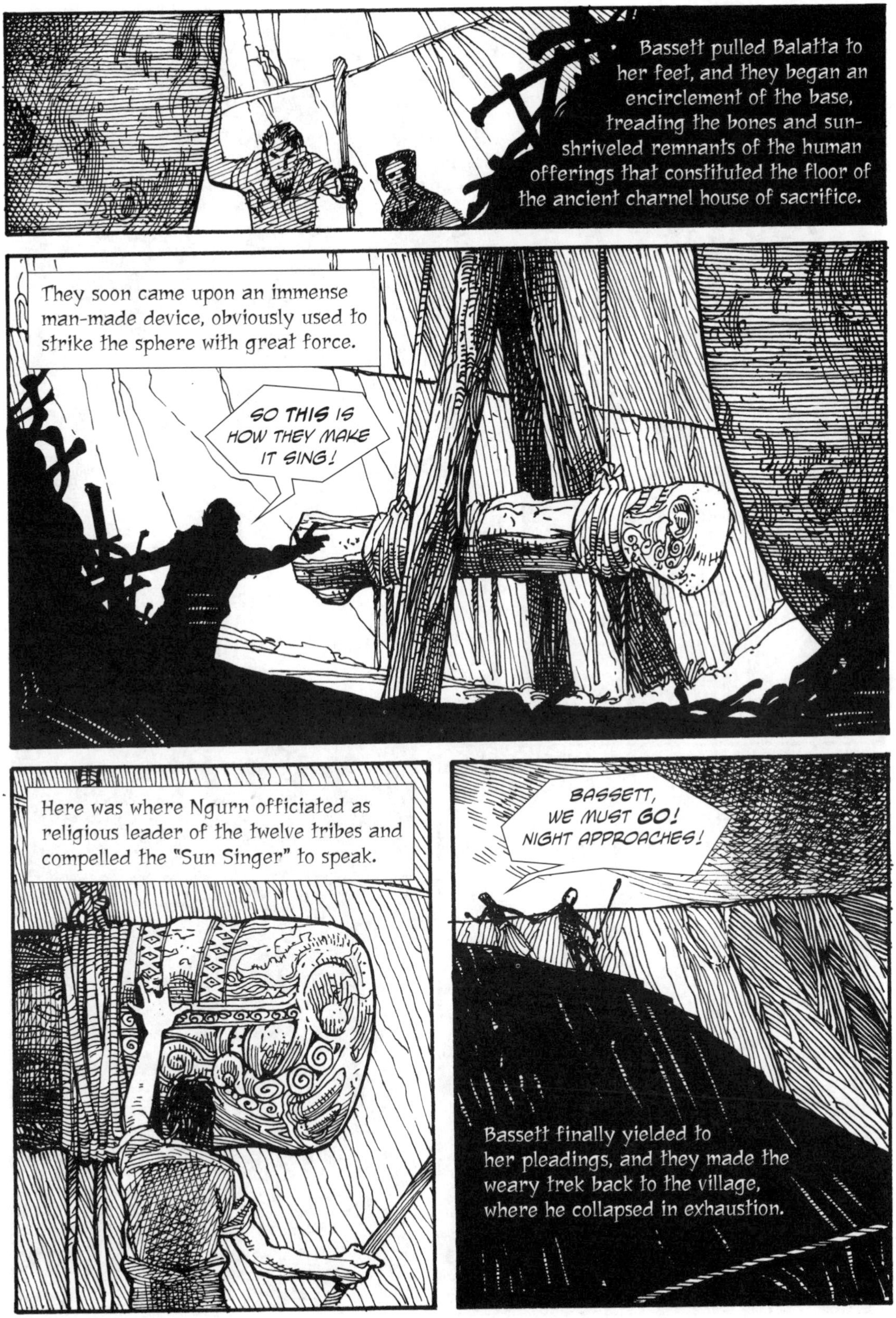
Bassett pulled Balatta to her feet, and they began an encirclement of the base, treading the bones and sun-shriveled remnants of the human offerings that constituted the floor of the ancient charnel house of sacrifice.
They soon came upon an immense man-made device, obviously used to strike the sphere with great force.
SO THIS IS HOW THEY MAKE IT SING!
Here was where Ngurn officiated as religious leader of the twelve tribes and compelled the "Sun Singer" to speak.
BASSETT, WE MUST GO! NIGHT APPROACHES!
Bassett finally yielded to her pleadings, and they made the weary trek back to the village, where he collapsed in exhaustion.

The slow weeks passed, and Bassett struggled against his increasing attacks of fever, sometimes laying for days and nights in a coma. He was determined to recover from his weakness, and gain to civilization. Then would he lead an expedition back to the emissary from another world.

In his periods of recovery, he spent long hours in his hammock, watching the slow setting of the western stars, speculating as to the dwellers on the unseen worlds of those incredibly remote suns.

Who were they, who had bridged the sky with their heaven-singing message? And were their wisdoms shut even then in the huge, metallic heart of the Red One, waiting for the first earthman to read?

But Bassett's relapses grew more frequent, his brief convalescences less vigorous, until he came to know that he would never live to reach the sea.

Even Balatta knew that he would be dead ere the nuptial date determined by his taboo.

Came the day when all mists dissolved, when he found his brain clear as a bell, but neither hand nor foot could he lift. He knew the end was close, and Bassett stirred with resolve, calling Ngurn to him.

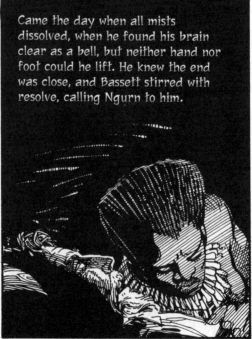

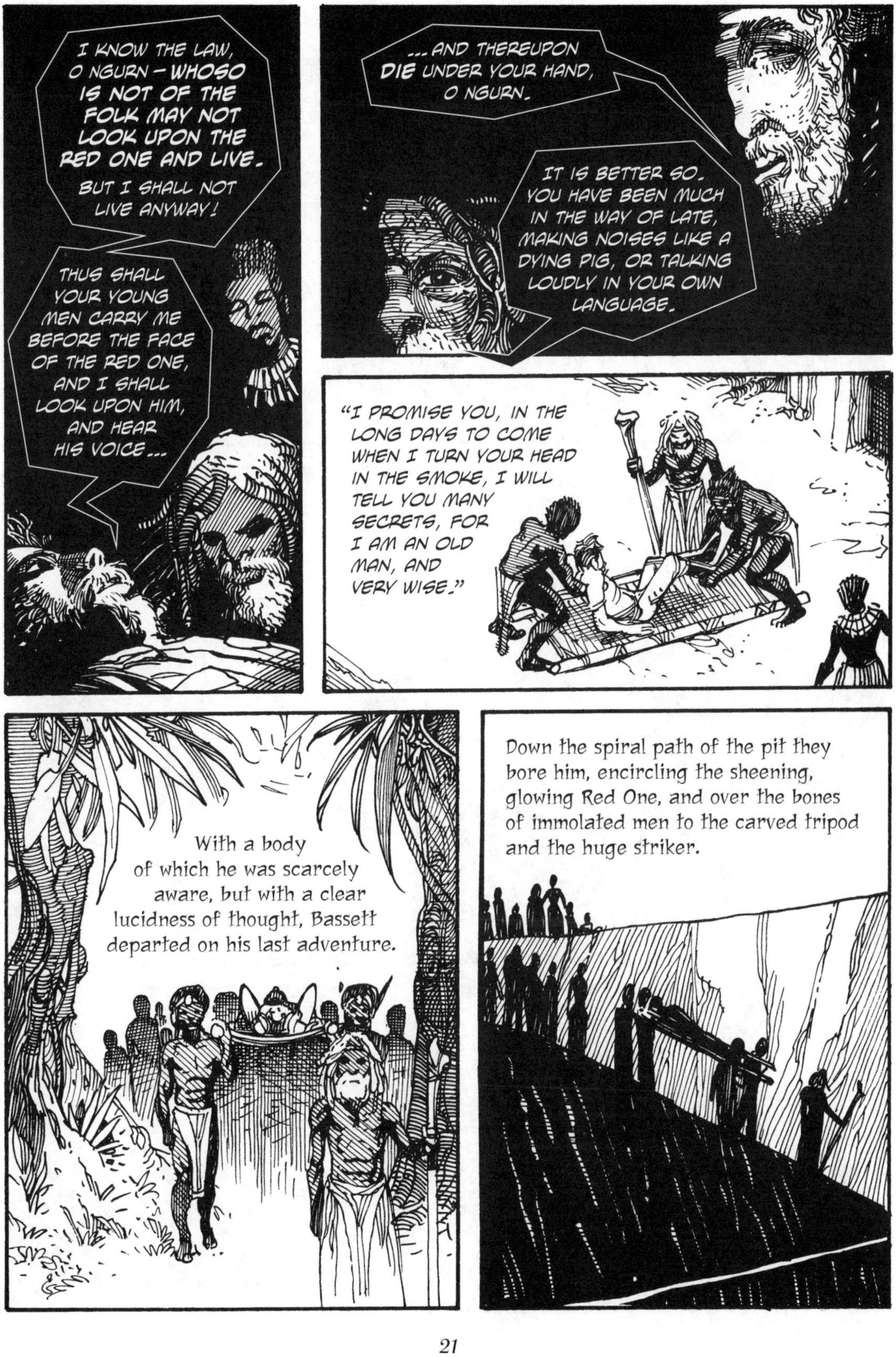
I KNOW THE LAW, O NGURN — WHOSO IS NOT OF THE FOLK MAY NOT LOOK UPON THE RED ONE AND LIVE.
BUT I SHALL NOT LIVE ANYWAY!
THUS SHALL YOUR YOUNG MEN CARRY ME BEFORE THE FACE OF THE RED ONE, AND I SHALL LOOK UPON HIM, AND HEAR HIS VOICE...
...AND THEREUPON DIE UNDER YOUR HAND, O NGURN.
IT IS BETTER SO. YOU HAVE BEEN MUCH IN THE WAY OF LATE, MAKING NOISES LIKE A DYING PIG, OR TALKING LOUDLY IN YOUR OWN LANGUAGE.
"I PROMISE YOU, IN THE LONG DAYS TO COME WHEN I TURN YOUR HEAD IN THE SMOKE, I WILL TELL YOU MANY SECRETS, FOR I AM AN OLD MAN, AND VERY WISE."
With a body of which he was scarcely aware, but with a clear lucidness of thought, Bassett departed on his last adventure.
Down the spiral path of the pit they bore him, encircling the sheening, glowing Red One, and over the bones of immolated men to the carved tripod and the huge striker.

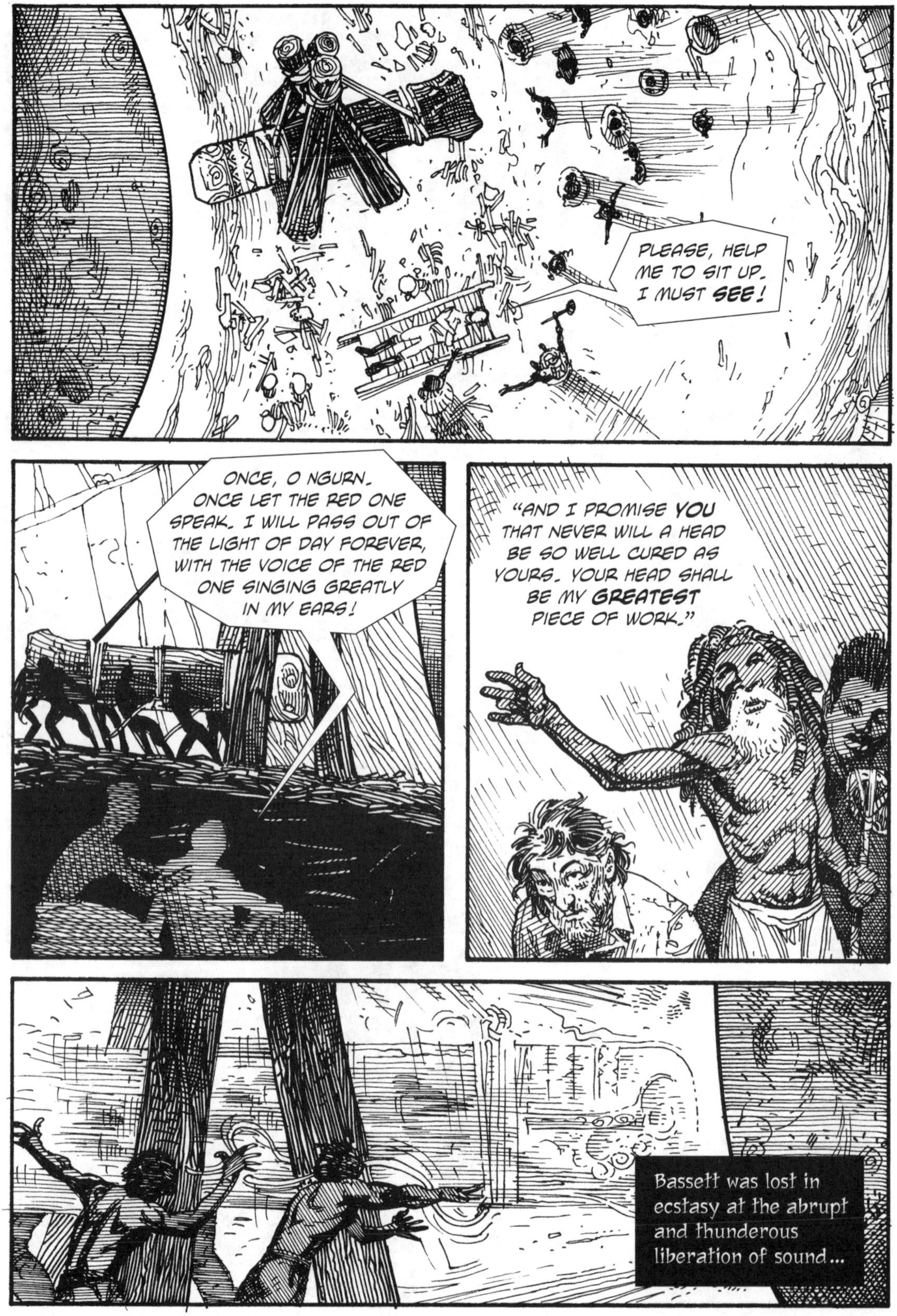
PLEASE, HELP ME TO SIT UP. I MUST SEE!
ONCE, O NGURN. ONCE LET THE RED ONE SPEAK. I WILL PASS OUT OF THE LIGHT OF DAY FOREVER, WITH THE VOICE OF THE RED ONE SINGING GREATLY IN MY EARS!
"AND I PROMISE YOU THAT NEVER WILL A HEAD BE SO WELL CURED AS YOURS. YOUR HEAD SHALL BE MY GREATEST PIECE OF WORK."
Bassett was lost in ecstasy at the abrupt and thunderous liberation of sound...

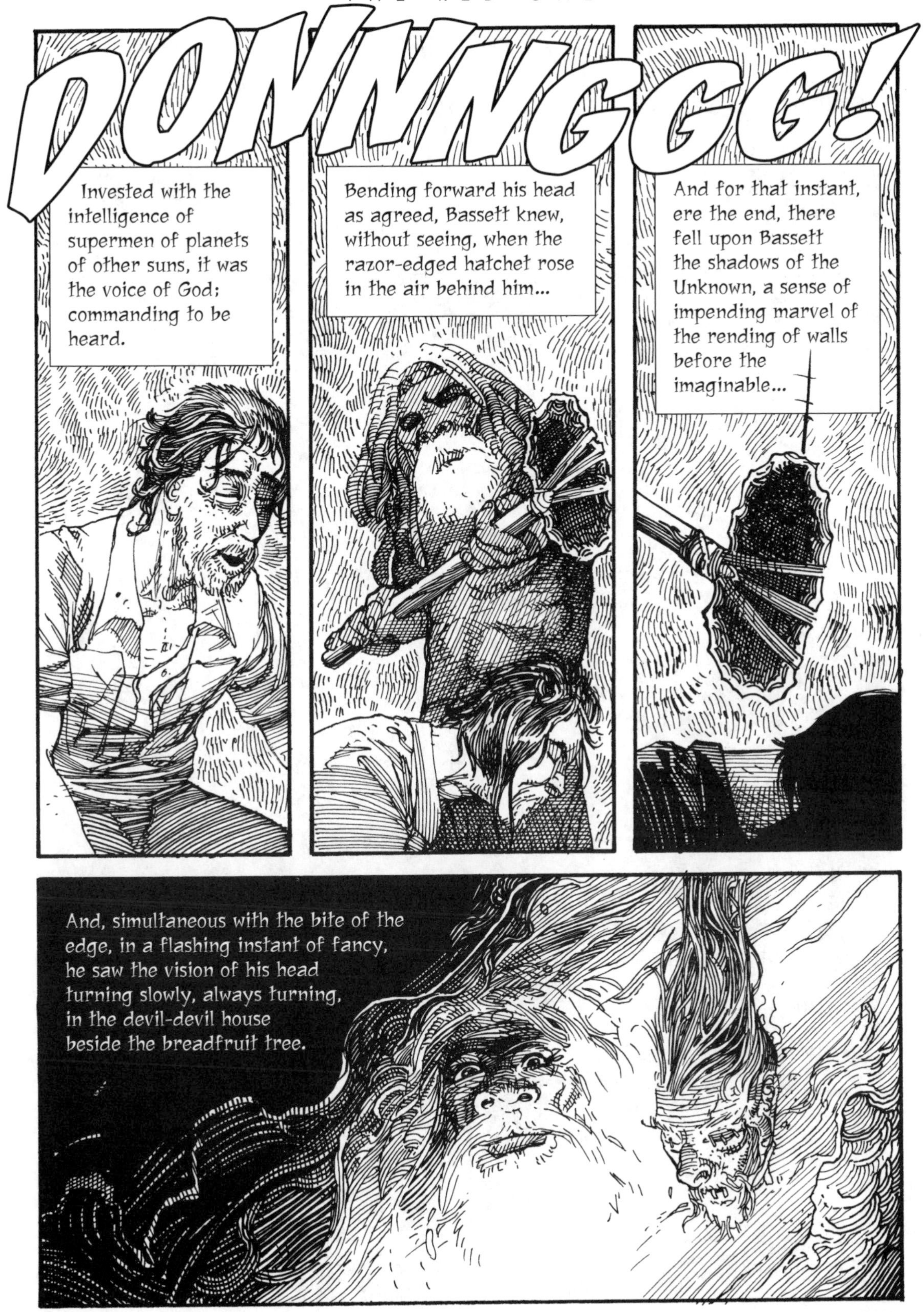
DONNNGGG!
Invested with the intelligence of supermen of planets of other suns, it was the voice of God; commanding to be heard.
Bending forward his head as agreed, Bassett knew, without seeing, when the razor-edged hatchet rose in the air behind him...
And for that instant, ere the end, there fell upon Bassett the shadows of the Unknown, a sense of impending marvel of the rending of walls before the imaginable...
And, simultaneous with the bite of the edge, in a flashing instant of fancy, he saw the vision of his head turning slowly, always turning, in the devil-devil house beside the breadfruit tree.

TYPOGRAPHY: TOM POMPLUN

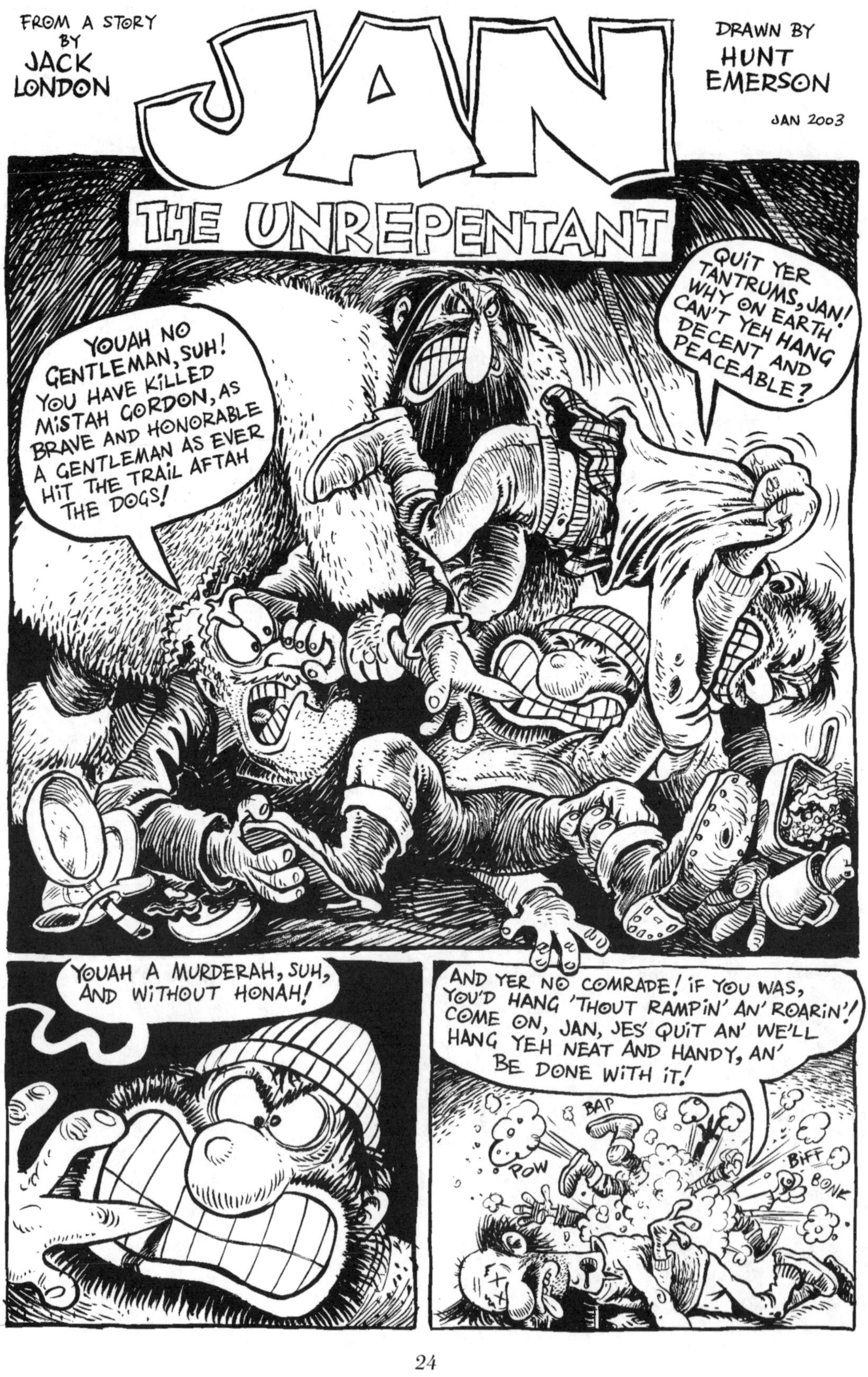
FROM A STORY BY JACK LONDON
JAN THE UNREPENTANT
DRAWN BY HUNT EMERSON
JAN 2003
YOUAH NO GENTLEMAN, SUH! YOU HAVE KILLED MISTAH GORDON, AS BRAVE AND HONORABLE A GENTLEMAN AS EVER HIT THE TRAIL AFTAH THE DOGS!
QUIT YER TANTRUMS, JAN! WHY ON EARTH CAN'T YEH HANG DECENT AND PEACEABLE?
YOUAH A MURDERAH, SUH, AND WITHOUT HONAH!
AND YER NO COMRADE! IF YOU WAS, YOU'D HANG 'THOUT RAMPIN' AN' ROARIN'! COME ON, JAN, JES' QUIT AN' WE'LL HANG YEH NEAT AND HANDY, AN' BE DONE WITH IT!
BAP
POW
BIFF
BONK

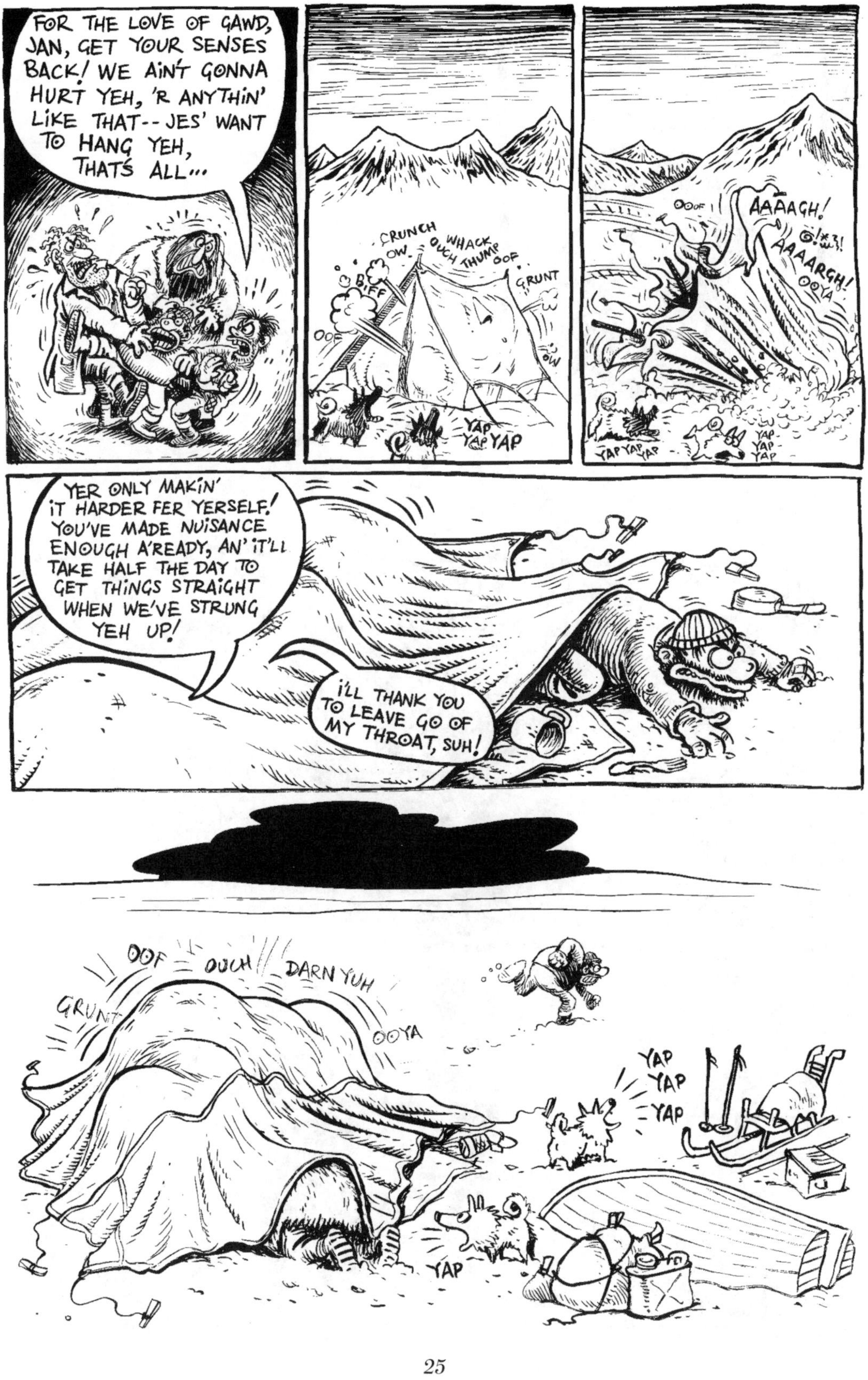
FOR THE LOVE OF GAWD, JAN, GET YOUR SENSES BACK! WE AIN'T GONNA HURT YEH, 'R ANYTHIN' LIKE THAT-- JES' WANT TO HANG YEH, THAT'S ALL...
CRUNCH WHACK
OW OUCH THUMP OOF
BIFF
OOF
GRUNT
OW
YAP YAP YAP
OOOF
AAAAGH!
AAAAARGH!
OOYA
YAP YAP YAP
YAP YAP YAP
YER ONLY MAKIN' IT HARDER FER YERSELF! YOU'VE MADE NUISANCE ENOUGH A'READY, AN' IT'LL TAKE HALF THE DAY TO GET THINGS STRAIGHT WHEN WE'VE STRUNG YEH UP!
I'LL THANK YOU TO LEAVE GO OF MY THROAT, SUH!
OOF
OUCH
DARN YUH
GRUNT
OOYA
YAP YAP YAP
YAP

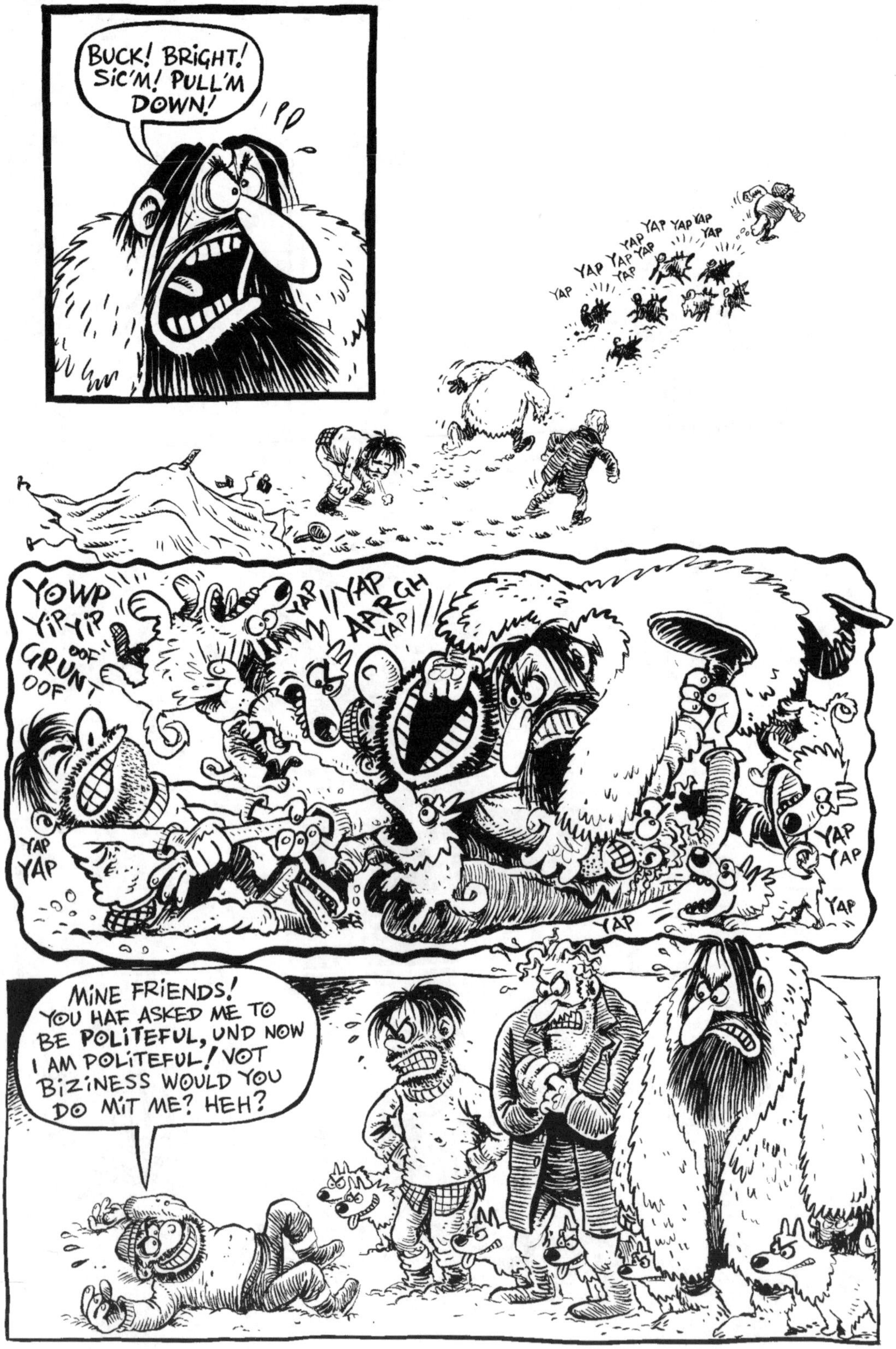
BUCK! BRIGHT! SIC'M! PULL'M DOWN!
YAP YAP YAP YAP YAP YAP YAP YAP YAP YAP YAP YAP
YOWP YIP YIP OOF GRUNT OOF
YAP YAP ARRGH YAP
YAP YAP
YAP YAP
YAP
YAP
MINE FRIENDS! YOU HAF ASKED ME TO BE POLITEFUL, UND NOW I AM POLITEFUL! VOT BIZINESS WOULD YOU DO MIT ME? HEH?

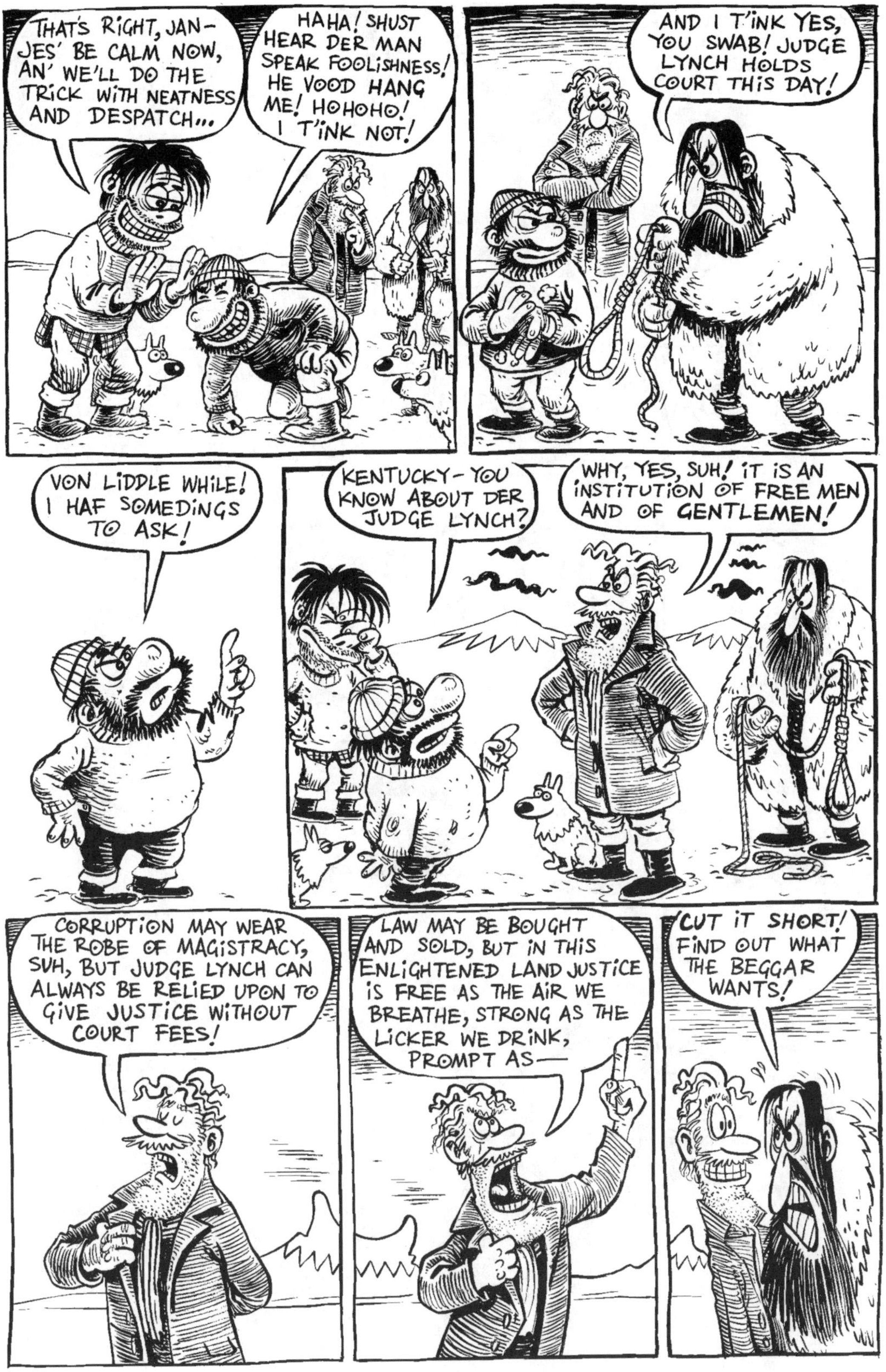
THAT'S RIGHT, JAN- JES' BE CALM NOW, AN' WE'LL DO THE TRICK WITH NEATNESS AND DESPATCH...
HAHA! SHUST HEAR DER MAN SPEAK FOOLISHNESS! HE VOOD HANG ME! HOHOHO! I T'INK NOT!
AND I T'INK YES, YOU SWAB! JUDGE LYNCH HOLDS COURT THIS DAY!
VON LIDDLE WHILE! I HAF SOMEDINGS TO ASK!
KENTUCKY- YOU KNOW ABOUT DER JUDGE LYNCH?
WHY, YES, SUH! IT IS AN INSTITUTION OF FREE MEN AND OF GENTLEMEN!
CORRUPTION MAY WEAR THE ROBE OF MAGISTRACY, SUH, BUT JUDGE LYNCH CAN ALWAYS BE RELIED UPON TO GIVE JUSTICE WITHOUT COURT FEES!
LAW MAY BE BOUGHT AND SOLD, BUT IN THIS ENLIGHTENED LAND JUSTICE IS FREE AS THE AIR WE BREATHE, STRONG AS THE LICKER WE DRINK, PROMPT AS—
CUT IT SHORT! FIND OUT WHAT THE BEGGAR WANTS!

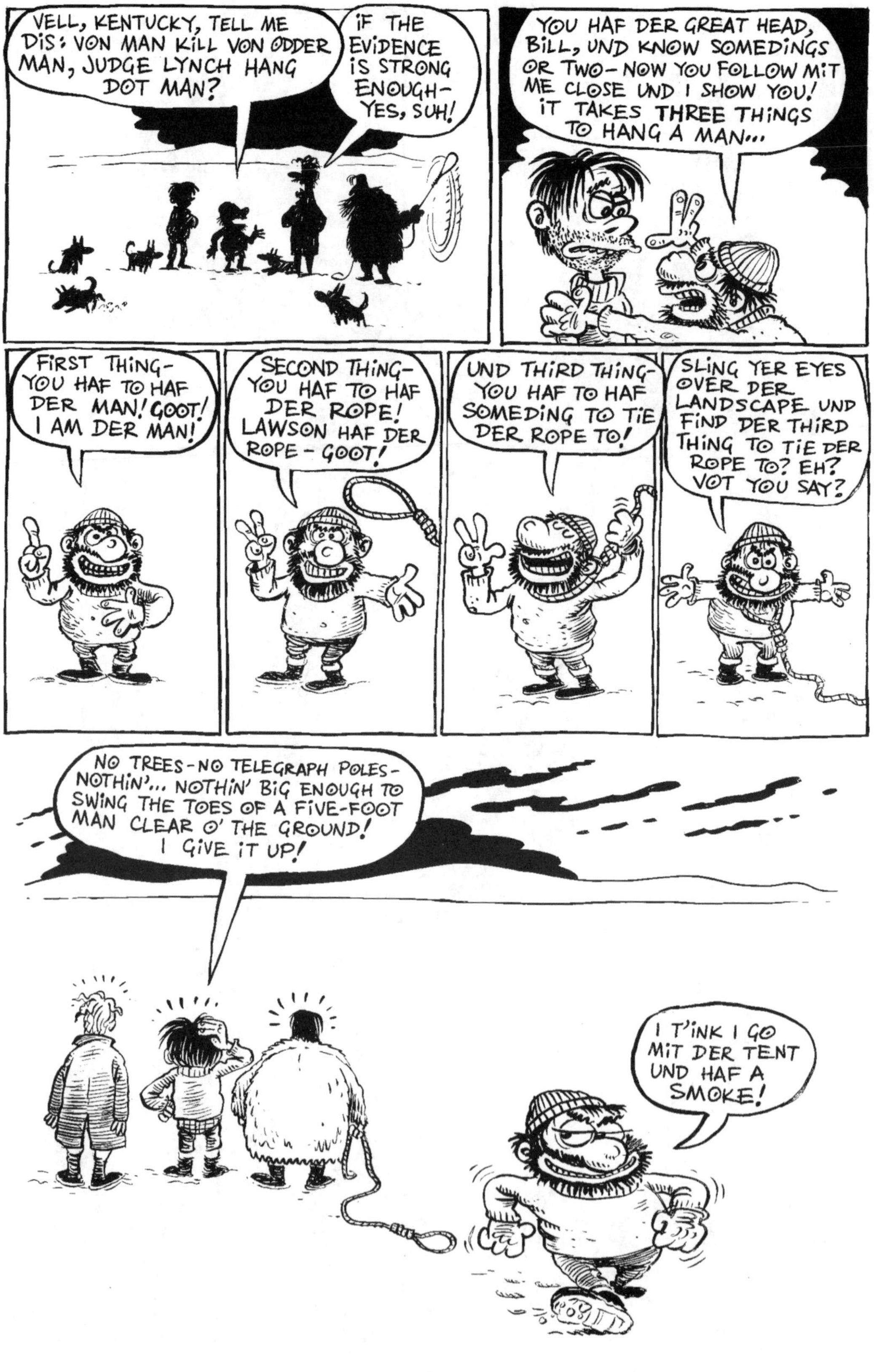
VELL, KENTUCKY, TELL ME DIS: VON MAN KILL VON ODDER MAN, JUDGE LYNCH HANG DOT MAN?
IF THE EVIDENCE IS STRONG ENOUGH- YES, SUH!
YOU HAF DER GREAT HEAD, BILL, UND KNOW SOMEDINGS OR TWO- NOW YOU FOLLOW MIT ME CLOSE UND I SHOW YOU! IT TAKES THREE THINGS TO HANG A MAN...
FIRST THING- YOU HAF TO HAF DER MAN! GOOT! I AM DER MAN!
SECOND THING- YOU HAF TO HAF DER ROPE! LAWSON HAF DER ROPE - GOOT!
UND THIRD THING- YOU HAF TO HAF SOMEDING TO TIE DER ROPE TO!
SLING YER EYES OVER DER LANDSCAPE UND FIND DER THIRD THING TO TIE DER ROPE TO? EH? VOT YOU SAY?
NO TREES-NO TELEGRAPH POLES- NOTHIN'... NOTHIN' BIG ENOUGH TO SWING THE TOES OF A FIVE-FOOT MAN CLEAR O' THE GROUND! I GIVE IT UP!
I T'INK I GO MIT DER TENT UND HAF A SMOKE!

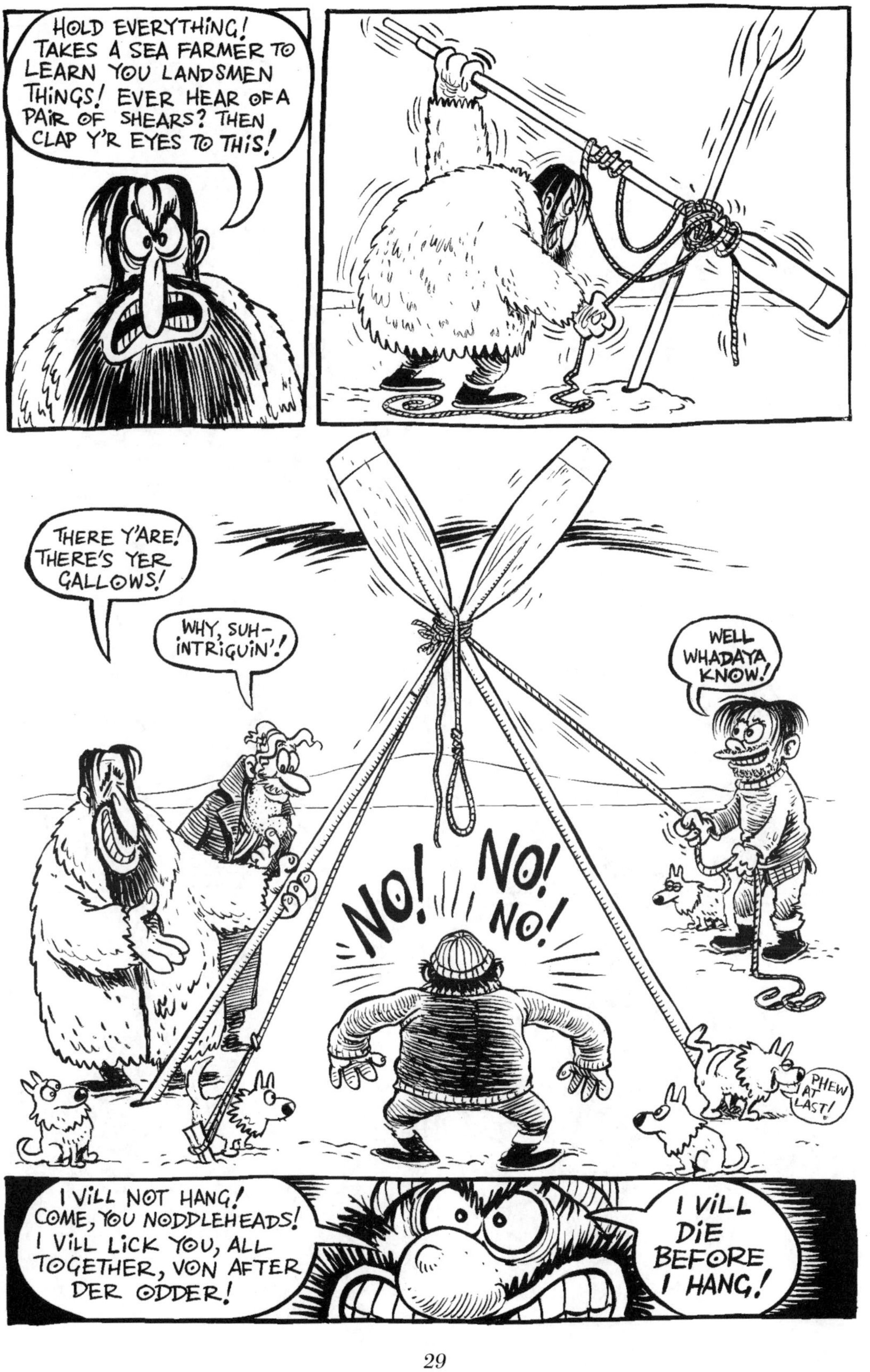
HOLD EVERYTHING! TAKES A SEA FARMER TO LEARN YOU LANDSMEN THINGS! EVER HEAR OF A PAIR OF SHEARS? THEN CLAP Y'R EYES TO THIS!
THERE Y'ARE! THERE'S YER GALLOWS!
WHY, SUH-INTRIGUIN'!
WELL WHADAYA KNOW!
NO! NO! NO!
PHEW AT LAST!
I VILL NOT HANG! COME, YOU NODDLEHEADS! I VILL LICK YOU, ALL TOGETHER, VON AFTER DER ODDER!
I VILL DIE BEFORE I HANG!

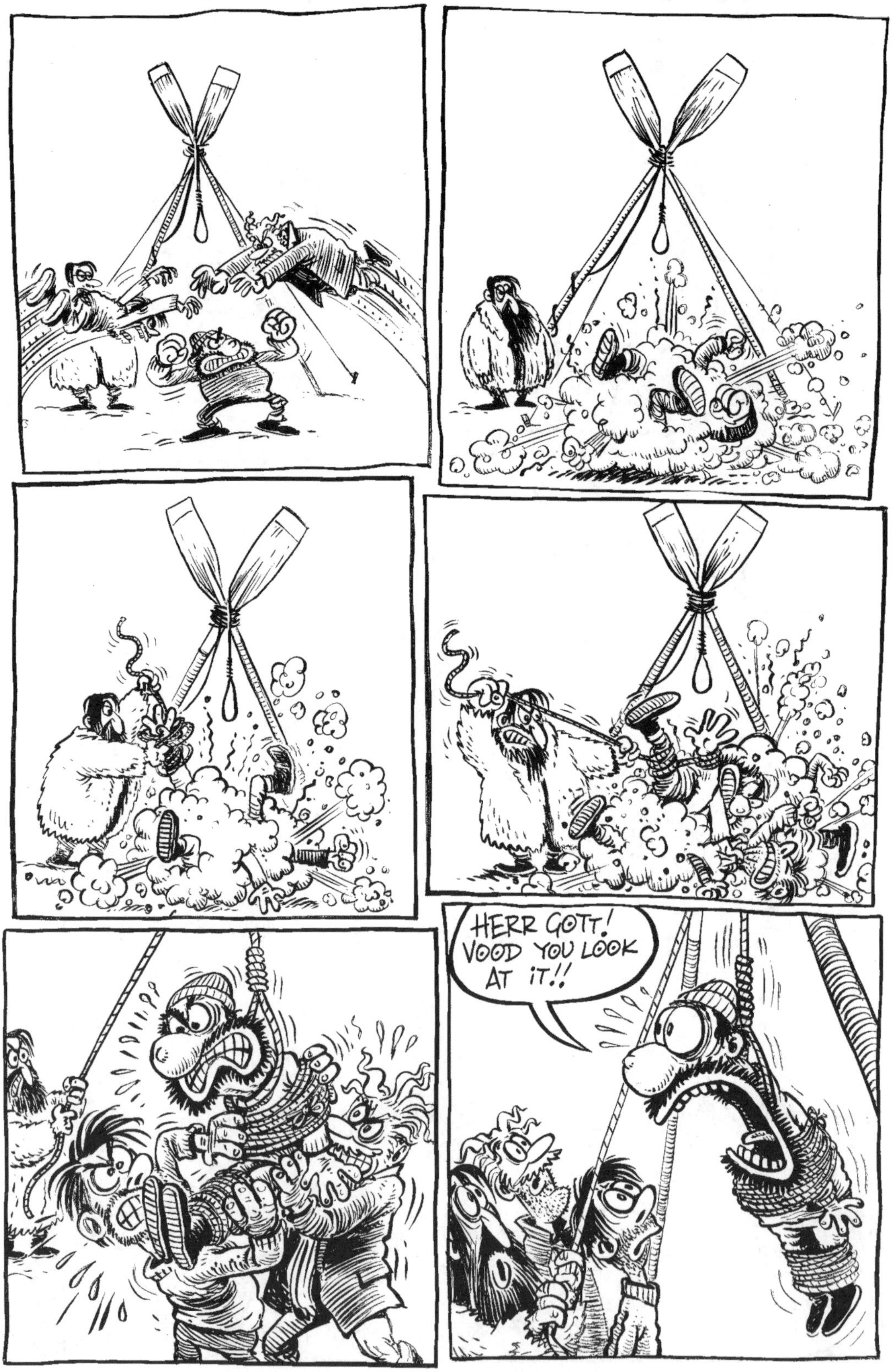
HERR GOTT! VOOD YOU LOOK AT IT!!

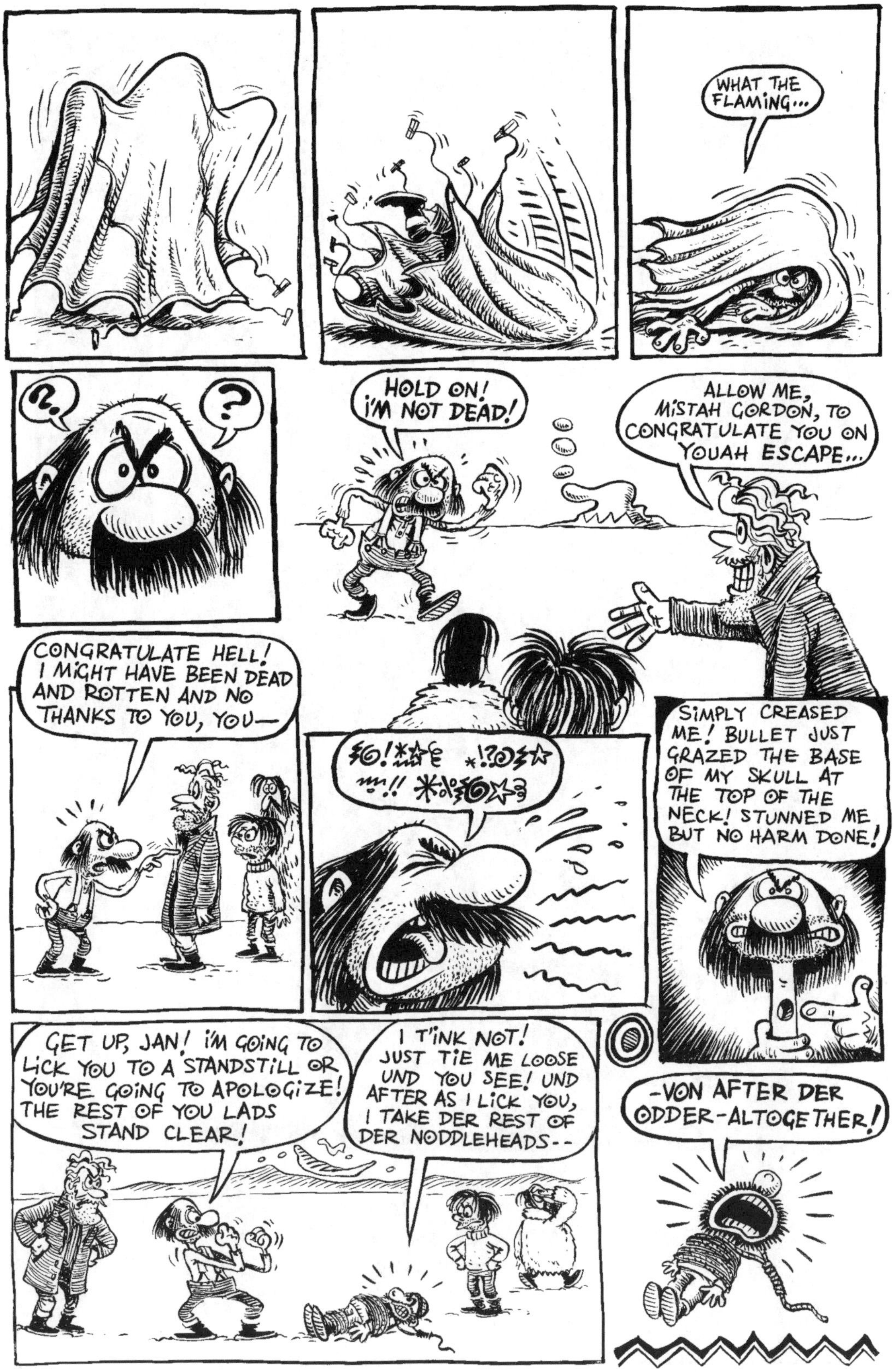
WHAT THE FLAMING...
HOLD ON! I'M NOT DEAD!
ALLOW ME, MISTAH GORDON, TO CONGRATULATE YOU ON YOUAH ESCAPE...
CONGRATULATE HELL! I MIGHT HAVE BEEN DEAD AND ROTTEN AND NO THANKS TO YOU, YOU—
SIMPLY CREASED ME! BULLET JUST GRAZED THE BASE OF MY SKULL AT THE TOP OF THE NECK! STUNNED ME BUT NO HARM DONE!
GET UP, JAN! I'M GOING TO LICK YOU TO A STANDSTILL OR YOU'RE GOING TO APOLOGIZE! THE REST OF YOU LADS STAND CLEAR!
I T'INK NOT! JUST TIE ME LOOSE UND YOU SEE! UND AFTER AS I LICK YOU, I TAKE DER REST OF DER NODDLEHEADS--
-VON AFTER DER ODDER-ALTOGETHER!

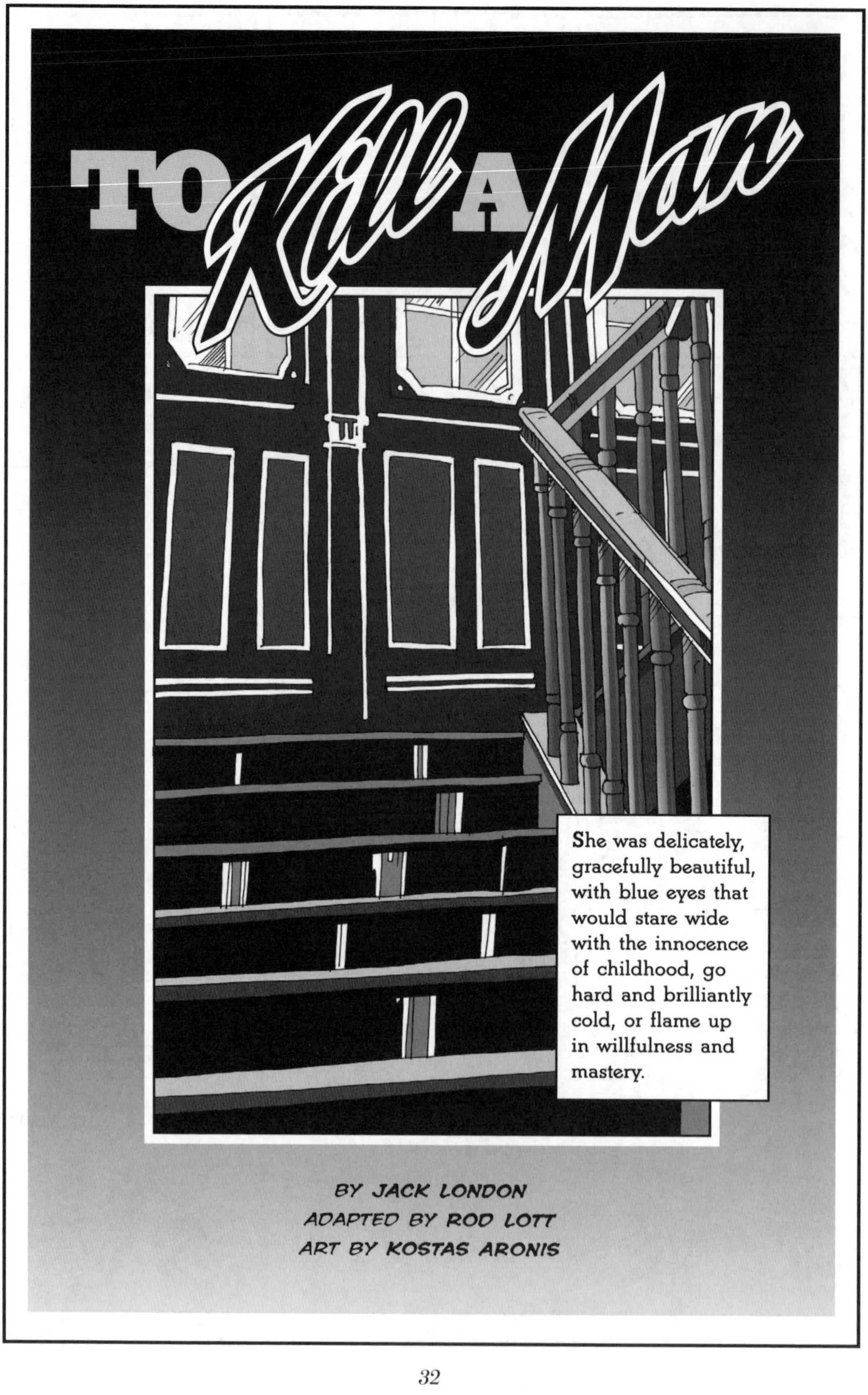
TO Kill A Man
She was delicately, gracefully beautiful, with blue eyes that would stare wide with the innocence of childhood, go hard and brilliantly cold, or flame up in willfulness and mastery.
BY JACK LONDON
ADAPTED BY ROD LOTT
ART BY KOSTAS ARONIS

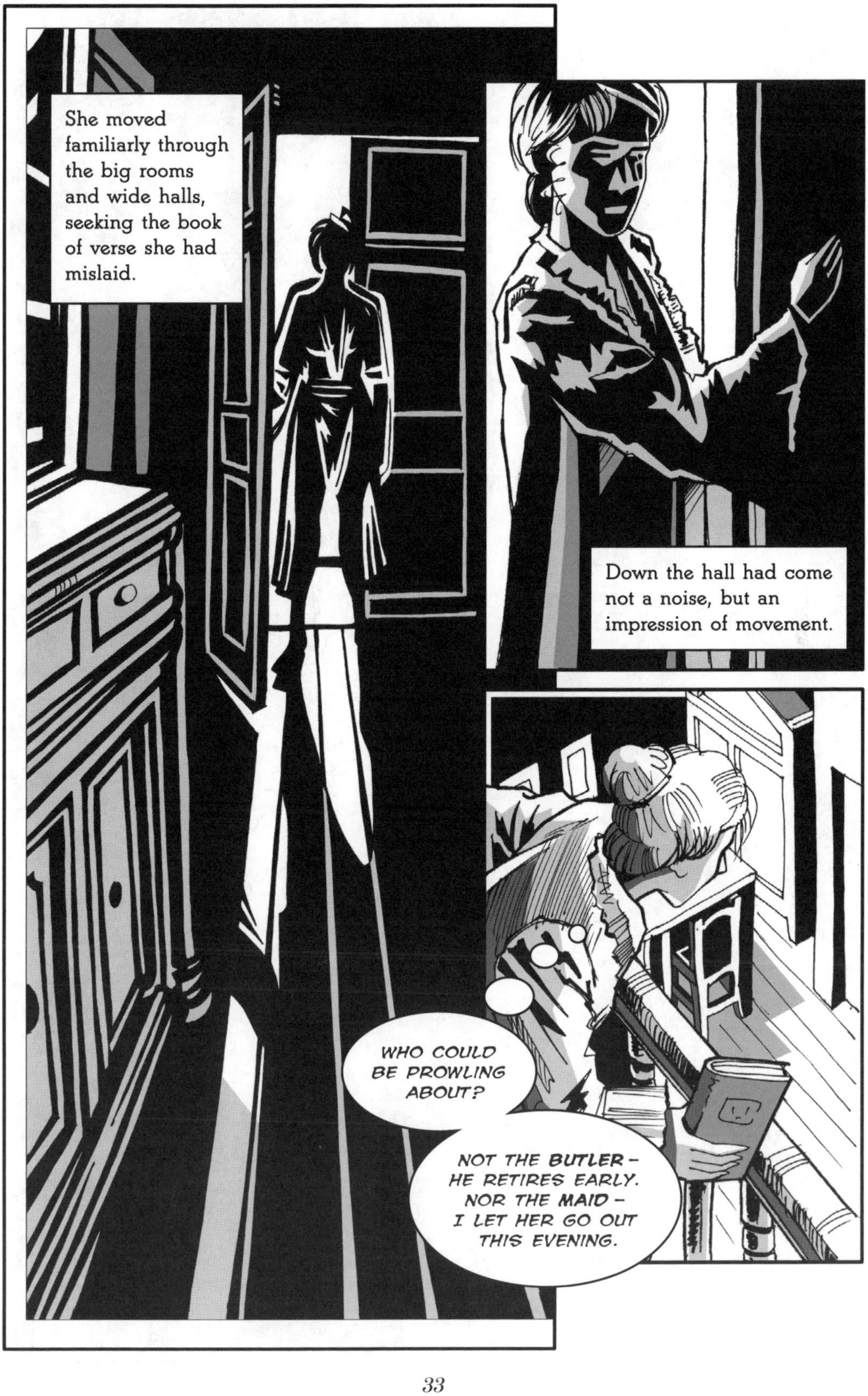
She moved familiarly through the big rooms and wide halls, seeking the book of verse she had mislaid.
Down the hall had come not a noise, but an impression of movement.
WHO COULD BE PROWLING ABOUT?
NOT THE BUTLER - HE RETIRES EARLY. NOR THE MAID - I LET HER GO OUT THIS EVENING.

She passed cautiously on to the dining room...

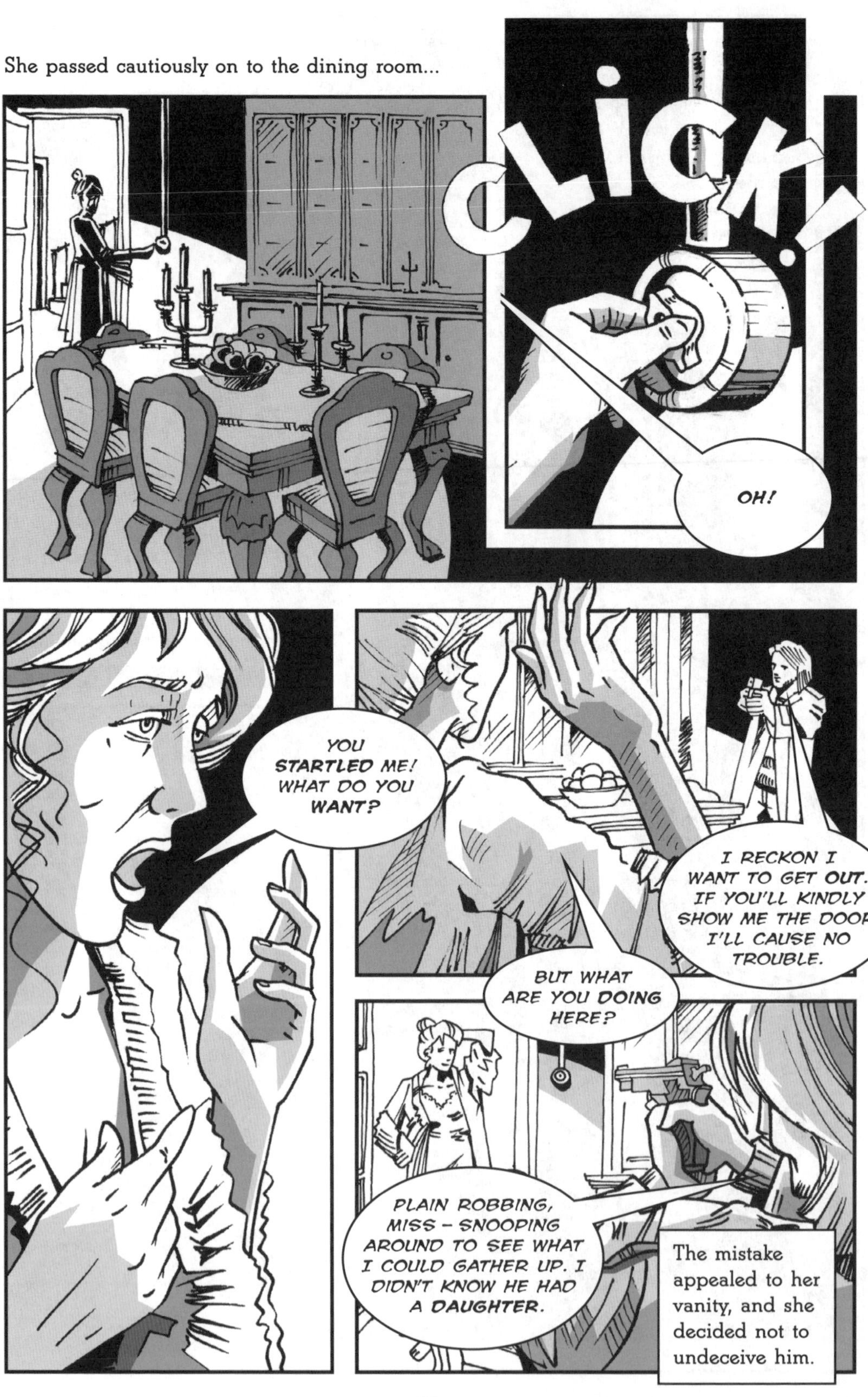
CLICK!
OH!
YOU STARTLED ME! WHAT DO YOU WANT?
I RECKON I WANT TO GET OUT. IF YOU'LL KINDLY SHOW ME THE DOOR, I'LL CAUSE NO TROUBLE.
BUT WHAT ARE YOU DOING HERE?
PLAIN ROBBING, MISS – SNOOPING AROUND TO SEE WHAT I COULD GATHER UP. I DIDN'T KNOW HE HAD A DAUGHTER.

The mistake appealed to her vanity, and she decided not to undeceive him.

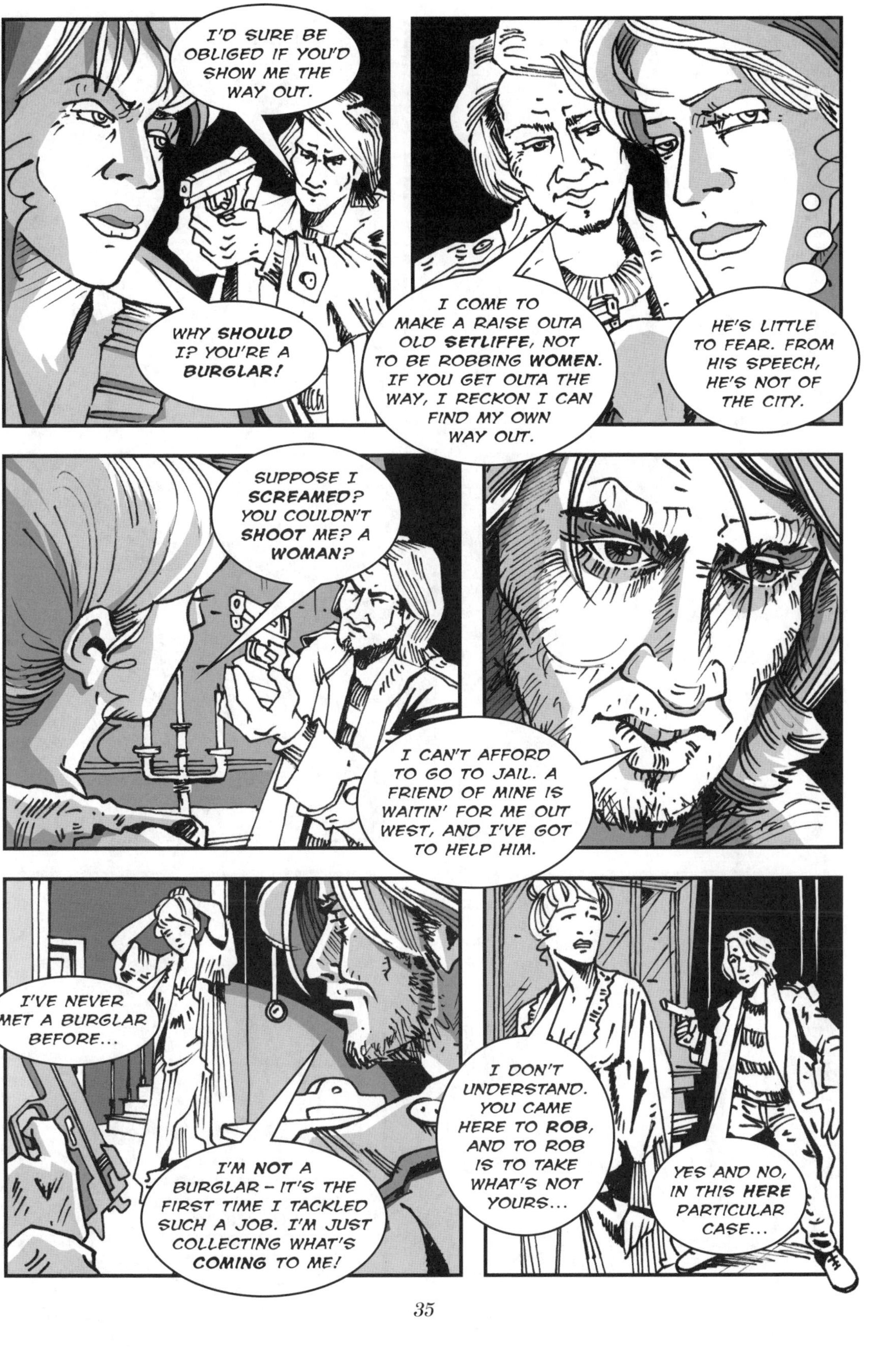
I'D SURE BE OBLIGED IF YOU'D SHOW ME THE WAY OUT.
WHY SHOULD I? YOU'RE A BURGLAR!
I COME TO MAKE A RAISE OUTA OLD SETLIFFE, NOT TO BE ROBBING WOMEN. IF YOU GET OUTA THE WAY, I RECKON I CAN FIND MY OWN WAY OUT.
HE'S LITTLE TO FEAR. FROM HIS SPEECH, HE'S NOT OF THE CITY.
SUPPOSE I SCREAMED? YOU COULDN'T SHOOT ME? A WOMAN?
I CAN'T AFFORD TO GO TO JAIL. A FRIEND OF MINE IS WAITIN' FOR ME OUT WEST, AND I'VE GOT TO HELP HIM.
I'VE NEVER MET A BURGLAR BEFORE...
I'M NOT A BURGLAR – IT'S THE FIRST TIME I TACKLED SUCH A JOB. I'M JUST COLLECTING WHAT'S COMING TO ME!
I DON'T UNDERSTAND. YOU CAME HERE TO ROB, AND TO ROB IS TO TAKE WHAT'S NOT YOURS...
YES AND NO, IN THIS HERE PARTICULAR CASE...

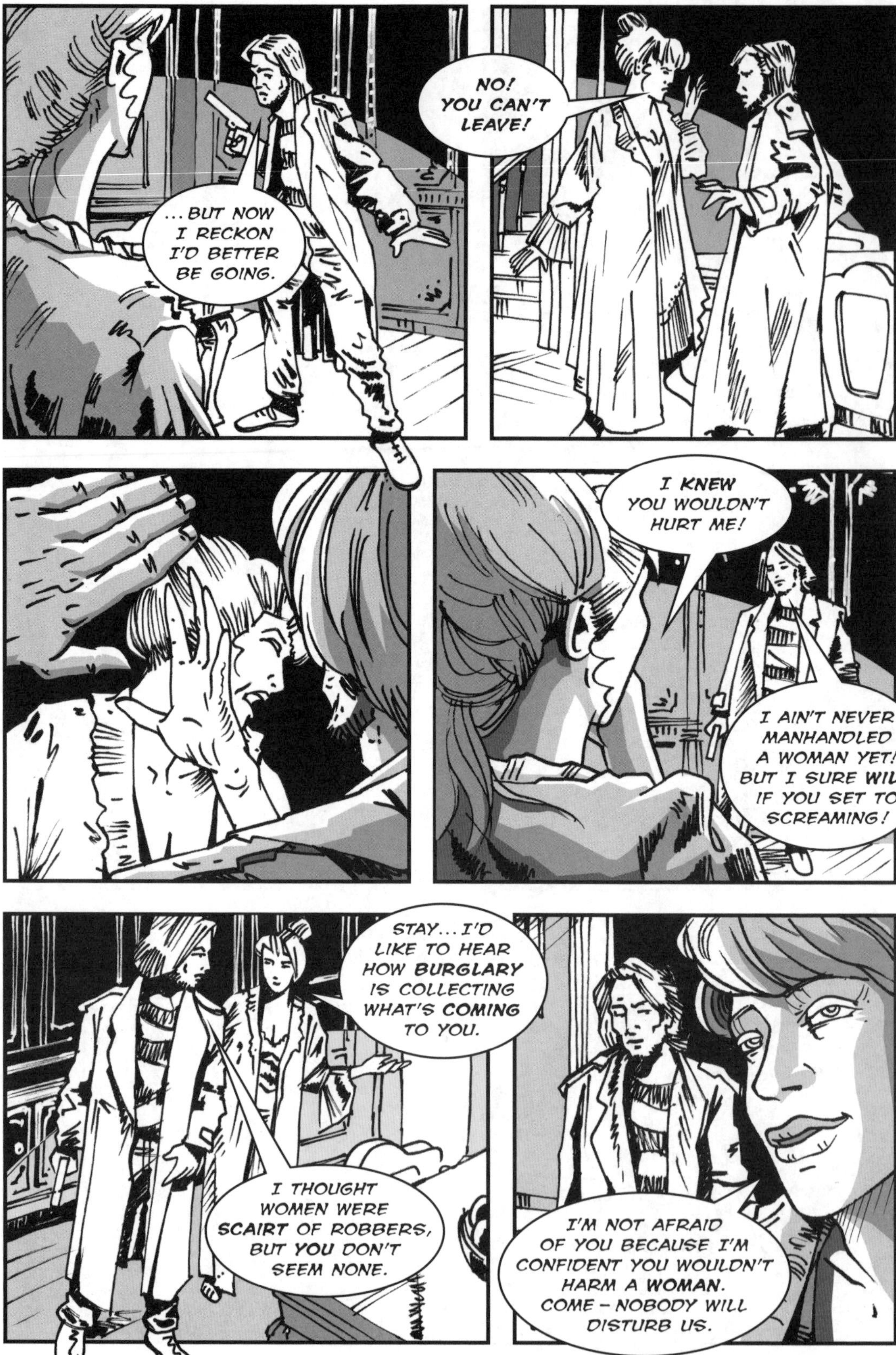
...BUT NOW I RECKON I'D BETTER BE GOING.
NO! YOU CAN'T LEAVE!
I KNEW YOU WOULDN'T HURT ME!
I AIN'T NEVER MANHANDLED A WOMAN YET! BUT I SURE WILL, IF YOU SET TO SCREAMING!
STAY... I'D LIKE TO HEAR HOW BURGLARY IS COLLECTING WHAT'S COMING TO YOU.
I THOUGHT WOMEN WERE SCAIRT OF ROBBERS, BUT YOU DON'T SEEM NONE.
I'M NOT AFRAID OF YOU BECAUSE I'M CONFIDENT YOU WOULDN'T HARM A WOMAN. COME – NOBODY WILL DISTURB US.

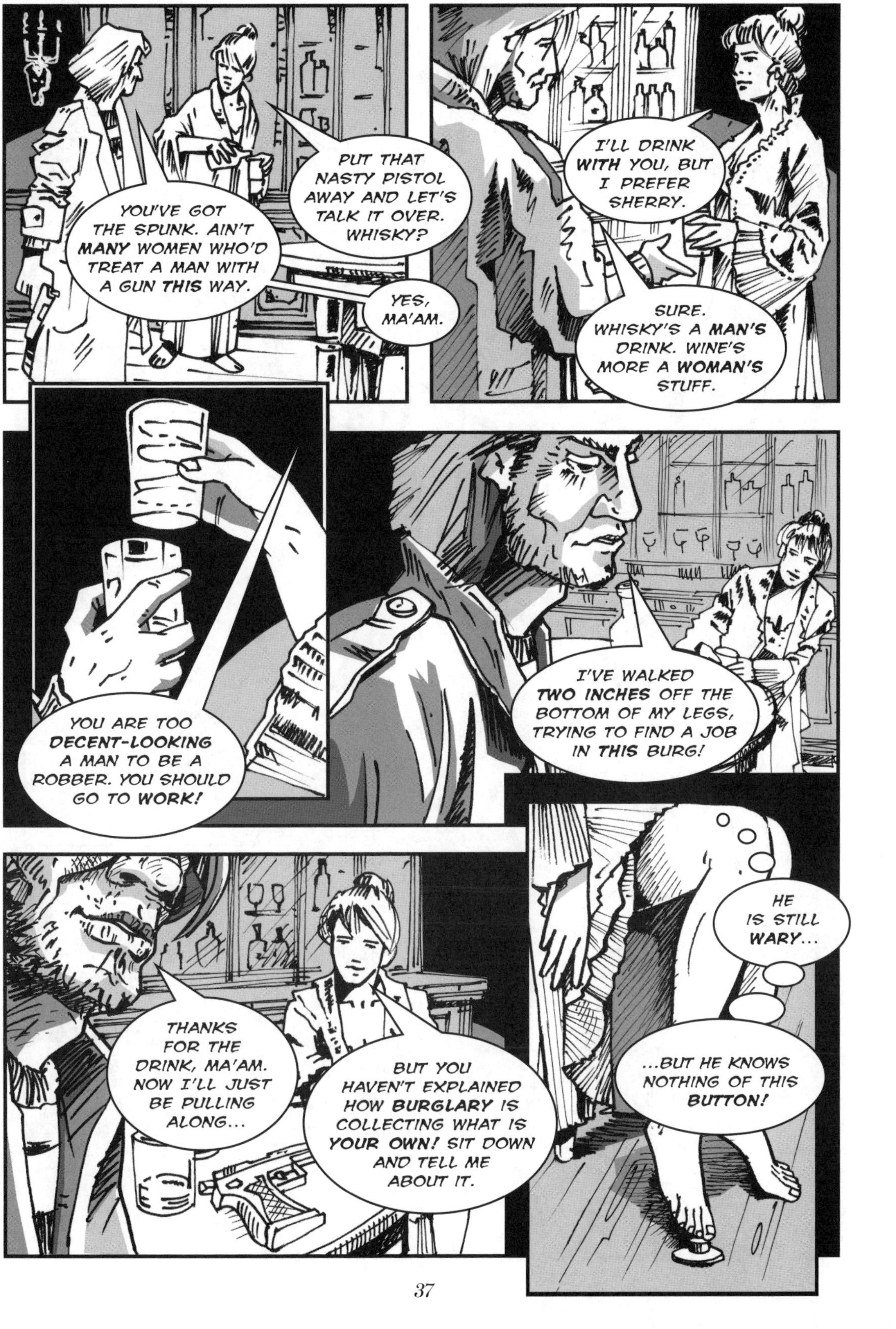
YOU'VE GOT THE SPUNK. AIN'T MANY WOMEN WHO'D TREAT A MAN WITH A GUN THIS WAY.
PUT THAT NASTY PISTOL AWAY AND LET'S TALK IT OVER. WHISKY?
YES, MA'AM.
I'LL DRINK WITH YOU, BUT I PREFER SHERRY.
SURE. WHISKY'S A MAN'S DRINK. WINE'S MORE A WOMAN'S STUFF.
YOU ARE TOO DECENT-LOOKING A MAN TO BE A ROBBER. YOU SHOULD GO TO WORK!
I'VE WALKED TWO INCHES OFF THE BOTTOM OF MY LEGS, TRYING TO FIND A JOB IN THIS BURG!
THANKS FOR THE DRINK, MA'AM. NOW I'LL JUST BE PULLING ALONG...
BUT YOU HAVEN'T EXPLAINED HOW BURGLARY IS COLLECTING WHAT IS YOUR OWN! SIT DOWN AND TELL ME ABOUT IT.
HE IS STILL WARY...
...BUT HE KNOWS NOTHING OF THIS BUTTON!

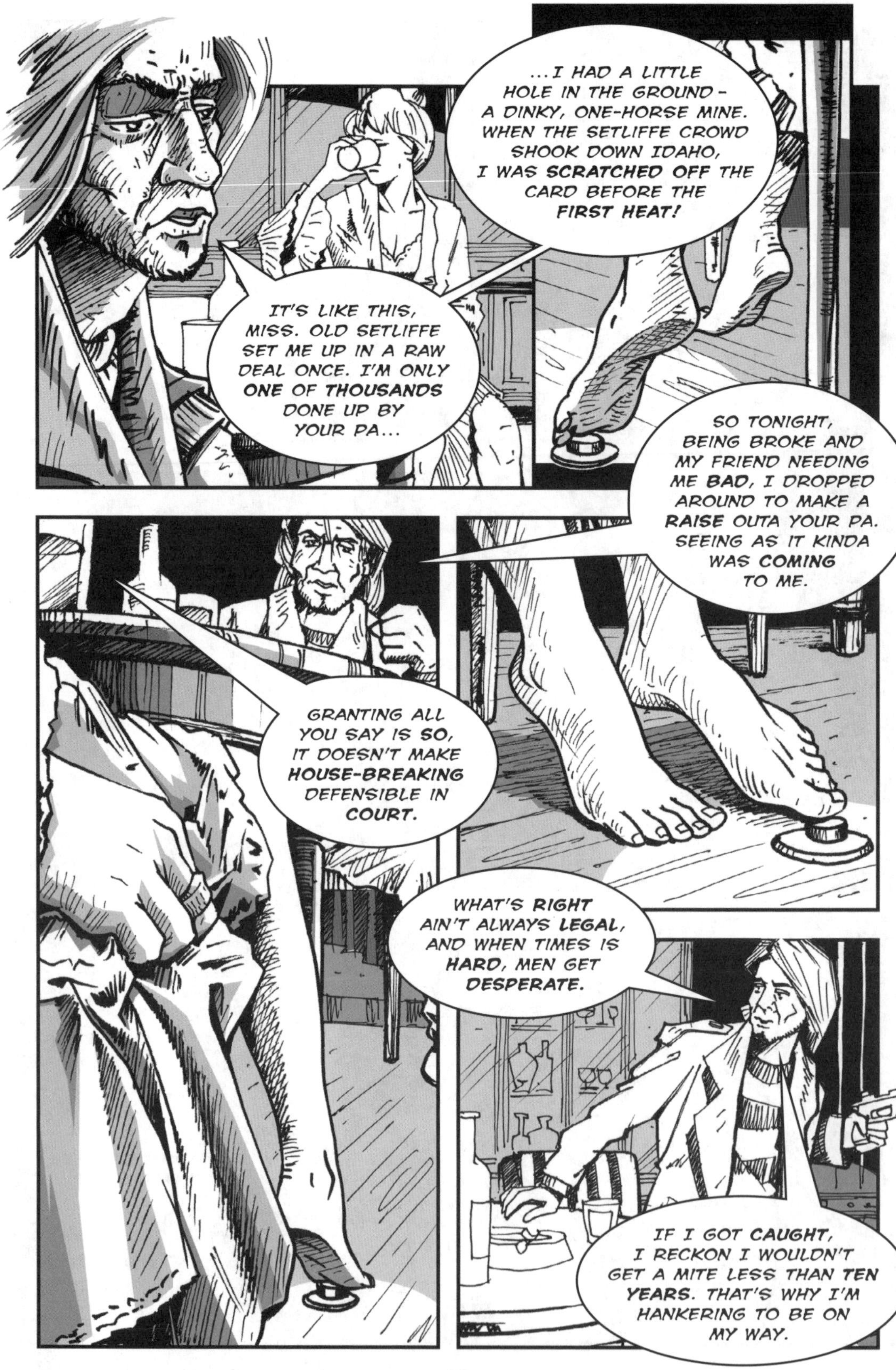
IT'S LIKE THIS, MISS. OLD SETLIFFE SET ME UP IN A RAW DEAL ONCE. I'M ONLY ONE OF THOUSANDS DONE UP BY YOUR PA...
...I HAD A LITTLE HOLE IN THE GROUND – A DINKY, ONE-HORSE MINE. WHEN THE SETLIFFE CROWD SHOOK DOWN IDAHO, I WAS SCRATCHED OFF THE CARD BEFORE THE FIRST HEAT!
SO TONIGHT, BEING BROKE AND MY FRIEND NEEDING ME BAD, I DROPPED AROUND TO MAKE A RAISE OUTA YOUR PA. SEEING AS IT KINDA WAS COMING TO ME.
GRANTING ALL YOU SAY IS SO, IT DOESN'T MAKE HOUSE-BREAKING DEFENSIBLE IN COURT.
WHAT'S RIGHT AIN'T ALWAYS LEGAL, AND WHEN TIMES IS HARD, MEN GET DESPERATE.
IF I GOT CAUGHT, I RECKON I WOULDN'T GET A MITE LESS THAN TEN YEARS. THAT'S WHY I'M HANKERING TO BE ON MY WAY.

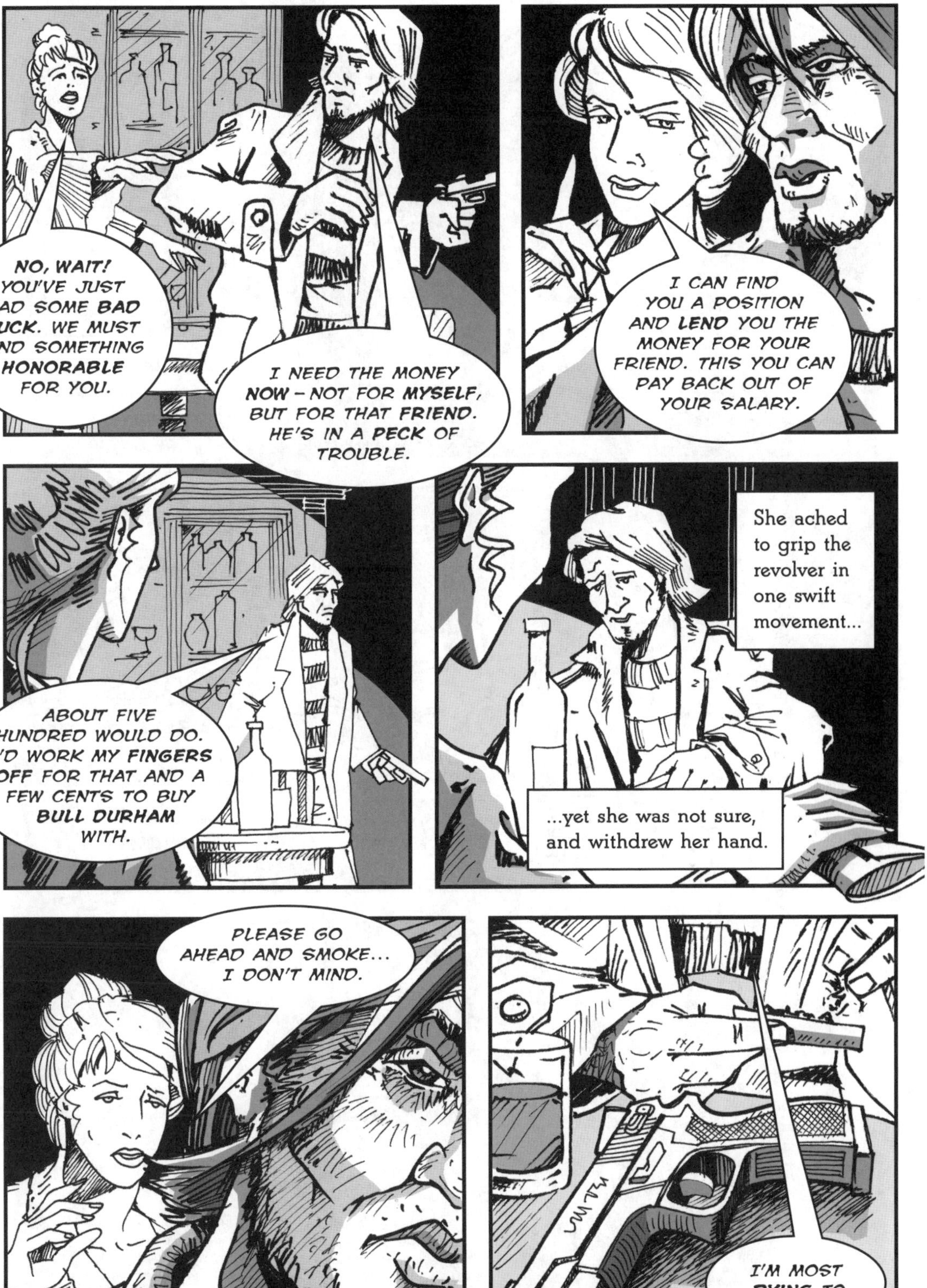
NO, WAIT! YOU'VE JUST HAD SOME BAD LUCK. WE MUST FIND SOMETHING HONORABLE FOR YOU.
I NEED THE MONEY NOW – NOT FOR MYSELF, BUT FOR THAT FRIEND. HE'S IN A PECK OF TROUBLE.
I CAN FIND YOU A POSITION AND LEND YOU THE MONEY FOR YOUR FRIEND. THIS YOU CAN PAY BACK OUT OF YOUR SALARY.
ABOUT FIVE HUNDRED WOULD DO. I'D WORK MY FINGERS OFF FOR THAT AND A FEW CENTS TO BUY BULL DURHAM WITH.
She ached to grip the revolver in one swift movement...
...yet she was not sure, and withdrew her hand.
PLEASE GO AHEAD AND SMOKE... I DON'T MIND.
I'M MOST DYING TO.

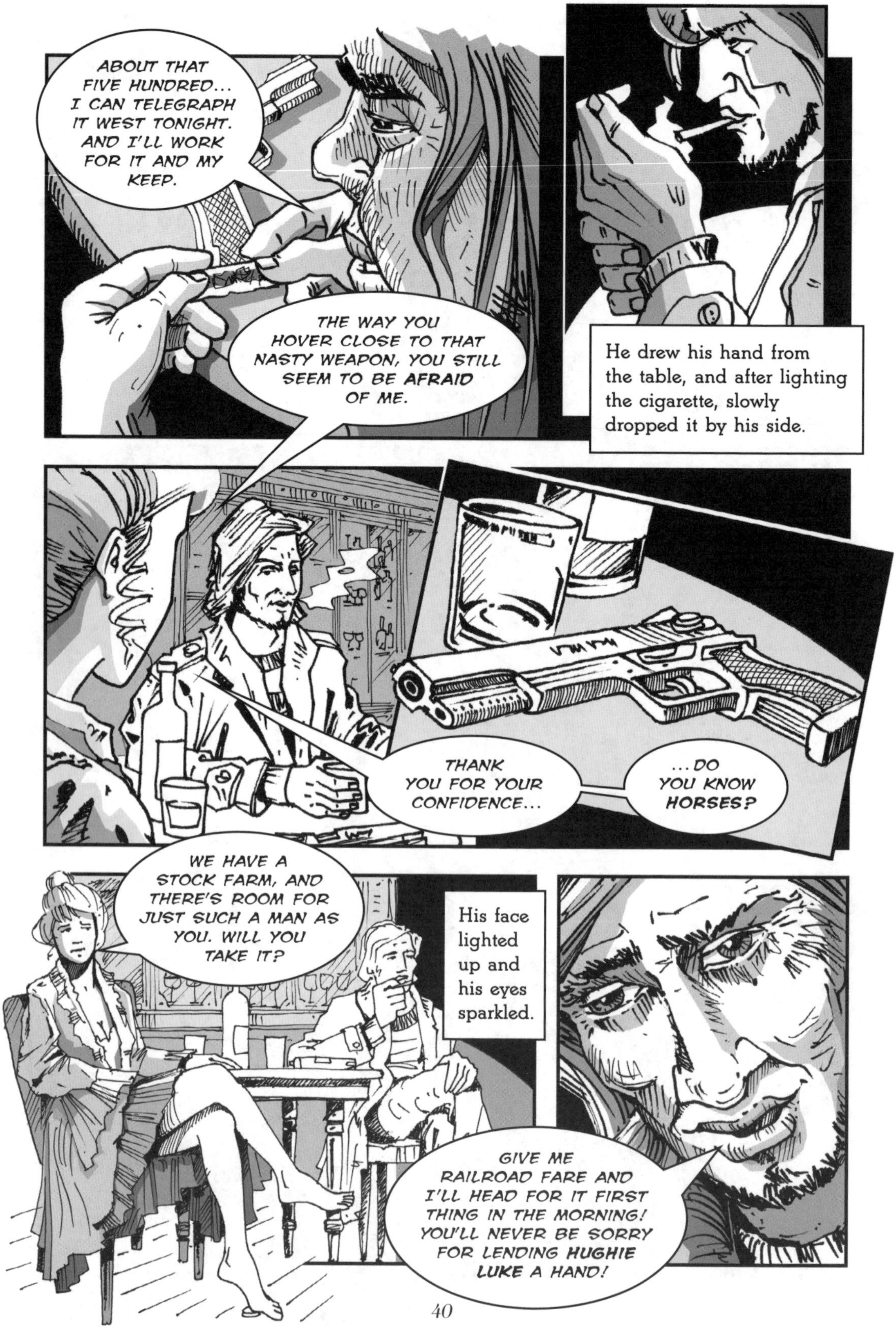
ABOUT THAT FIVE HUNDRED... I CAN TELEGRAPH IT WEST TONIGHT. AND I'LL WORK FOR IT AND MY KEEP.
He drew his hand from the table, and after lighting the cigarette, slowly dropped it by his side.
THE WAY YOU HOVER CLOSE TO THAT NASTY WEAPON, YOU STILL SEEM TO BE **AFRAID** OF ME.
THANK YOU FOR YOUR CONFIDENCE...
...DO YOU KNOW **HORSES?**
WE HAVE A STOCK FARM, AND THERE'S ROOM FOR JUST SUCH A MAN AS YOU. WILL YOU TAKE IT?
His face lighted up and his eyes sparkled.
GIVE ME RAILROAD FARE AND I'LL HEAD FOR IT FIRST THING IN THE MORNING! YOU'LL NEVER BE SORRY FOR LENDING **HUGHIE LUKE** A HAND!

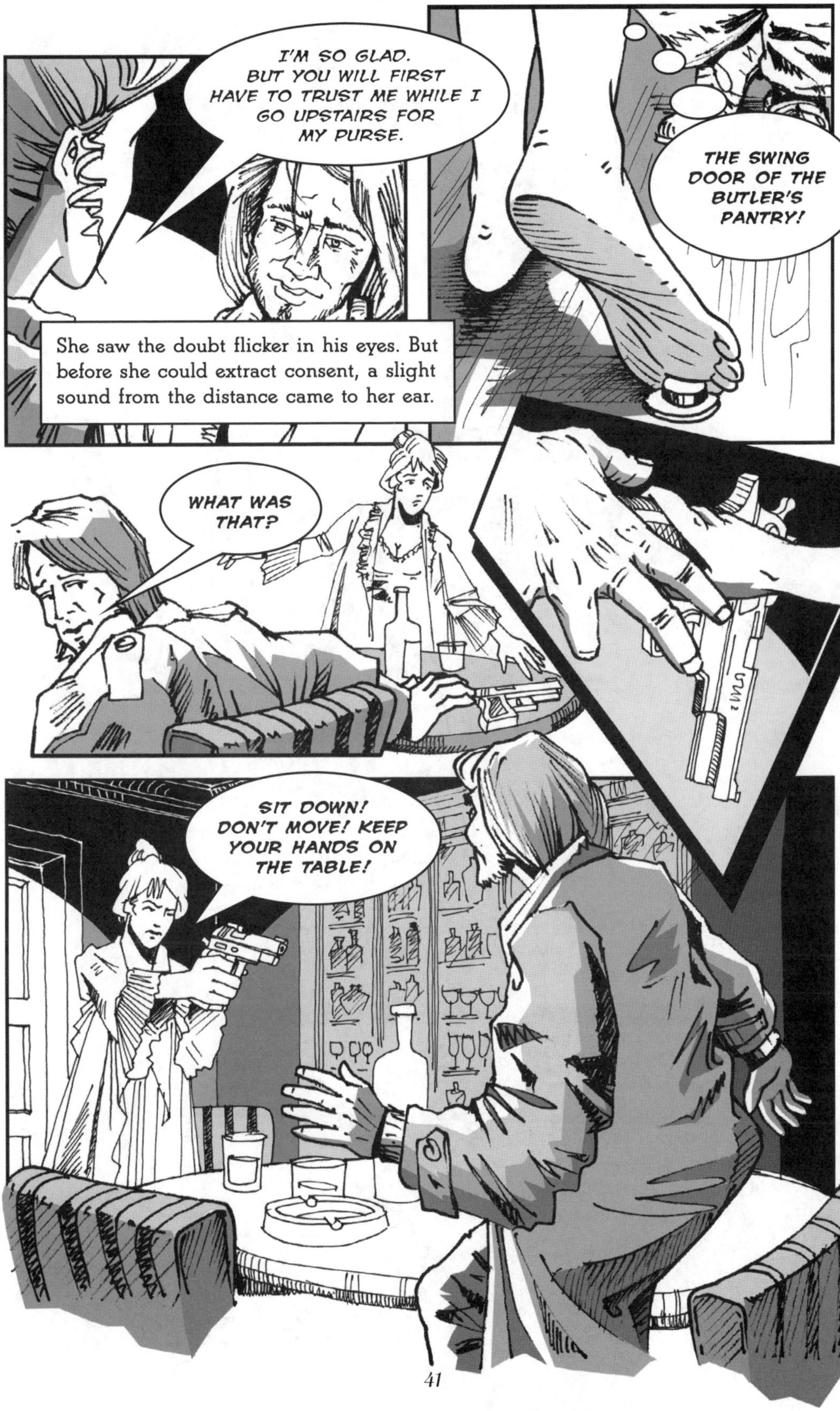
I'M SO GLAD. BUT YOU WILL FIRST HAVE TO TRUST ME WHILE I GO UPSTAIRS FOR MY PURSE.
She saw the doubt flicker in his eyes. But before she could extract consent, a slight sound from the distance came to her ear.
THE SWING DOOR OF THE BUTLER'S PANTRY!
WHAT WAS THAT?
SIT DOWN! DON'T MOVE! KEEP YOUR HANDS ON THE TABLE!

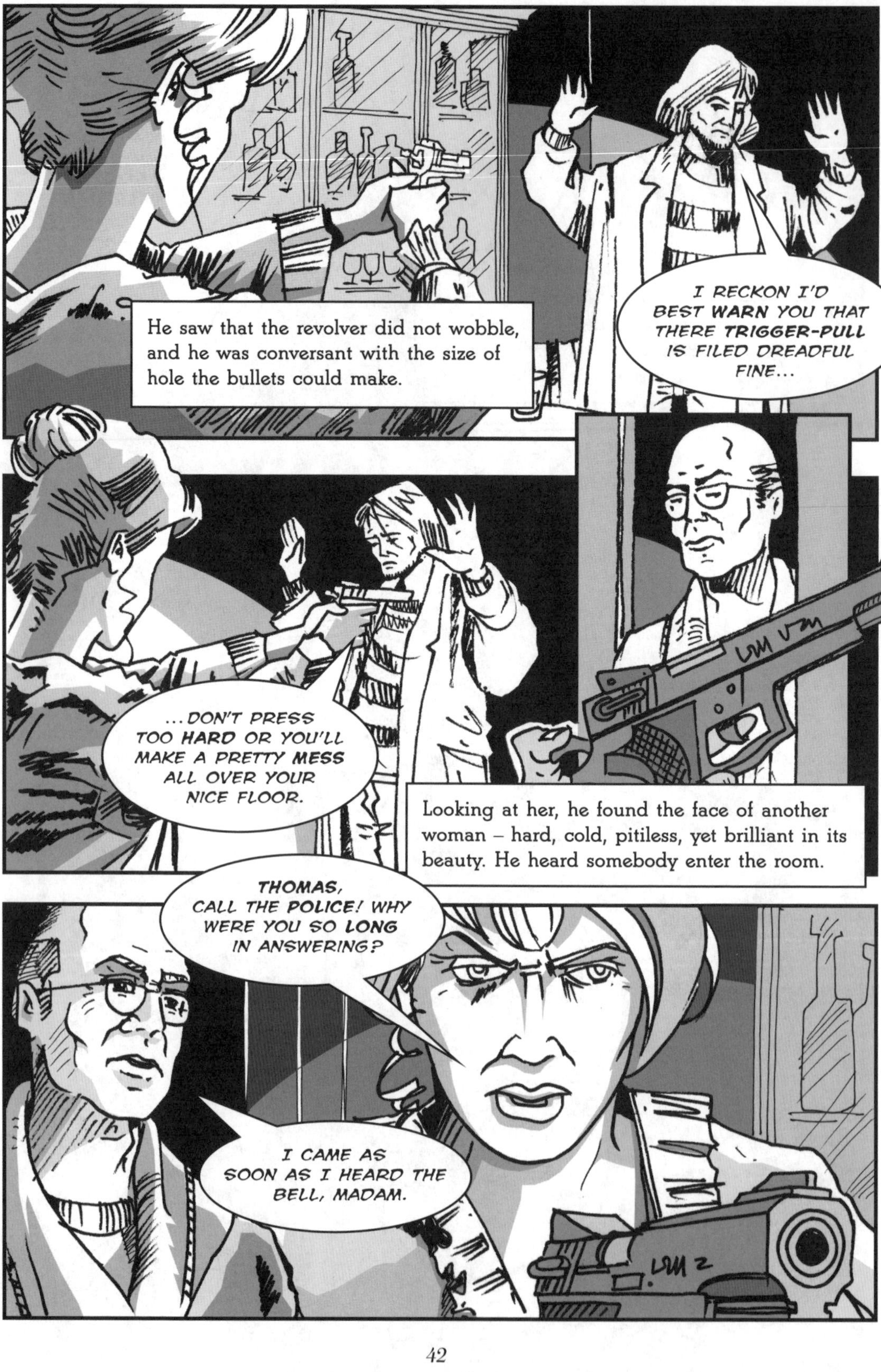
He saw that the revolver did not wobble, and he was conversant with the size of hole the bullets could make.
I RECKON I'D BEST WARN YOU THAT THERE TRIGGER-PULL IS FILED DREADFUL FINE...
...DON'T PRESS TOO HARD OR YOU'LL MAKE A PRETTY MESS ALL OVER YOUR NICE FLOOR.
Looking at her, he found the face of another woman – hard, cold, pitiless, yet brilliant in its beauty. He heard somebody enter the room.
THOMAS, CALL THE POLICE! WHY WERE YOU SO LONG IN ANSWERING?
I CAME AS SOON AS I HEARD THE BELL, MADAM.

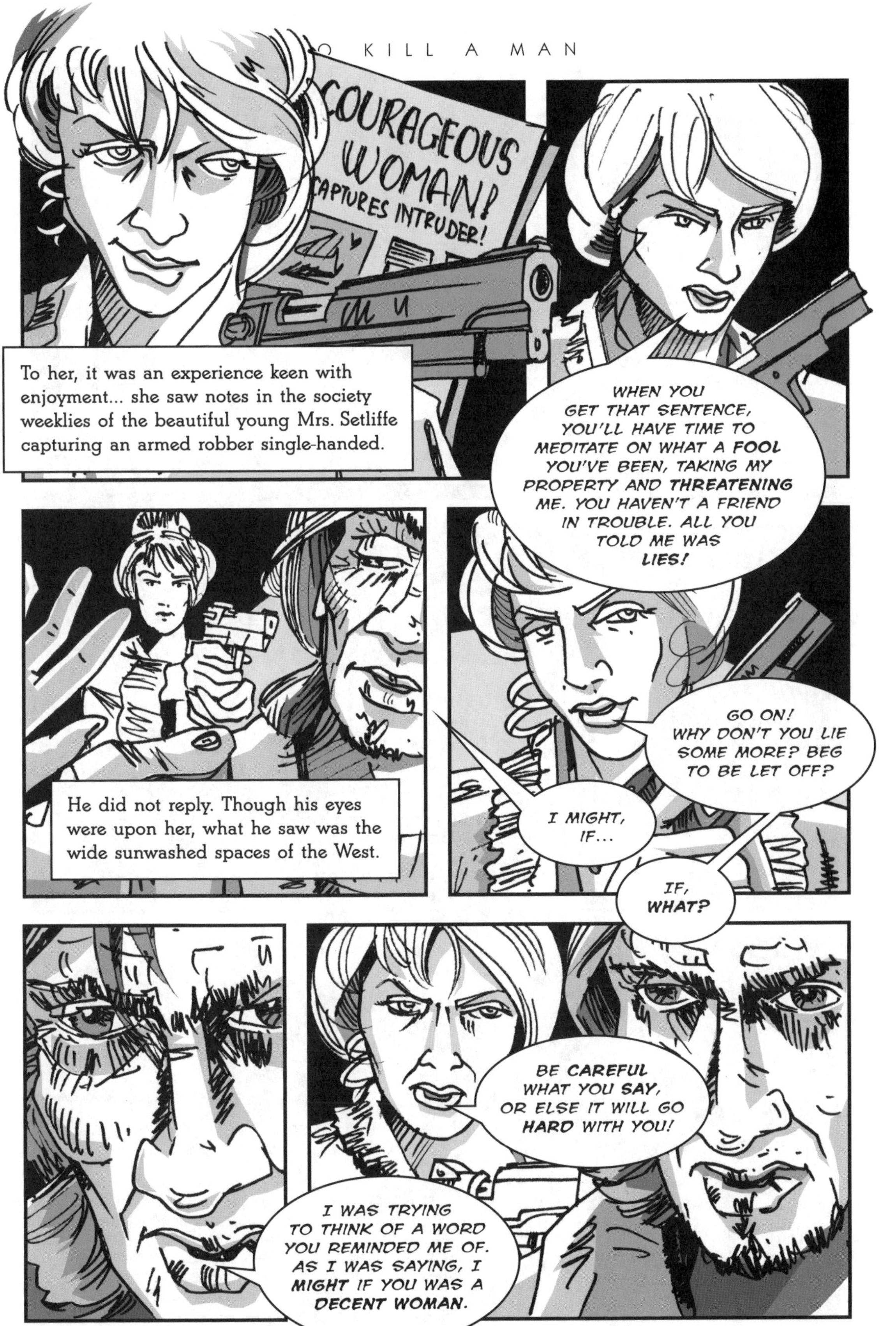
COURAGEOUS WOMAN! CAPTURES INTRUDER!
To her, it was an experience keen with enjoyment... she saw notes in the society weeklies of the beautiful young Mrs. Setliffe capturing an armed robber single-handed.
WHEN YOU GET THAT SENTENCE, YOU'LL HAVE TIME TO MEDITATE ON WHAT A FOOL YOU'VE BEEN, TAKING MY PROPERTY AND THREATENING ME. YOU HAVEN'T A FRIEND IN TROUBLE. ALL YOU TOLD ME WAS LIES!
He did not reply. Though his eyes were upon her, what he saw was the wide sunwashed spaces of the West.
GO ON! WHY DON'T YOU LIE SOME MORE? BEG TO BE LET OFF?
I MIGHT, IF...
IF, WHAT?
BE CAREFUL WHAT YOU SAY, OR ELSE IT WILL GO HARD WITH YOU!
I WAS TRYING TO THINK OF A WORD YOU REMINDED ME OF. AS I WAS SAYING, I MIGHT IF YOU WAS A DECENT WOMAN.

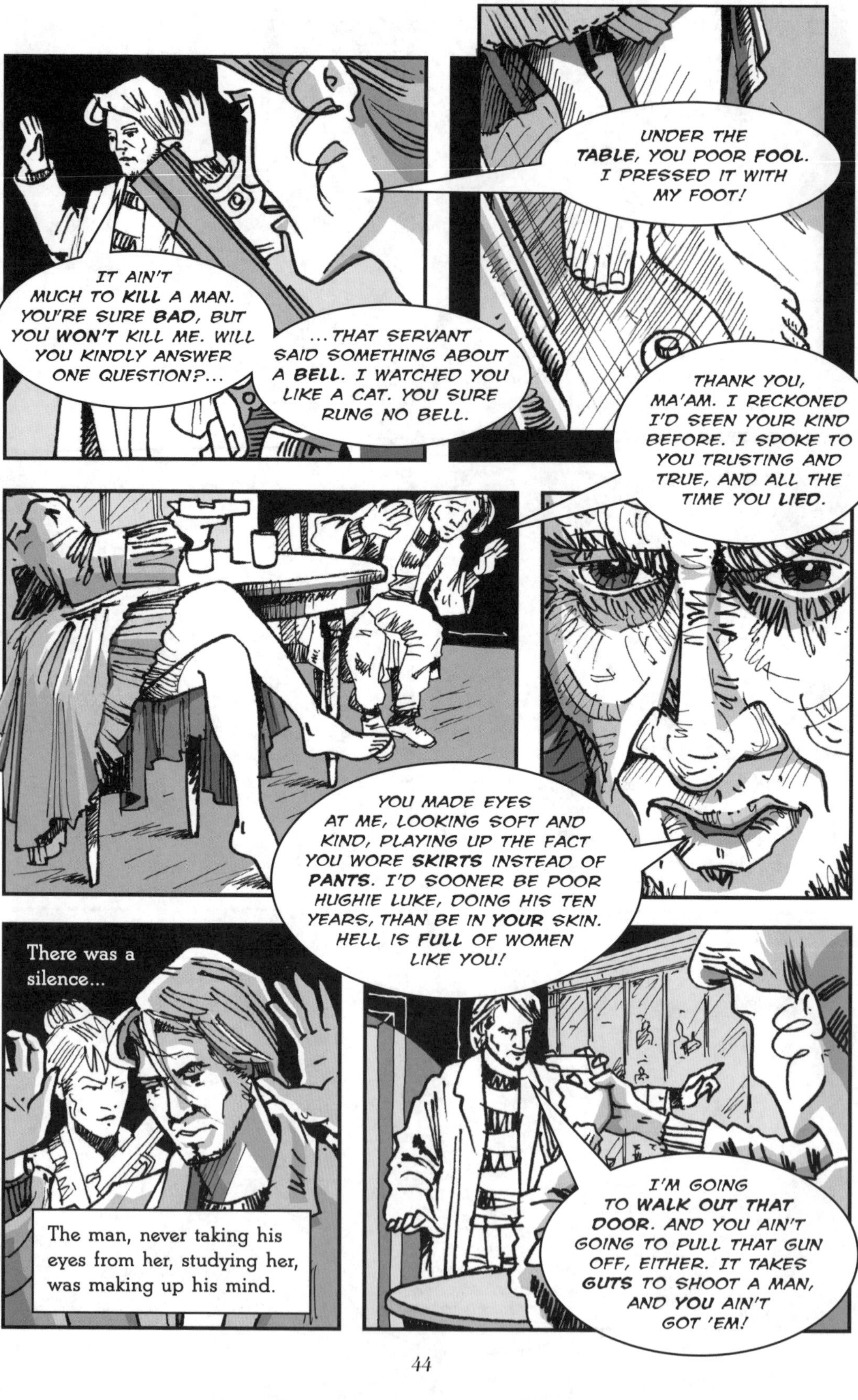
IT AIN'T MUCH TO KILL A MAN. YOU'RE SURE BAD, BUT YOU WON'T KILL ME. WILL YOU KINDLY ANSWER ONE QUESTION?...
...THAT SERVANT SAID SOMETHING ABOUT A BELL. I WATCHED YOU LIKE A CAT. YOU SURE RUNG NO BELL.
UNDER THE TABLE, YOU POOR FOOL. I PRESSED IT WITH MY FOOT!
THANK YOU, MA'AM. I RECKONED I'D SEEN YOUR KIND BEFORE. I SPOKE TO YOU TRUSTING AND TRUE, AND ALL THE TIME YOU LIED.
YOU MADE EYES AT ME, LOOKING SOFT AND KIND, PLAYING UP THE FACT YOU WORE SKIRTS INSTEAD OF PANTS. I'D SOONER BE POOR HUGHIE LUKE, DOING HIS TEN YEARS, THAN BE IN YOUR SKIN. HELL IS FULL OF WOMEN LIKE YOU!
There was a silence...
The man, never taking his eyes from her, studying her, was making up his mind.
I'M GOING TO WALK OUT THAT DOOR. AND YOU AIN'T GOING TO PULL THAT GUN OFF, EITHER. IT TAKES GUTS TO SHOOT A MAN, AND YOU AIN'T GOT 'EM!

The hammer rose halfway...

PULL *HARDER!* GO ON AND SPATTER MY *BRAINS* OUT ON THE *FLOOR!* SLAP A *HOLE* IN ME THE SIZE OF YOUR *FIST!* *THAT'S WHAT KILLING A MAN MEANS!*

The hammer lowered gently. Twice again, it came up halfway and was reluctantly eased down.

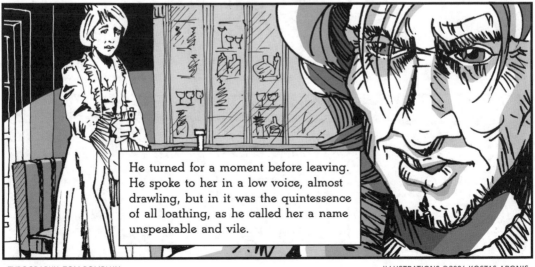

He turned for a moment before leaving. He spoke to her in a low voice, almost drawling, but in it was the quintessence of all loathing, as he called her a name unspeakable and vile.

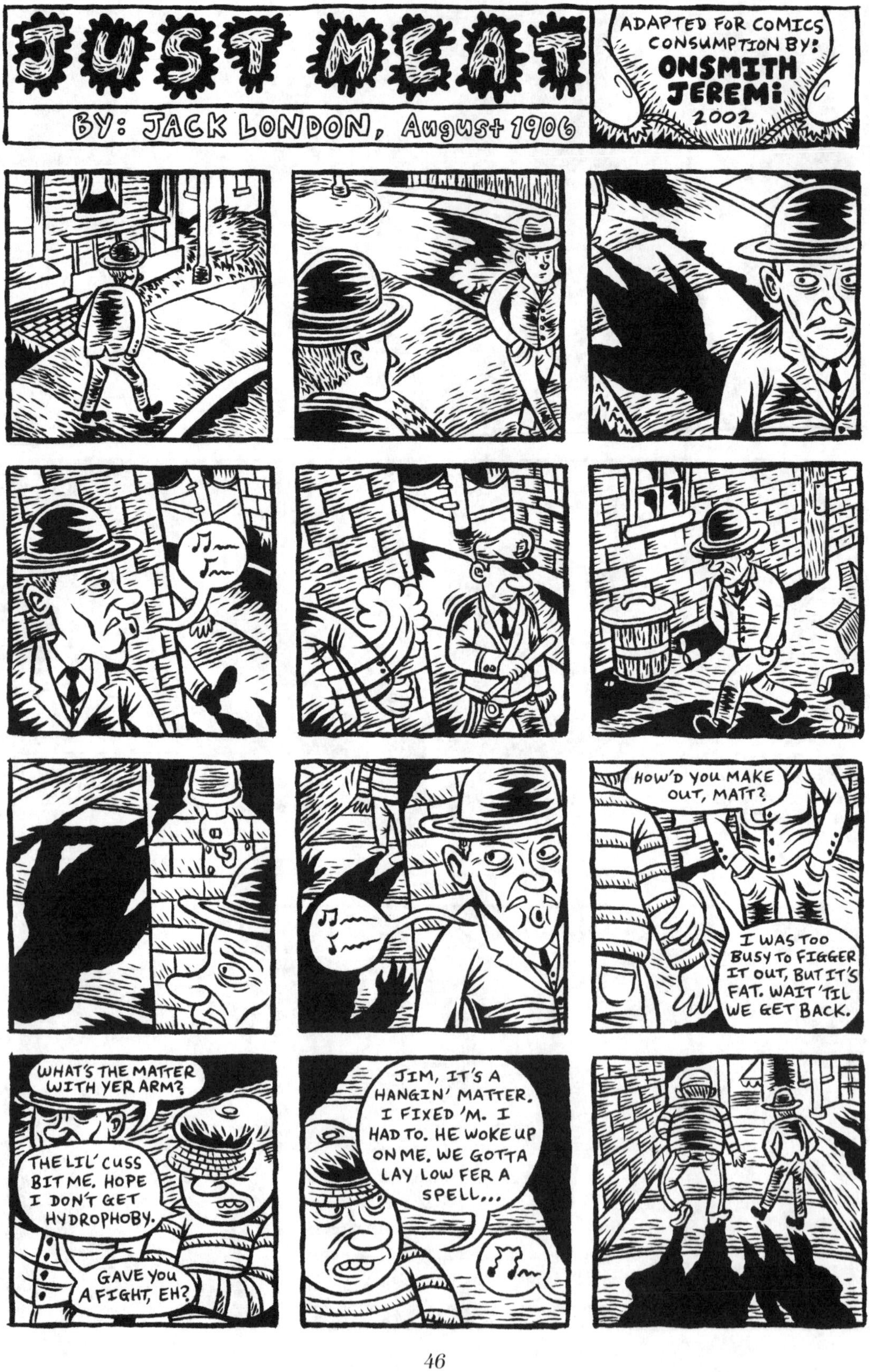
JUST MEAT
ADAPTED FOR COMICS CONSUMPTION BY:
ONSMITH JEREMI
2002
BY: JACK LONDON, August 1906
HOW'D YOU MAKE OUT, MATT?
I WAS TOO BUSY TO FIGGER IT OUT, BUT IT'S FAT. WAIT 'TIL WE GET BACK.
WHAT'S THE MATTER WITH YER ARM?
THE LIL' CUSS BIT ME. HOPE I DON'T GET HYDROPHOBY.
GAVE YOU A FIGHT, EH?
JIM, IT'S A HANGIN' MATTER. I FIXED 'M. I HAD TO. HE WOKE UP ON ME. WE GOTTA LAY LOW FER A SPELL...

OH MY!

THAT'S NOTHIN! I AIN'T BEGUN YET.

WAKE ME UP! I'M DREAMIN'!

WE'RE RICH MEN, MATT. WE'LL BE REGULAR SWELLS!

THE BUNCH IS WORTH FIFTY THOUSAN'...

A HUNDRED THOUSAN'!

WHAT IN HELL WAS HE DOIN' WITH 'EM ALL AT THE HOUSE? I'D A-THOUGHT HE'D KEEP 'EM IN A SAFE DOWN AT THE STORE.

THERE'S NO TELLIN'.

HE MIGHT A-BEN GETTIN' READY TO CHUCK HIS PARDNER...

HE MIGHT A-PULLED OUT IN THE MORNIN' FOR PARTS UNKNOWN IF WE HADN'T HAPPENED ALONG.

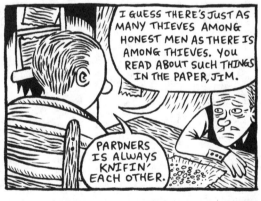
I GUESS THERE'S JUST AS MANY THIEVES AMONG HONEST MEN AS THERE IS AMONG THIEVES. YOU READ ABOUT SUCH THINGS IN THE PAPER, JIM.

PARDNERS IS ALWAYS KNIFIN' EACH OTHER.

I GUESS WE MIGHT AS WELL COUNT 'EM. YOU WATCH AN' SEE THAT IT'S SQUARE, BECAUSE YOU AN' ME GOTTA BE ON THE SQUARE, JIM. UNDERSTAND?

AIN'T WE ALWAYS BEEN SQUARE?

IT DON'T COST NOTHIN' BEIN' SQUARE IN HARD TIMES. IT'S BEIN' SQUARE IN PROSPERITY THAT COUNTS.

WE'RE PROSPEROUS NOW, AN' WE'VE GOTTA BE BUSINESS MEN~ HONEST BUSINESS MEN, UNDERSTAND?

THAT'S THE TALK FOR ME!

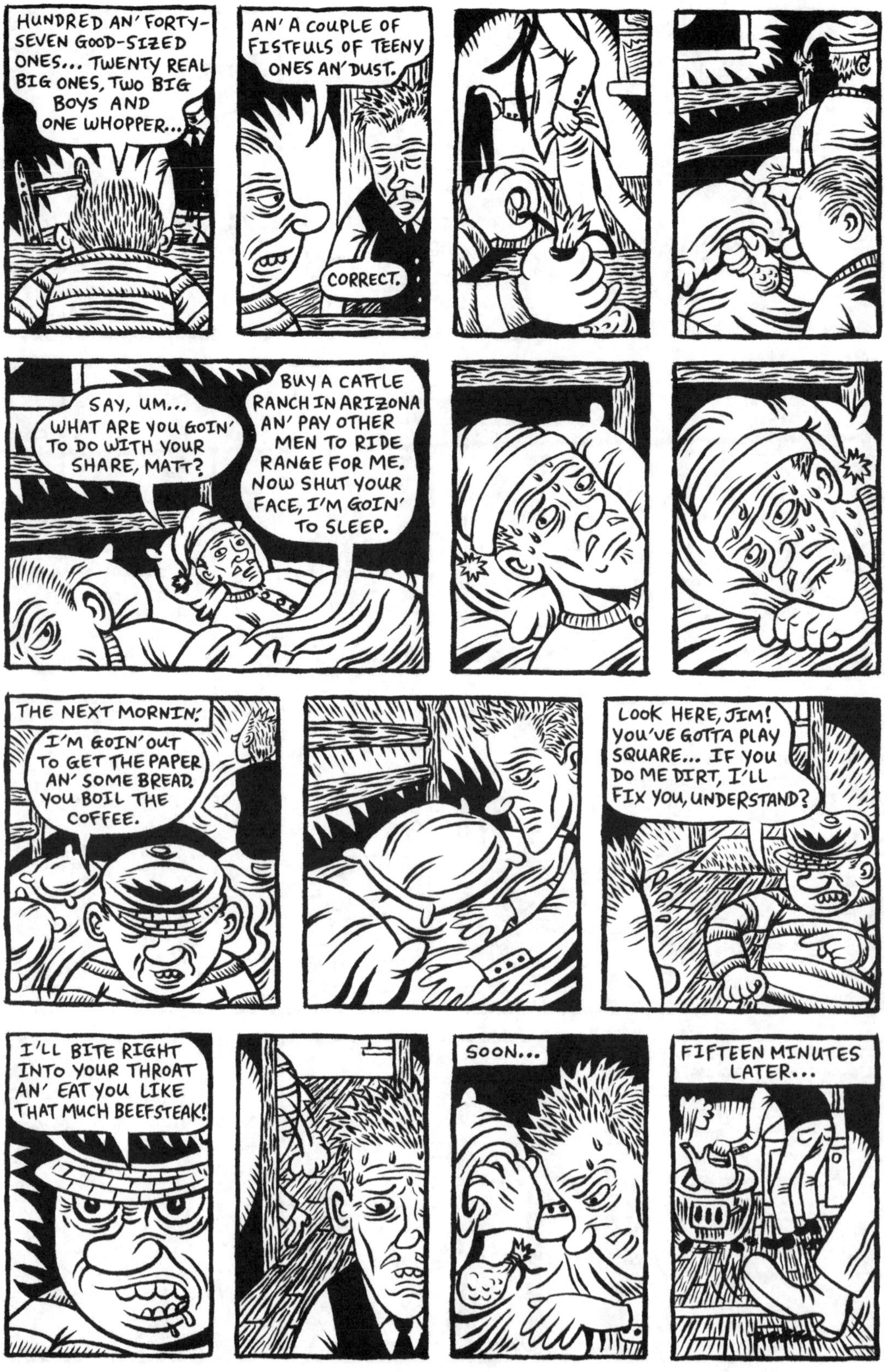
HUNDRED AN' FORTY-SEVEN GOOD-SIZED ONES... TWENTY REAL BIG ONES, TWO BIG BOYS AND ONE WHOPPER...
AN' A COUPLE OF FISTFULS OF TEENY ONES AN' DUST.
CORRECT.
SAY, UM... WHAT ARE YOU GOIN' TO DO WITH YOUR SHARE, MATT?
BUY A CATTLE RANCH IN ARIZONA AN' PAY OTHER MEN TO RIDE RANGE FOR ME. NOW SHUT YOUR FACE, I'M GOIN' TO SLEEP.
THE NEXT MORNIN'
I'M GOIN' OUT TO GET THE PAPER AN' SOME BREAD. YOU BOIL THE COFFEE.
LOOK HERE, JIM! YOU'VE GOTTA PLAY SQUARE... IF YOU DO ME DIRT, I'LL FIX YOU, UNDERSTAND?
I'LL BITE RIGHT INTO YOUR THROAT AN' EAT YOU LIKE THAT MUCH BEEFSTEAK!
SOON...
FIFTEEN MINUTES LATER...

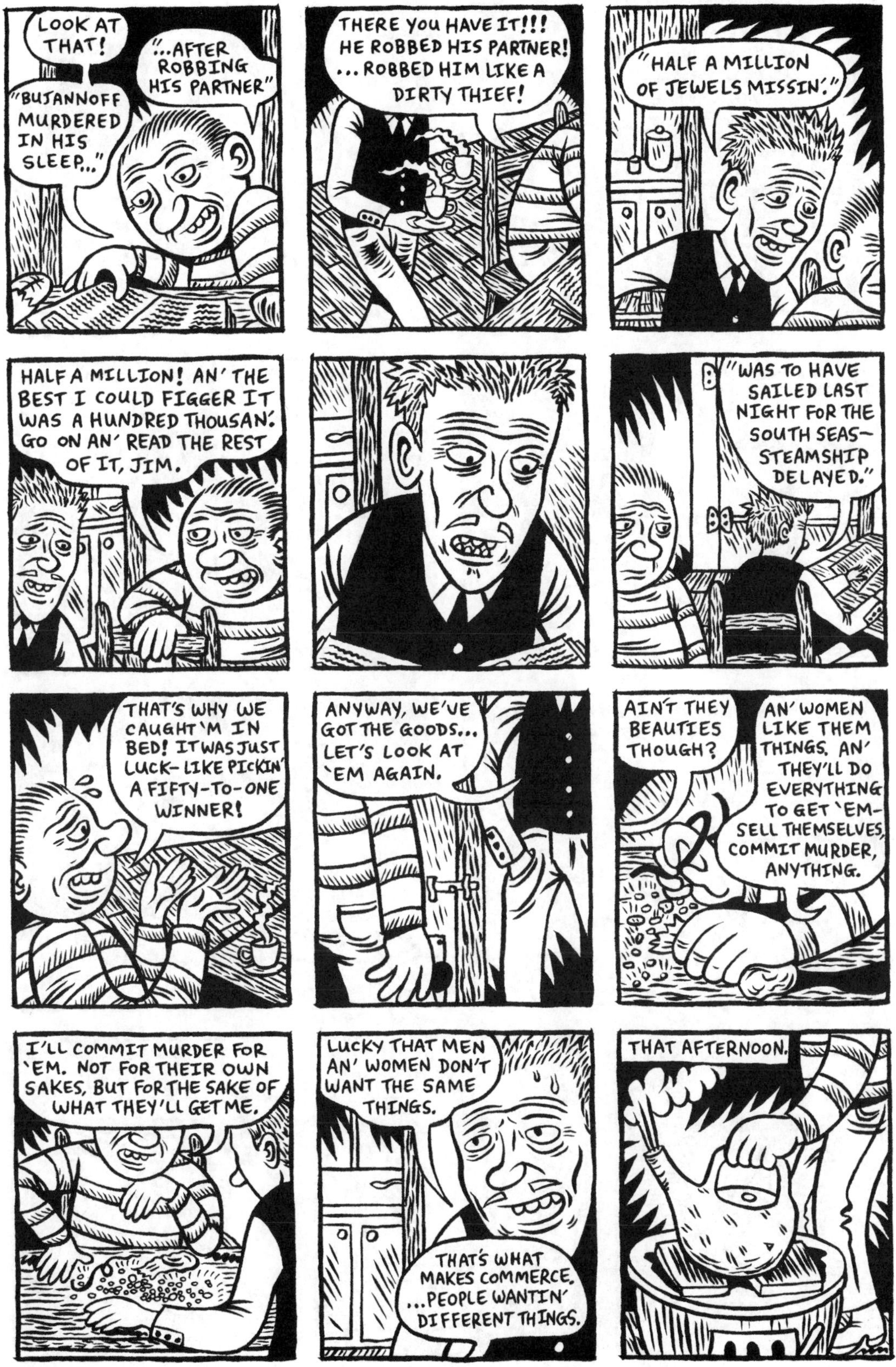
LOOK AT THAT!
"BUJANNOFF MURDERED IN HIS SLEEP..."
"...AFTER ROBBING HIS PARTNER"
THERE YOU HAVE IT!!! HE ROBBED HIS PARTNER! ...ROBBED HIM LIKE A DIRTY THIEF!
"HALF A MILLION OF JEWELS MISSIN'."
HALF A MILLION! AN' THE BEST I COULD FIGGER IT WAS A HUNDRED THOUSAN'. GO ON AN' READ THE REST OF IT, JIM.
"WAS TO HAVE SAILED LAST NIGHT FOR THE SOUTH SEAS— STEAMSHIP DELAYED."
THAT'S WHY WE CAUGHT 'M IN BED! IT WAS JUST LUCK- LIKE PICKIN' A FIFTY-TO-ONE WINNER!
ANYWAY, WE'VE GOT THE GOODS... LET'S LOOK AT 'EM AGAIN.
AIN'T THEY BEAUTIES THOUGH?
AN' WOMEN LIKE THEM THINGS. AN' THEY'LL DO EVERYTHING TO GET 'EM- SELL THEMSELVES, COMMIT MURDER, ANYTHING.
I'LL COMMIT MURDER FOR 'EM. NOT FOR THEIR OWN SAKES, BUT FOR THE SAKE OF WHAT THEY'LL GET ME.
LUCKY THAT MEN AN' WOMEN DON'T WANT THE SAME THINGS.
THAT'S WHAT MAKES COMMERCE. ...PEOPLE WANTIN' DIFFERENT THINGS.
THAT AFTERNOON.

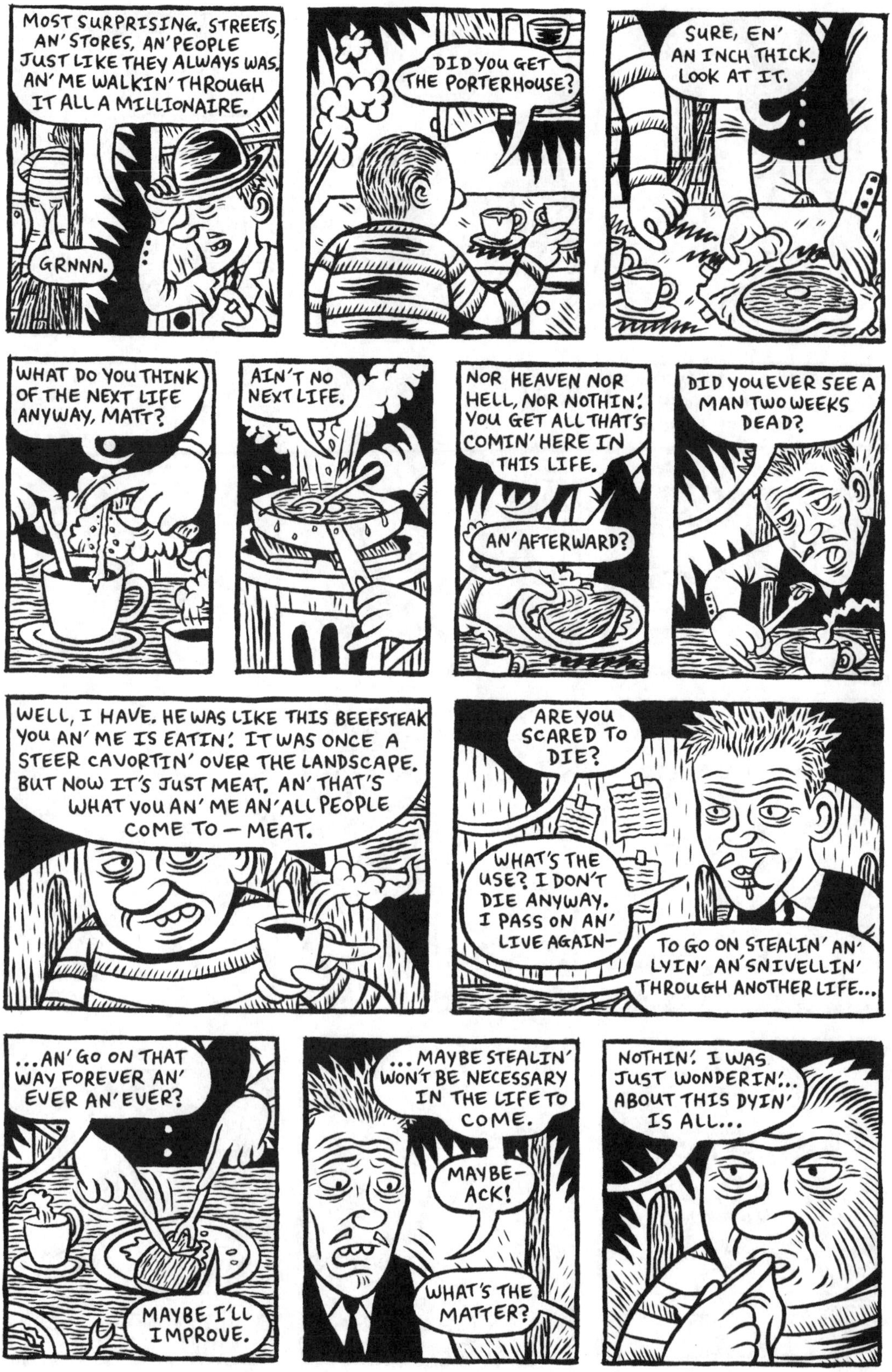
MOST SURPRISING. STREETS, AN' STORES, AN' PEOPLE JUST LIKE THEY ALWAYS WAS. AN' ME WALKIN' THROUGH IT ALL A MILLIONAIRE.
GRNNN.
DID YOU GET THE PORTERHOUSE?
SURE, EN' AN INCH THICK. LOOK AT IT.
WHAT DO YOU THINK OF THE NEXT LIFE ANYWAY, MATT?
AIN'T NO NEXT LIFE.
NOR HEAVEN NOR HELL, NOR NOTHIN'. YOU GET ALL THAT'S COMIN' HERE IN THIS LIFE.
AN' AFTERWARD?
DID YOU EVER SEE A MAN TWO WEEKS DEAD?
WELL, I HAVE. HE WAS LIKE THIS BEEFSTEAK YOU AN' ME IS EATIN'. IT WAS ONCE A STEER CAVORTIN' OVER THE LANDSCAPE. BUT NOW IT'S JUST MEAT. AN' THAT'S WHAT YOU AN' ME AN' ALL PEOPLE COME TO — MEAT.
ARE YOU SCARED TO DIE?
WHAT'S THE USE? I DON'T DIE ANYWAY. I PASS ON AN' LIVE AGAIN–
TO GO ON STEALIN' AN' LYIN' AN' SNIVELLIN' THROUGH ANOTHER LIFE...
...AN' GO ON THAT WAY FOREVER AN' EVER AN' EVER?
MAYBE I'LL IMPROVE.
...MAYBE STEALIN' WON'T BE NECESSARY IN THE LIFE TO COME.
MAYBE– ACK!
WHAT'S THE MATTER?
NOTHIN'. I WAS JUST WONDERIN'... ABOUT THIS DYIN' IS ALL...

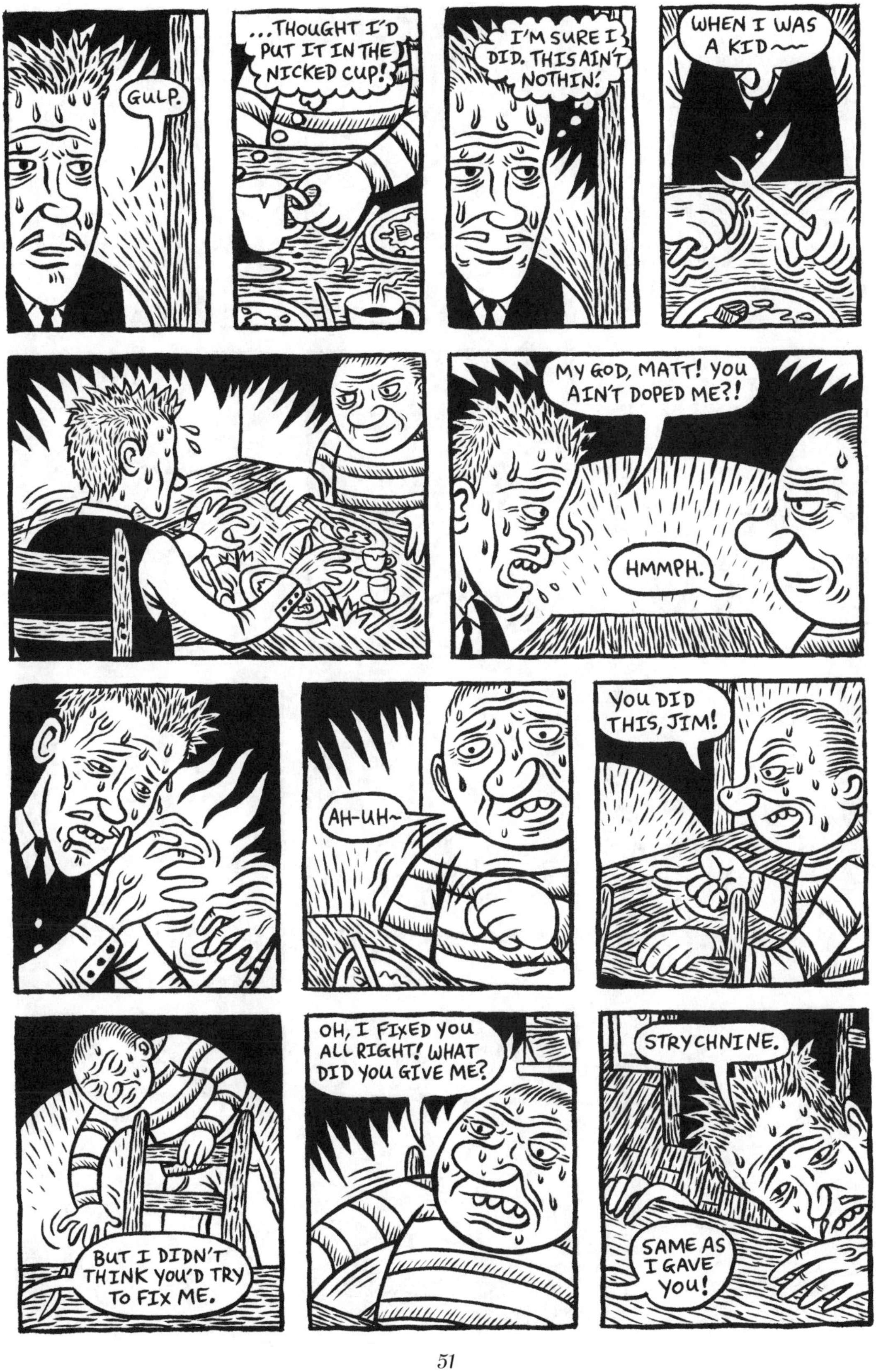
GULP.
...THOUGHT I'D PUT IT IN THE NICKED CUP!
I'M SURE I DID. THIS AIN'T NOTHIN'.
WHEN I WAS A KID~~
MY GOD, MATT! YOU AIN'T DOPED ME?!
HMMPH.
AH-UH~
YOU DID THIS, JIM!
BUT I DIDN'T THINK YOU'D TRY TO FIX ME.
OH, I FIXED YOU ALL RIGHT! WHAT DID YOU GIVE ME?
STRYCHNINE.
SAME AS I GAVE YOU!

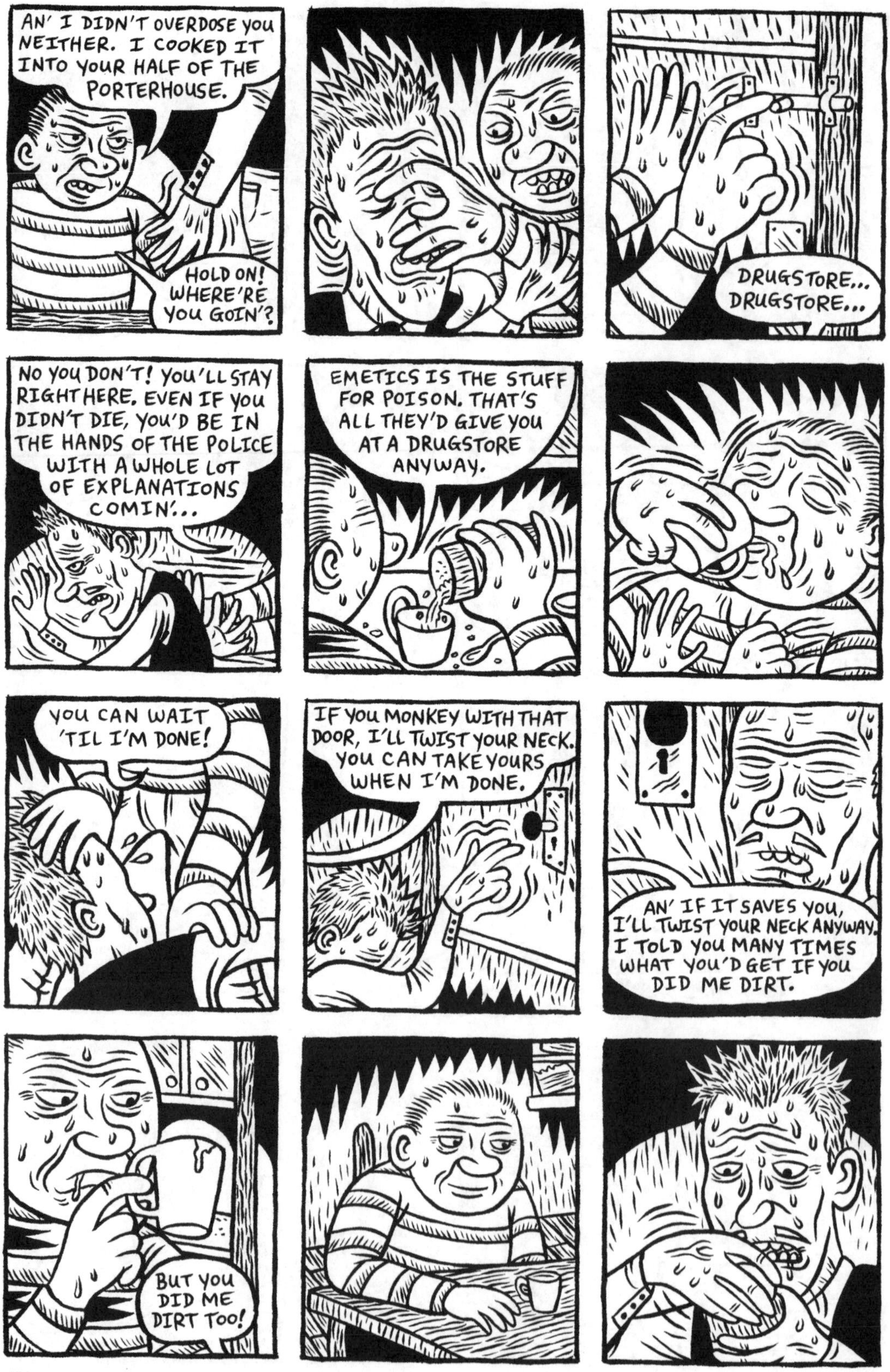
AN' I DIDN'T OVERDOSE YOU NEITHER. I COOKED IT INTO YOUR HALF OF THE PORTERHOUSE.
HOLD ON! WHERE'RE YOU GOIN'?
DRUGSTORE... DRUGSTORE...
NO YOU DON'T! YOU'LL STAY RIGHT HERE. EVEN IF YOU DIDN'T DIE, YOU'D BE IN THE HANDS OF THE POLICE WITH A WHOLE LOT OF EXPLANATIONS COMIN'...
EMETICS IS THE STUFF FOR POISON. THAT'S ALL THEY'D GIVE YOU AT A DRUGSTORE ANYWAY.
YOU CAN WAIT 'TIL I'M DONE!
IF YOU MONKEY WITH THAT DOOR, I'LL TWIST YOUR NECK. YOU CAN TAKE YOURS WHEN I'M DONE.
AN' IF IT SAVES YOU, I'LL TWIST YOUR NECK ANYWAY. I TOLD YOU MANY TIMES WHAT YOU'D GET IF YOU DID ME DIRT.
BUT YOU DID ME DIRT TOO!

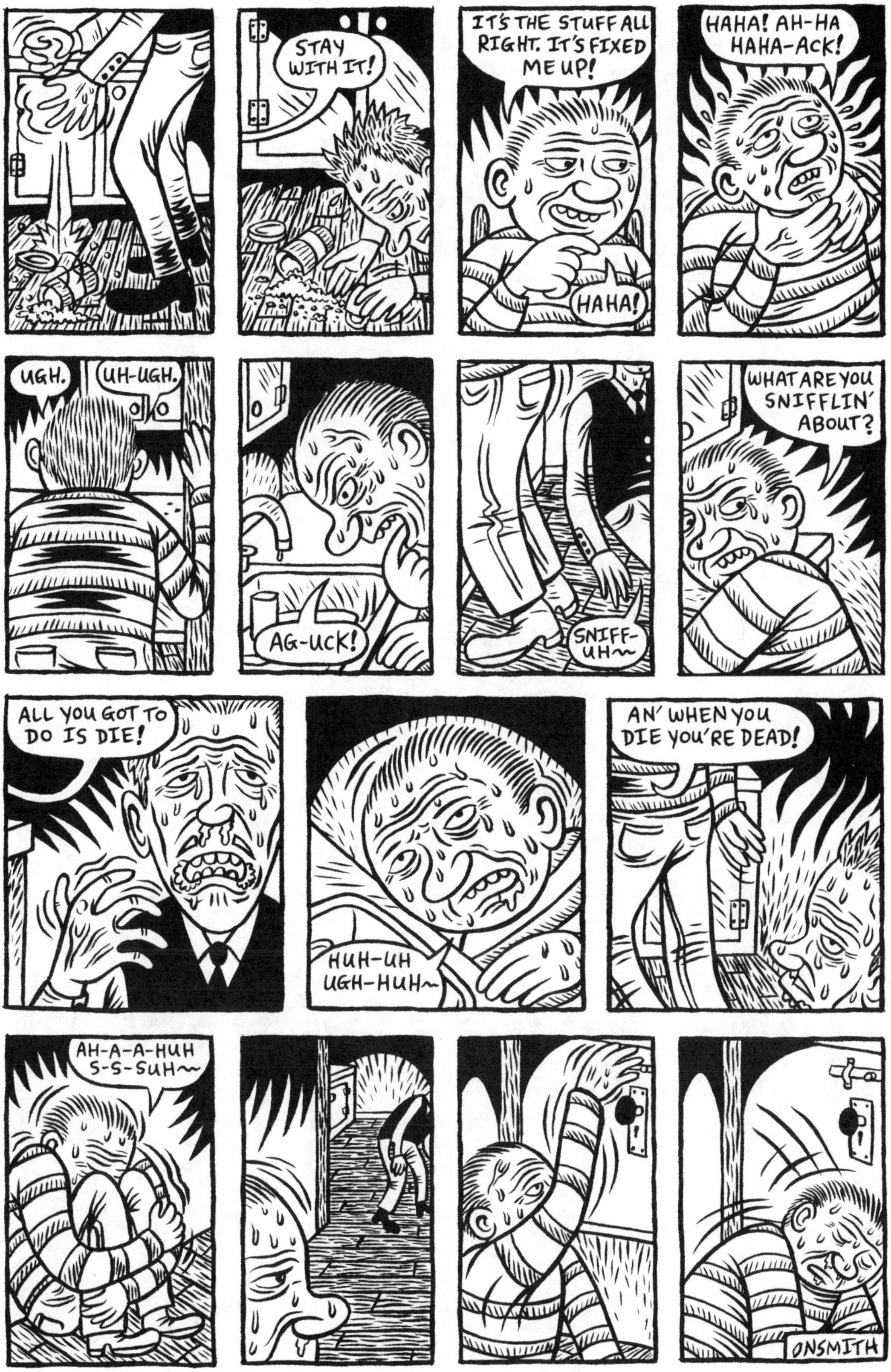
STAY WITH IT!
IT'S THE STUFF ALL RIGHT. IT'S FIXED ME UP!
HAHA!
HAHA! AH-HA HAHA-ACK!
UGH.
UH-UGH.
AG-UCK!
SNIFF-UH~
WHAT ARE YOU SNIFFLIN' ABOUT?
ALL YOU GOT TO DO IS DIE!
HUH-UH UGH-HUH~
AN' WHEN YOU DIE YOU'RE DEAD!
AH-A-A-HUH S-S-SUH~
ONSMITH

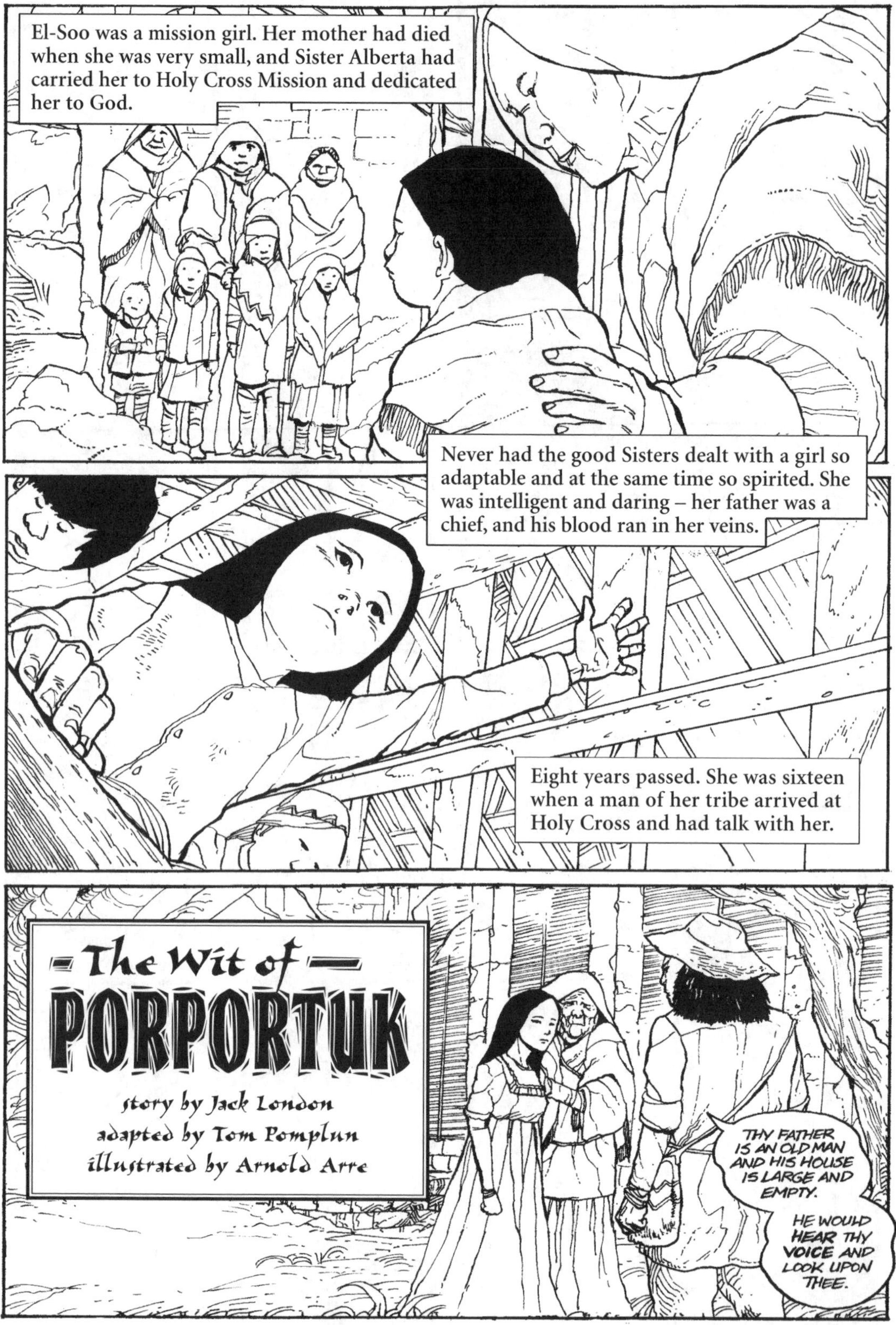
El-Soo was a mission girl. Her mother had died when she was very small, and Sister Alberta had carried her to Holy Cross Mission and dedicated her to God.
Never had the good Sisters dealt with a girl so adaptable and at the same time so spirited. She was intelligent and daring – her father was a chief, and his blood ran in her veins.
Eight years passed. She was sixteen when a man of her tribe arrived at Holy Cross and had talk with her.
The Wit of PORPORTUK
story by Jack London
adapted by Tom Pomplun
illustrated by Arnold Arre
THY FATHER IS AN OLD MAN AND HIS HOUSE IS LARGE AND EMPTY.
HE WOULD HEAR THY VOICE AND LOOK UPON THEE.

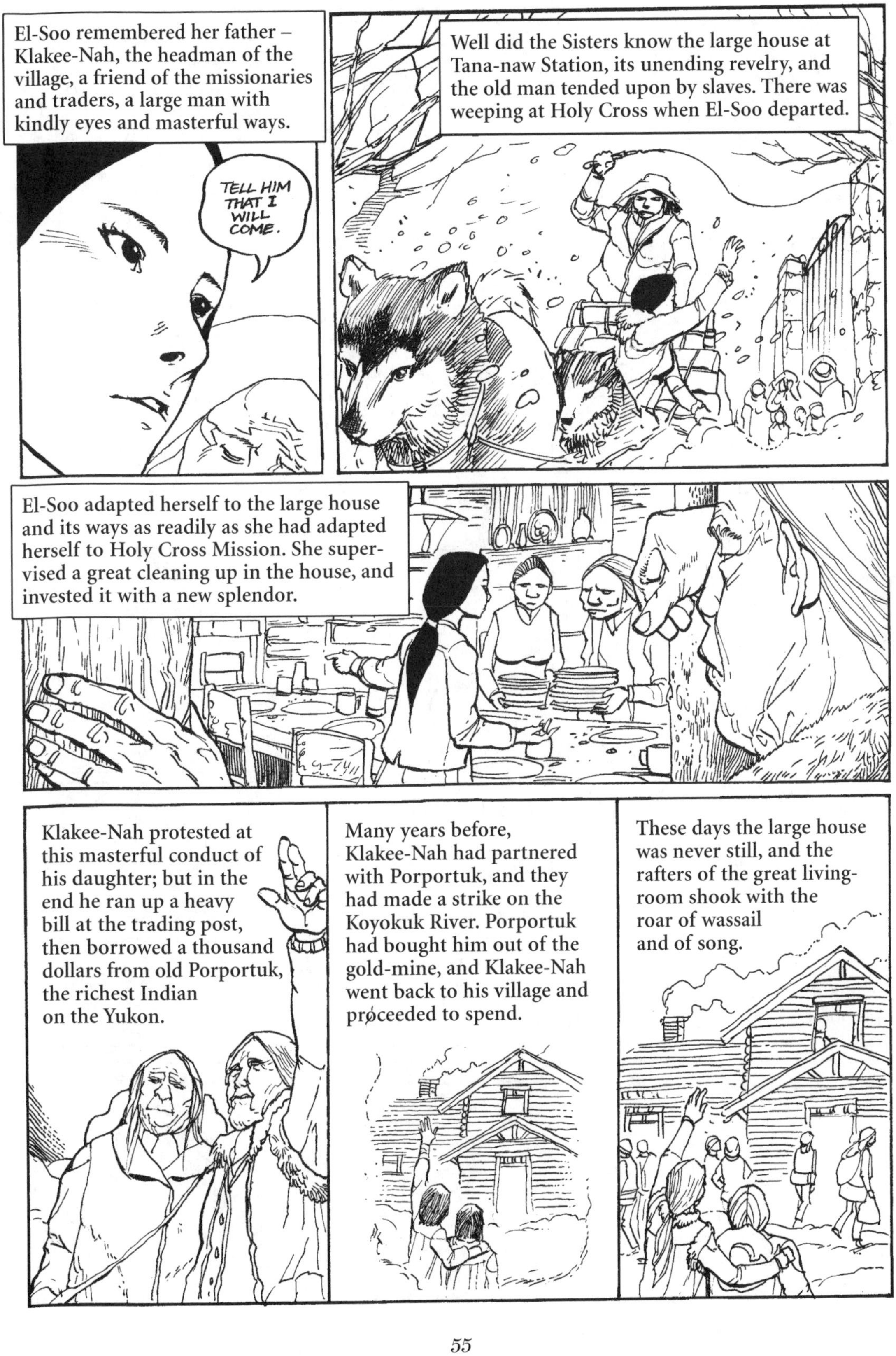
El-Soo remembered her father – Klakee-Nah, the headman of the village, a friend of the missionaries and traders, a large man with kindly eyes and masterful ways.
TELL HIM THAT I WILL COME.
Well did the Sisters know the large house at Tana-naw Station, its unending revelry, and the old man tended upon by slaves. There was weeping at Holy Cross when El-Soo departed.
El-Soo adapted herself to the large house and its ways as readily as she had adapted herself to Holy Cross Mission. She supervised a great cleaning up in the house, and invested it with a new splendor.
Klakee-Nah protested at this masterful conduct of his daughter; but in the end he ran up a heavy bill at the trading post, then borrowed a thousand dollars from old Porportuk, the richest Indian on the Yukon.
Many years before, Klakee-Nah had partnered with Porportuk, and they had made a strike on the Koyokuk River. Porportuk had bought him out of the gold-mine, and Klakee-Nah went back to his village and proceeded to spend.
These days the large house was never still, and the rafters of the great living-room shook with the roar of wassail and of song.

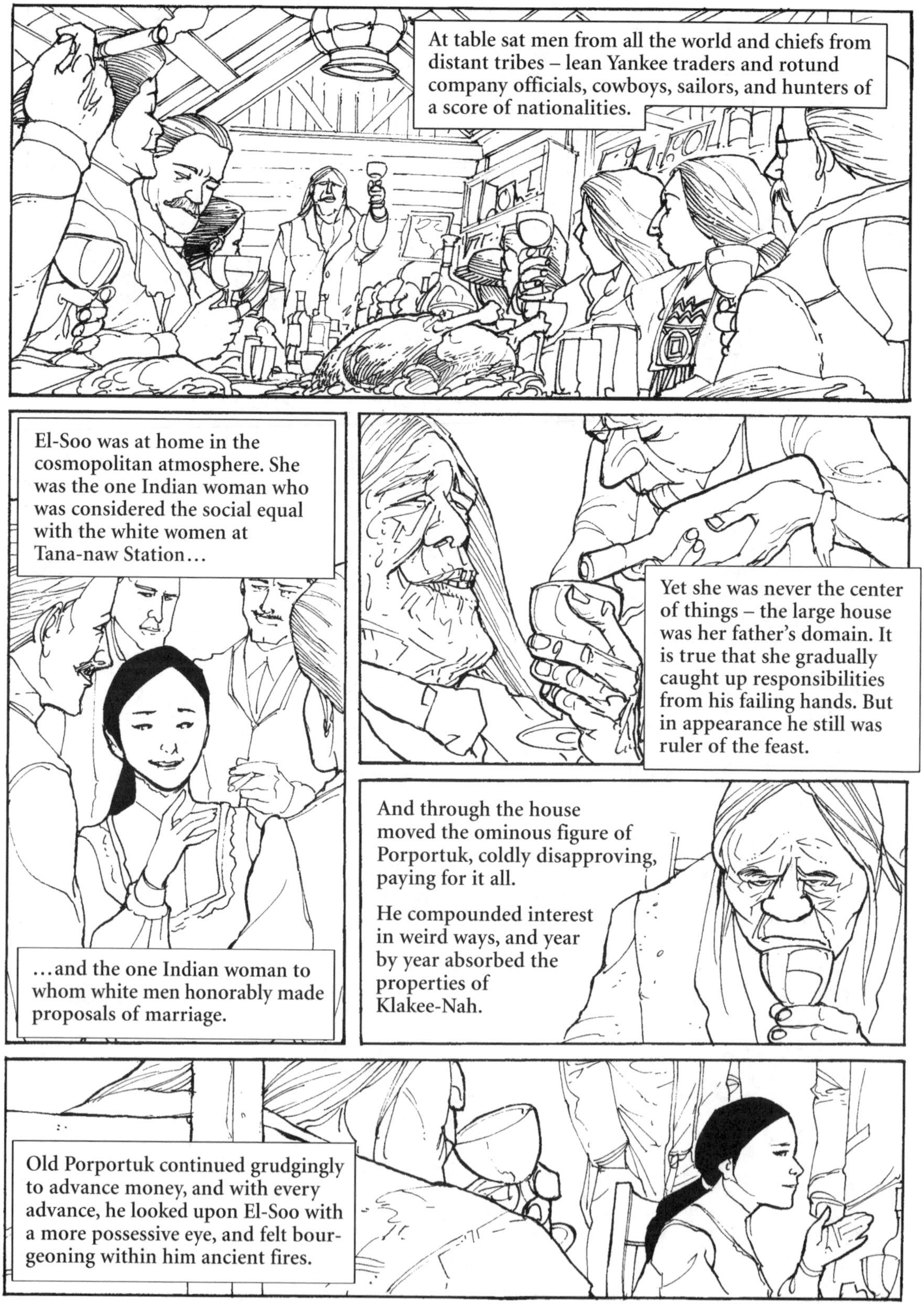
At table sat men from all the world and chiefs from distant tribes – lean Yankee traders and rotund company officials, cowboys, sailors, and hunters of a score of nationalities.
El-Soo was at home in the cosmopolitan atmosphere. She was the one Indian woman who was considered the social equal with the white women at Tana-naw Station…
…and the one Indian woman to whom white men honorably made proposals of marriage.
Yet she was never the center of things – the large house was her father's domain. It is true that she gradually caught up responsibilities from his failing hands. But in appearance he still was ruler of the feast.
And through the house moved the ominous figure of Porportuk, coldly disapproving, paying for it all.
He compounded interest in weird ways, and year by year absorbed the properties of Klakee-Nah.
Old Porportuk continued grudgingly to advance money, and with every advance, he looked upon El-Soo with a more possessive eye, and felt bourgeoning within him ancient fires.

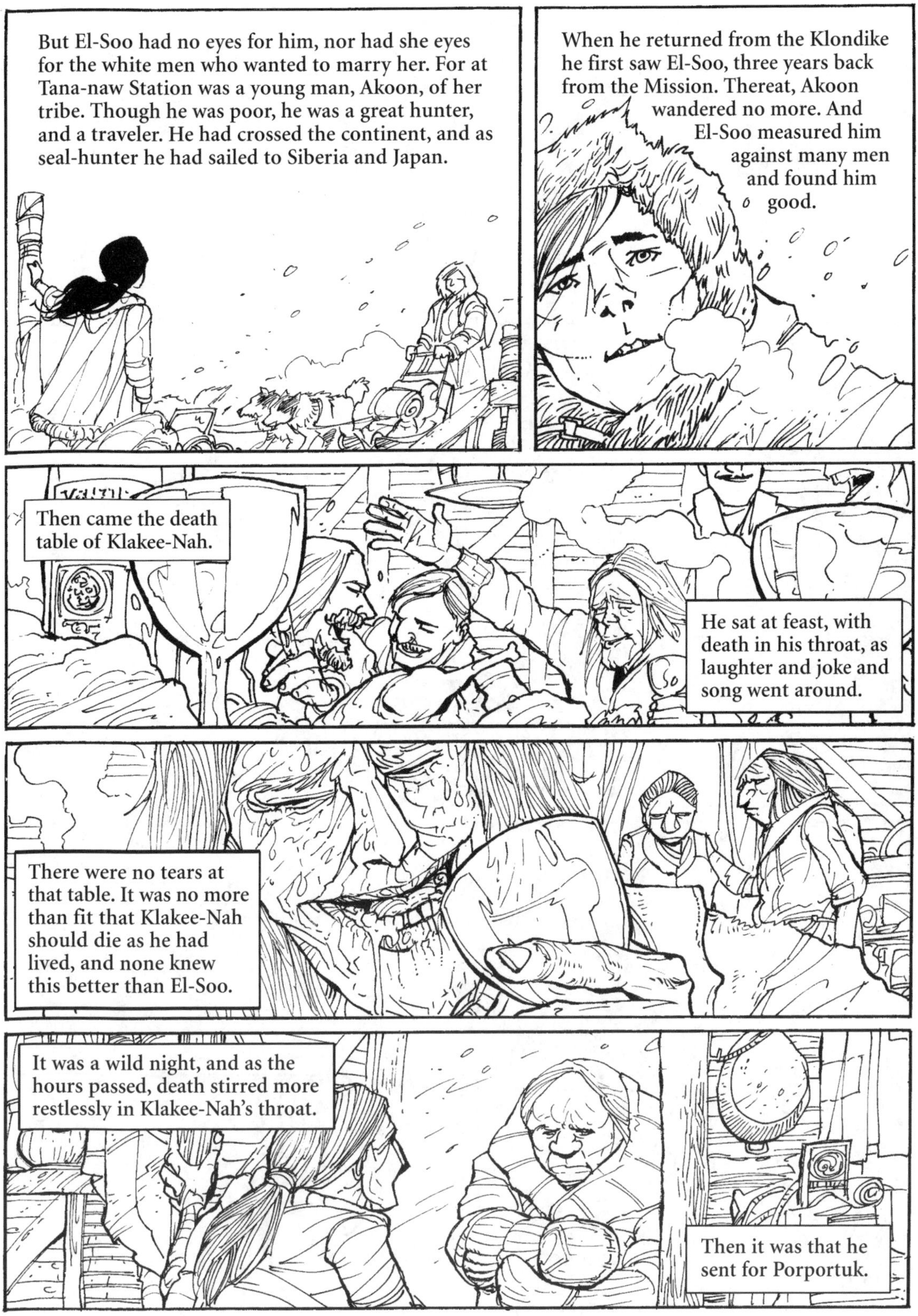
But El-Soo had no eyes for him, nor had she eyes for the white men who wanted to marry her. For at Tana-naw Station was a young man, Akoon, of her tribe. Though he was poor, he was a great hunter, and a traveler. He had crossed the continent, and as seal-hunter he had sailed to Siberia and Japan.
When he returned from the Klondike he first saw El-Soo, three years back from the Mission. Thereat, Akoon wandered no more. And El-Soo measured him against many men and found him good.
Then came the death table of Klakee-Nah.
He sat at feast, with death in his throat, as laughter and joke and song went around.
There were no tears at that table. It was no more than fit that Klakee-Nah should die as he had lived, and none knew this better than El-Soo.
It was a wild night, and as the hours passed, death stirred more restlessly in Klakee-Nah's throat.
Then it was that he sent for Porportuk.

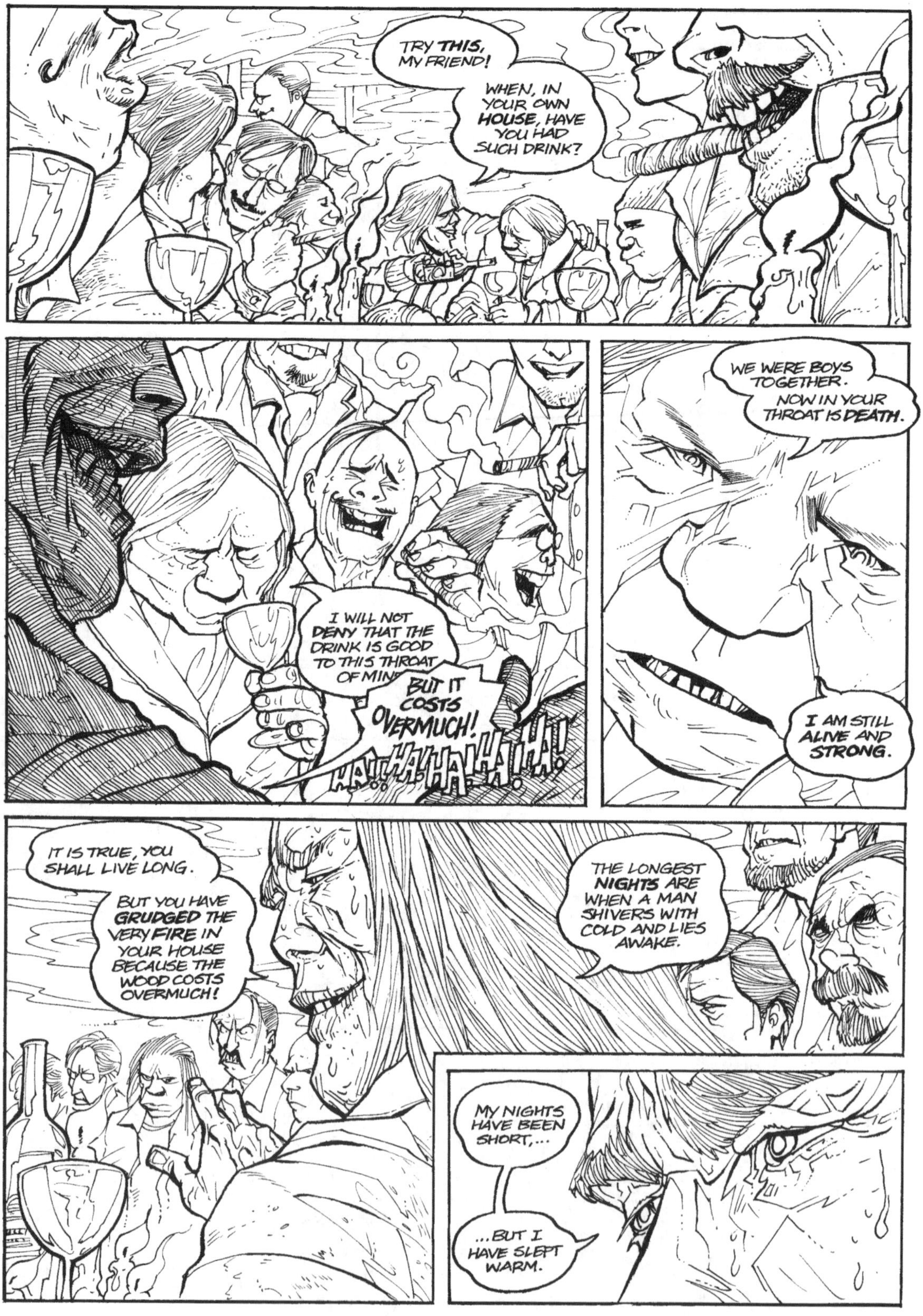
TRY THIS, MY FRIEND!
WHEN, IN YOUR OWN HOUSE, HAVE YOU HAD SUCH DRINK?
I WILL NOT DENY THAT THE DRINK IS GOOD TO THIS THROAT OF MINE,
BUT IT COSTS OVERMUCH!
HA! HA! HA! HA! HA!
WE WERE BOYS TOGETHER.
NOW IN YOUR THROAT IS DEATH.
I AM STILL ALIVE AND STRONG.
IT IS TRUE, YOU SHALL LIVE LONG.
BUT YOU HAVE GRUDGED THE VERY FIRE IN YOUR HOUSE BECAUSE THE WOOD COSTS OVERMUCH!
THE LONGEST NIGHTS ARE WHEN A MAN SHIVERS WITH COLD AND LIES AWAKE.
MY NIGHTS HAVE BEEN SHORT,...
...BUT I HAVE SLEPT WARM.

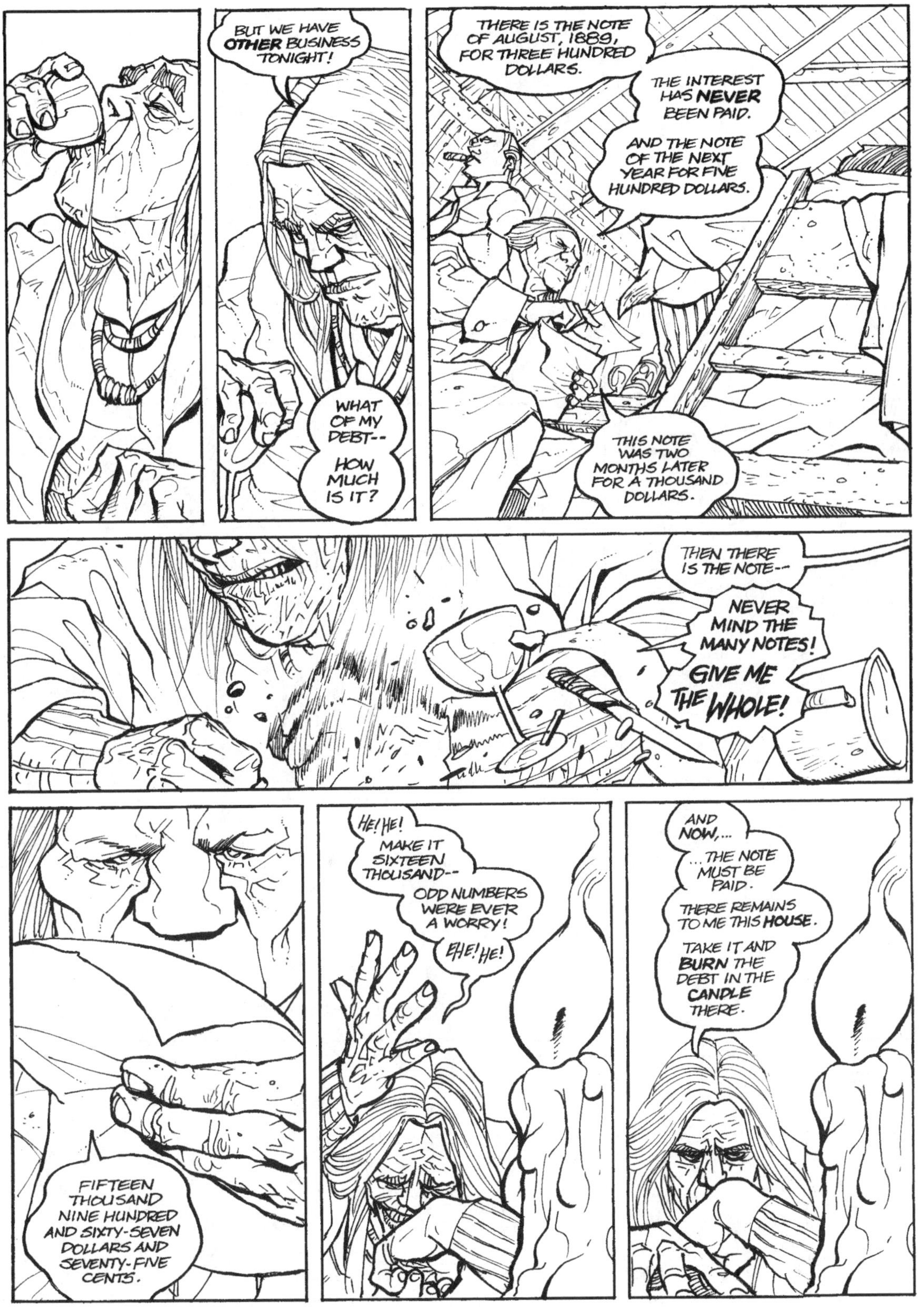
BUT WE HAVE OTHER BUSINESS TONIGHT!
WHAT OF MY DEBT--
HOW MUCH IS IT?
THERE IS THE NOTE OF AUGUST, 1889, FOR THREE HUNDRED DOLLARS.
THE INTEREST HAS NEVER BEEN PAID.
AND THE NOTE OF THE NEXT YEAR FOR FIVE HUNDRED DOLLARS.
THIS NOTE WAS TWO MONTHS LATER FOR A THOUSAND DOLLARS.
THEN THERE IS THE NOTE--
NEVER MIND THE MANY NOTES!
GIVE ME THE WHOLE!
FIFTEEN THOUSAND NINE HUNDRED AND SIXTY-SEVEN DOLLARS AND SEVENTY-FIVE CENTS.
HE! HE!
MAKE IT SIXTEEN THOUSAND--
ODD NUMBERS WERE EVER A WORRY!
EHE! HE!
AND NOW,...
...THE NOTE MUST BE PAID.
THERE REMAINS TO ME THIS HOUSE.
TAKE IT AND BURN THE DEBT IN THE CANDLE THERE.

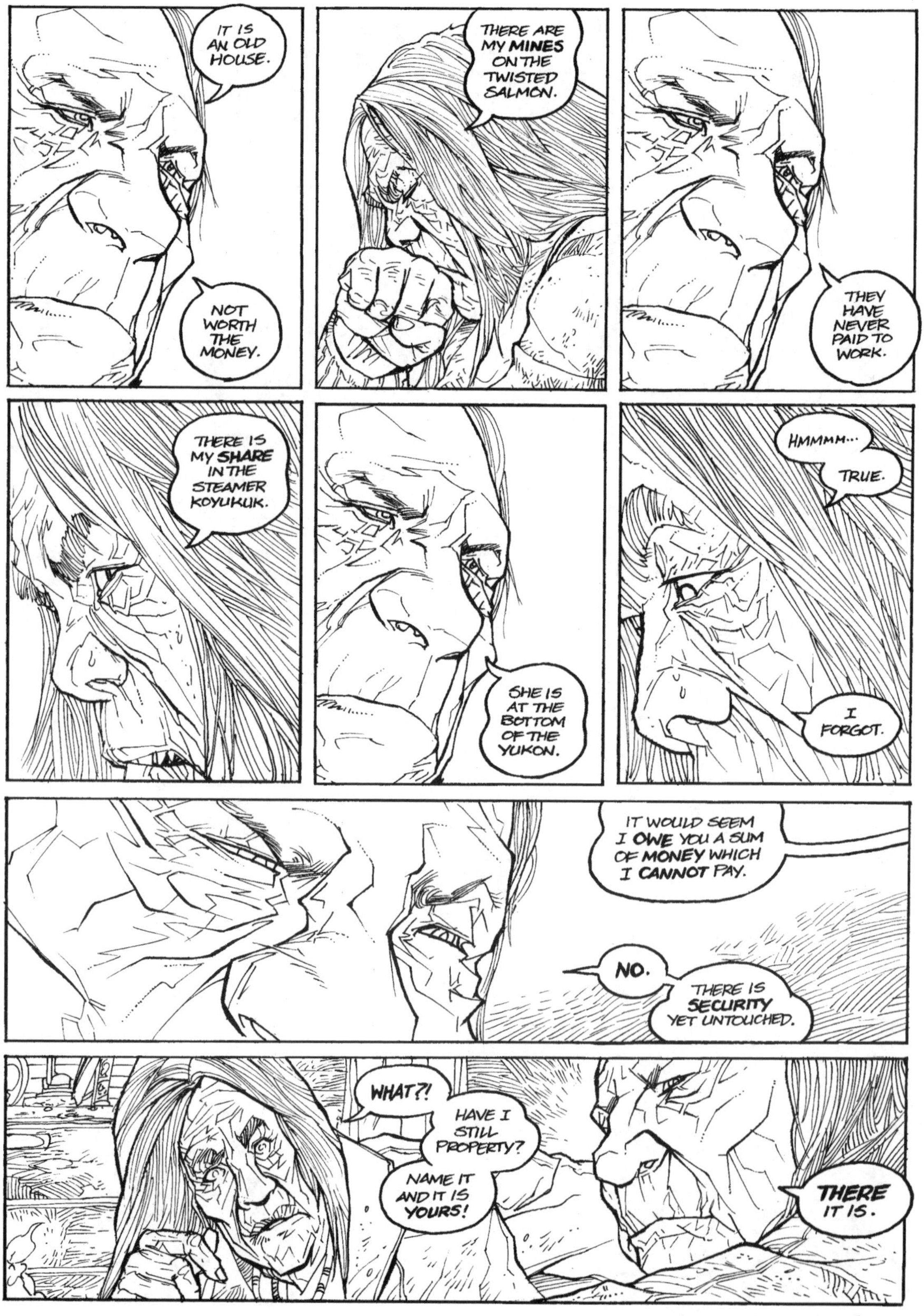
IT IS AN OLD HOUSE.
NOT WORTH THE MONEY.
THERE ARE MY MINES ON THE TWISTED SALMON.
THEY HAVE NEVER PAID TO WORK.
THERE IS MY SHARE IN THE STEAMER KOYUKUK.
SHE IS AT THE BOTTOM OF THE YUKON.
HMMMM...
TRUE.
I FORGOT.
IT WOULD SEEM I OWE YOU A SUM OF MONEY WHICH I CANNOT PAY.
NO.
THERE IS SECURITY YET UNTOUCHED.
WHAT?!
HAVE I STILL PROPERTY?
NAME IT AND IT IS YOURS!
THERE IT IS.

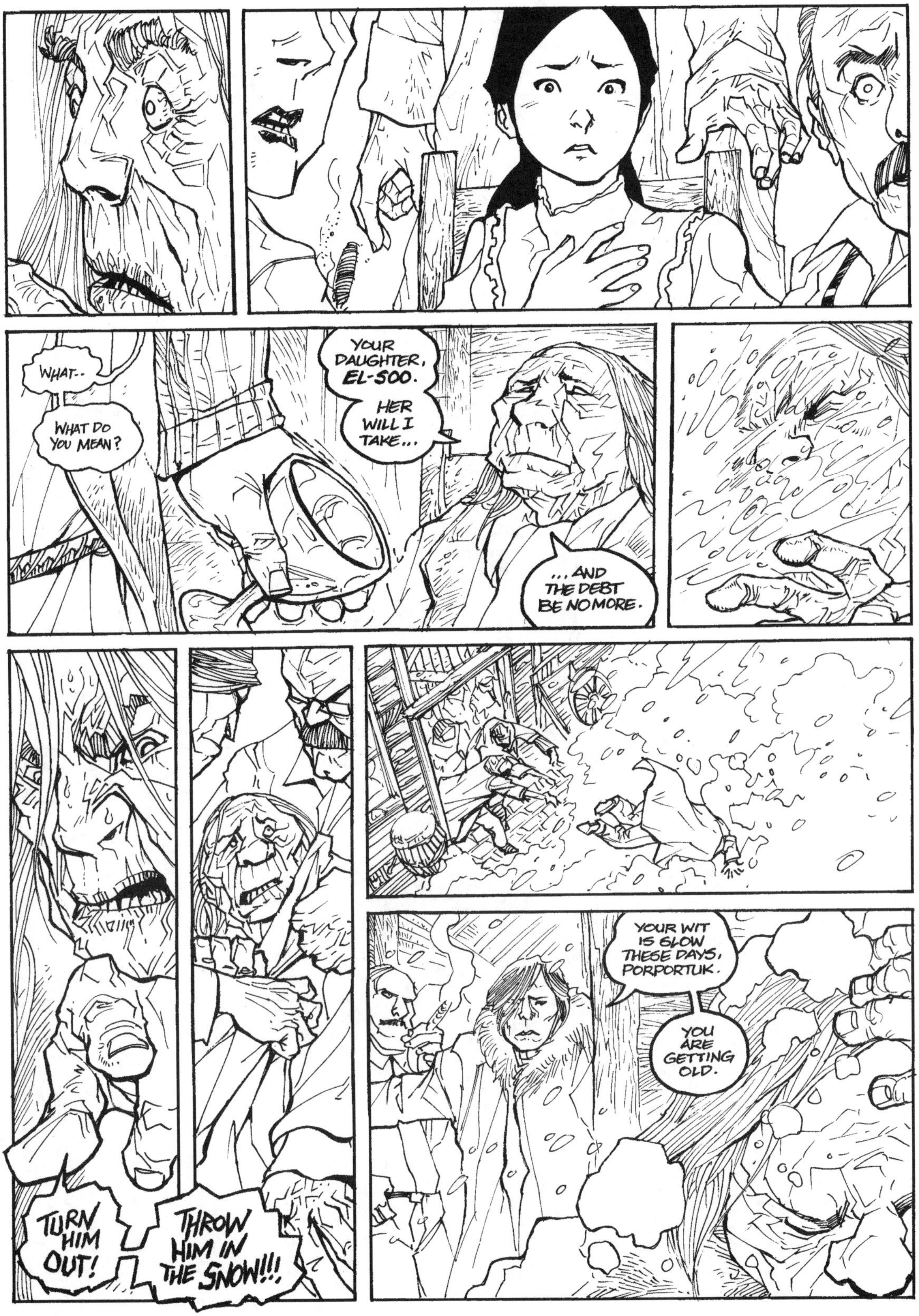
WHAT..
WHAT DO YOU MEAN?
YOUR DAUGHTER, EL-SOO.
HER WILL I TAKE...
...AND THE DEBT BE NO MORE.
TURN HIM OUT!
THROW HIM IN THE SNOW!!!
YOUR WIT IS SLOW THESE DAYS, PORPORTUK.
YOU ARE GETTING OLD.

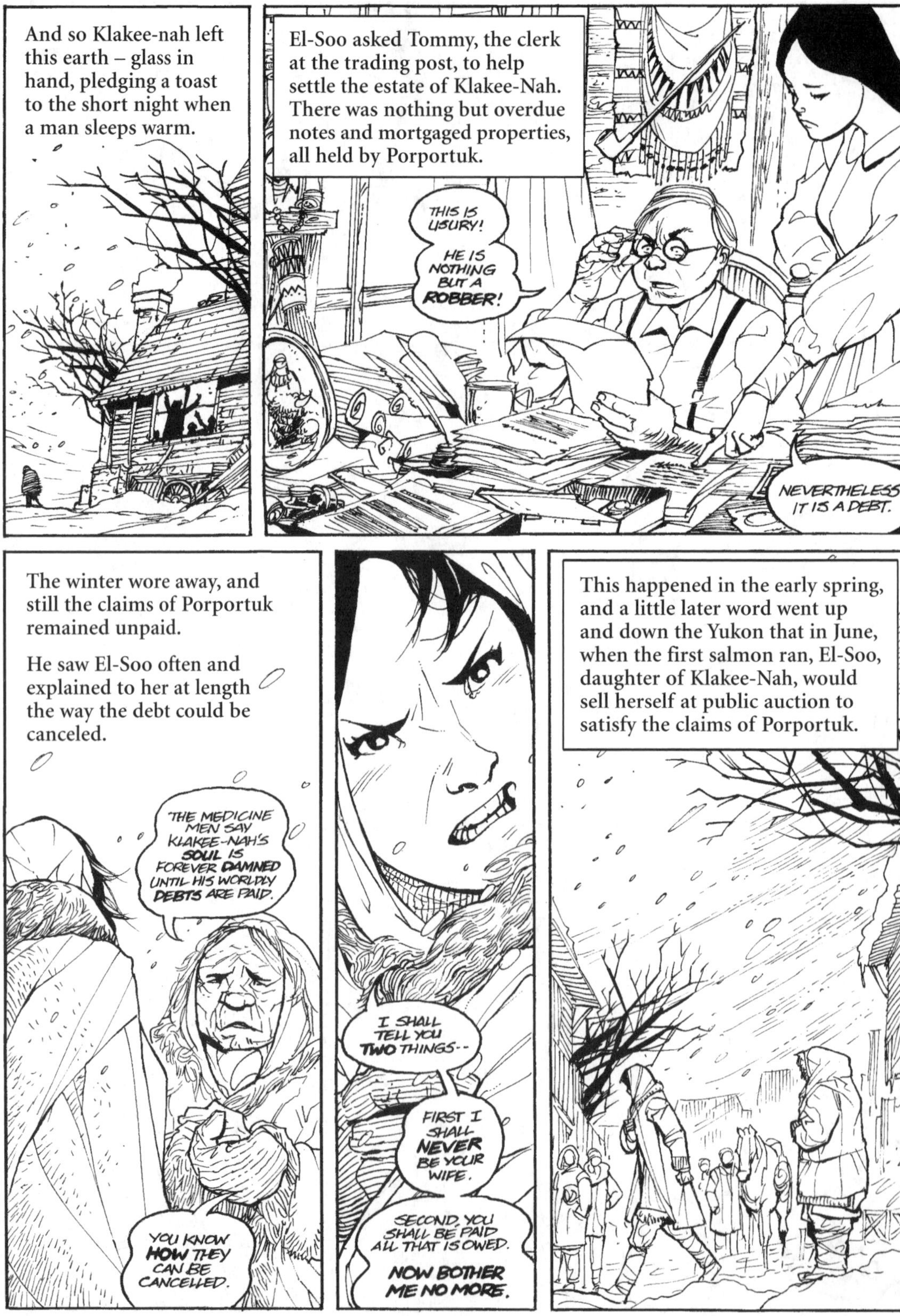
And so Klakee-nah left this earth – glass in hand, pledging a toast to the short night when a man sleeps warm.
El-Soo asked Tommy, the clerk at the trading post, to help settle the estate of Klakee-Nah. There was nothing but overdue notes and mortgaged properties, all held by Porportuk.
THIS IS USURY!
HE IS NOTHING BUT A ROBBER!
NEVERTHELESS IT IS A DEBT.
The winter wore away, and still the claims of Porportuk remained unpaid.
He saw El-Soo often and explained to her at length the way the debt could be canceled.
THE MEDICINE MEN SAY KLAKEE-NAH'S SOUL IS FOREVER DAMNED UNTIL HIS WORLDLY DEBTS ARE PAID.
YOU KNOW HOW THEY CAN BE CANCELLED.
I SHALL TELL YOU TWO THINGS--
FIRST I SHALL NEVER BE YOUR WIFE.
SECOND, YOU SHALL BE PAID ALL THAT IS OWED.
NOW BOTHER ME NO MORE.
This happened in the early spring, and a little later word went up and down the Yukon that in June, when the first salmon ran, El-Soo, daughter of Klakee-Nah, would sell herself at public auction to satisfy the claims of Porportuk.

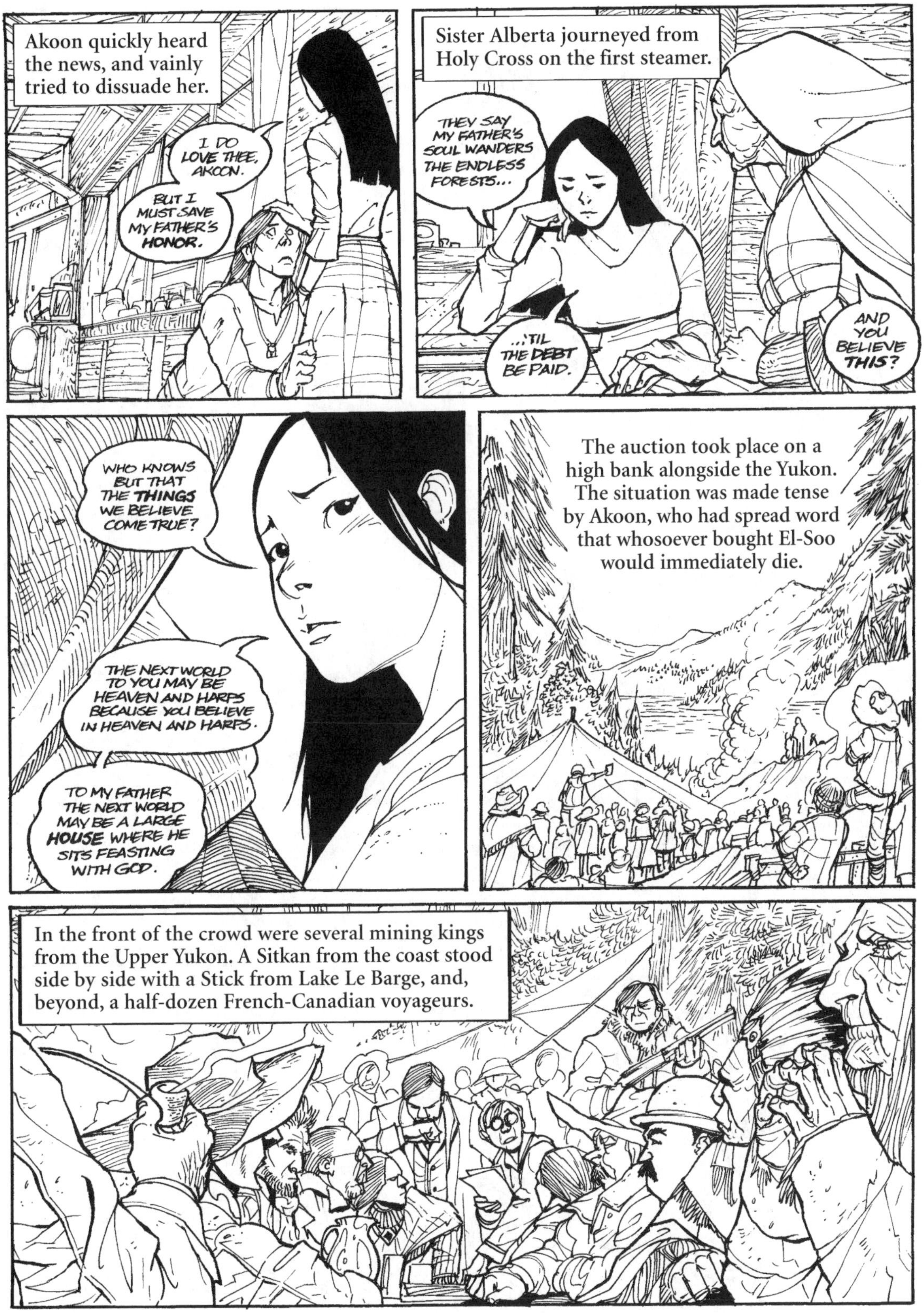
Akoon quickly heard the news, and vainly tried to dissuade her.
I DO LOVE THEE, AKOON.
BUT I MUST SAVE MY FATHER'S HONOR.
Sister Alberta journeyed from Holy Cross on the first steamer.
THEY SAY MY FATHER'S SOUL WANDERS THE ENDLESS FORESTS...
...'TIL THE DEBT BE PAID.
AND YOU BELIEVE THIS?
WHO KNOWS BUT THAT THE THINGS WE BELIEVE COME TRUE?
THE NEXT WORLD TO YOU MAY BE HEAVEN AND HARPS BECAUSE YOU BELIEVE IN HEAVEN AND HARPS.
TO MY FATHER THE NEXT WORLD MAY BE A LARGE HOUSE WHERE HE SITS FEASTING WITH GOD.
The auction took place on a high bank alongside the Yukon. The situation was made tense by Akoon, who had spread word that whosoever bought El-Soo would immediately die.
In the front of the crowd were several mining kings from the Upper Yukon. A Sitkan from the coast stood side by side with a Stick from Lake Le Barge, and, beyond, a half-dozen French-Canadian voyageurs.

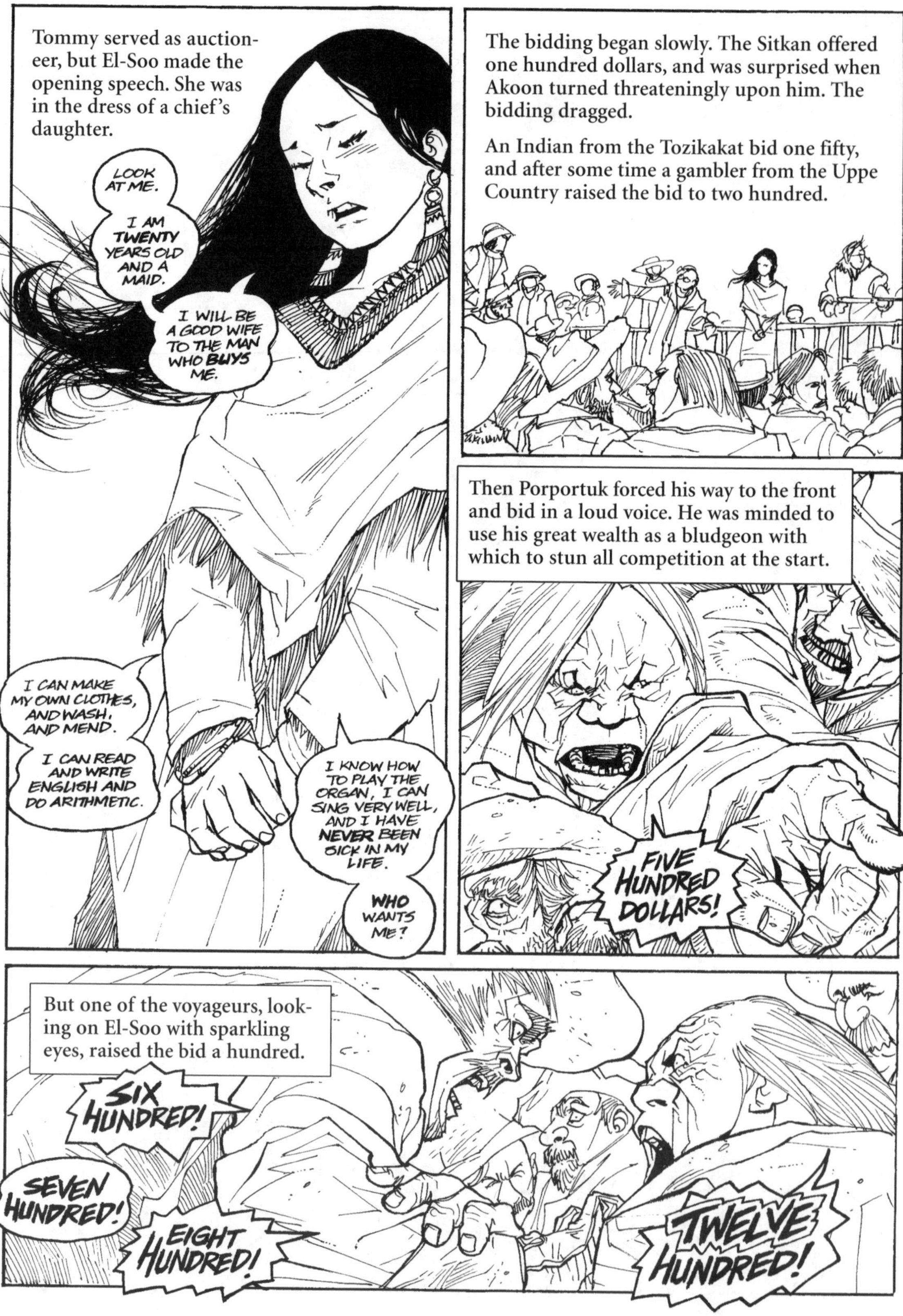
Tommy served as auctioneer, but El-Soo made the opening speech. She was in the dress of a chief's daughter.
LOOK AT ME.
I AM TWENTY YEARS OLD AND A MAID.
I WILL BE A GOOD WIFE TO THE MAN WHO BUYS ME.
I CAN MAKE MY OWN CLOTHES, AND WASH, AND MEND.
I CAN READ AND WRITE ENGLISH AND DO ARITHMETIC.
I KNOW HOW TO PLAY THE ORGAN, I CAN SING VERY WELL, AND I HAVE NEVER BEEN SICK IN MY LIFE.
WHO WANTS ME?
The bidding began slowly. The Sitkan offered one hundred dollars, and was surprised when Akoon turned threateningly upon him. The bidding dragged.
An Indian from the Tozikakat bid one fifty, and after some time a gambler from the Uppe Country raised the bid to two hundred.
Then Porportuk forced his way to the front and bid in a loud voice. He was minded to use his great wealth as a bludgeon with which to stun all competition at the start.
FIVE HUNDRED DOLLARS!
But one of the voyageurs, looking on El-Soo with sparkling eyes, raised the bid a hundred.
SIX HUNDRED!
SEVEN HUNDRED!
EIGHT HUNDRED!
TWELVE HUNDRED!

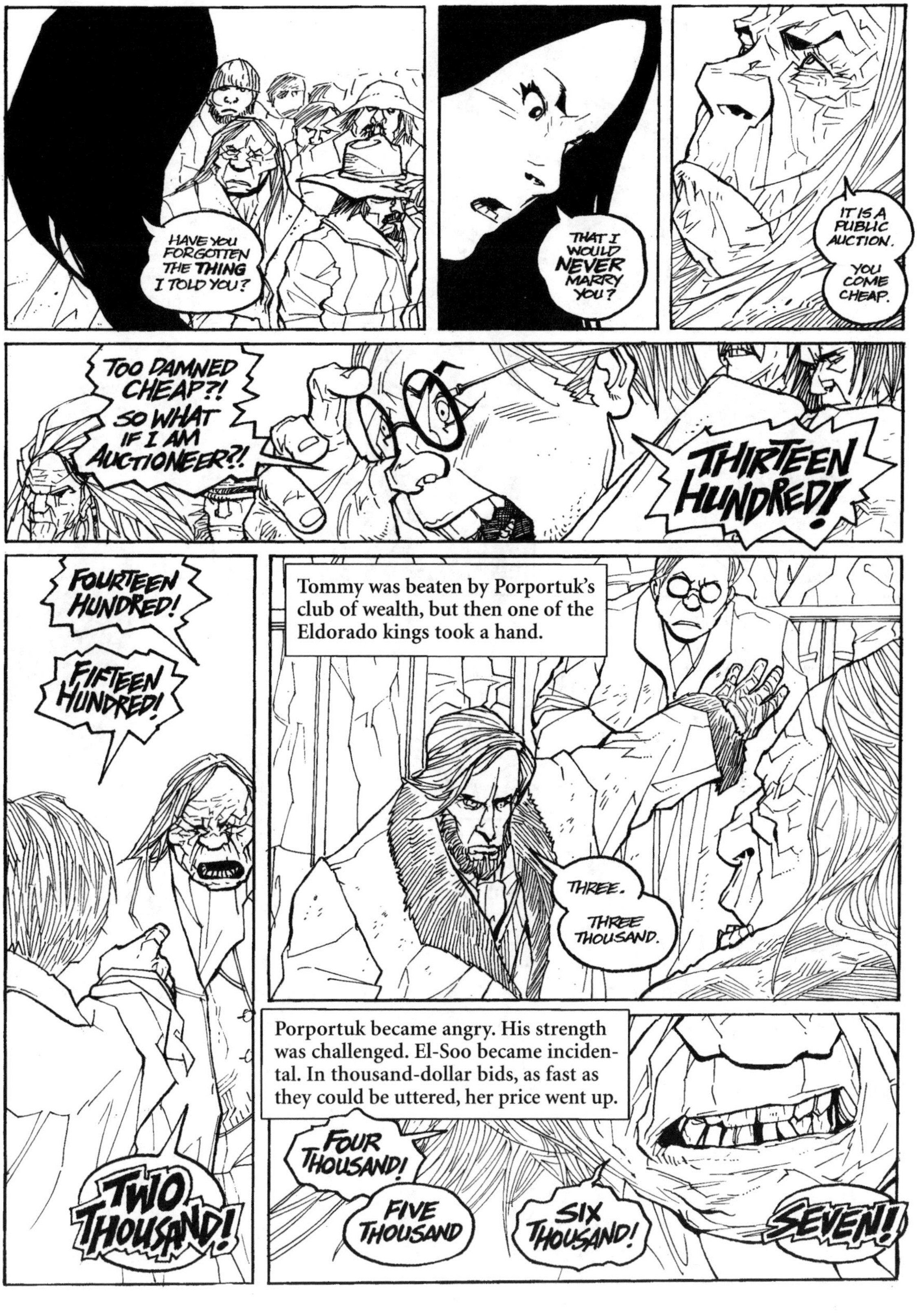
HAVE YOU FORGOTTEN THE THING I TOLD YOU?
THAT I WOULD NEVER MARRY YOU?
IT IS A PUBLIC AUCTION.
YOU COME CHEAP.
TOO DAMNED CHEAP?! SO WHAT IF I AM AUCTIONEER?!
THIRTEEN HUNDRED!
FOURTEEN HUNDRED!
FIFTEEN HUNDRED!
TWO THOUSAND!
Tommy was beaten by Porportuk's club of wealth, but then one of the Eldorado kings took a hand.
THREE.
THREE THOUSAND.
Porportuk became angry. His strength was challenged. El-Soo became incidental. In thousand-dollar bids, as fast as they could be uttered, her price went up.
FOUR THOUSAND!
FIVE THOUSAND
SIX THOUSAND!
SEVEN!

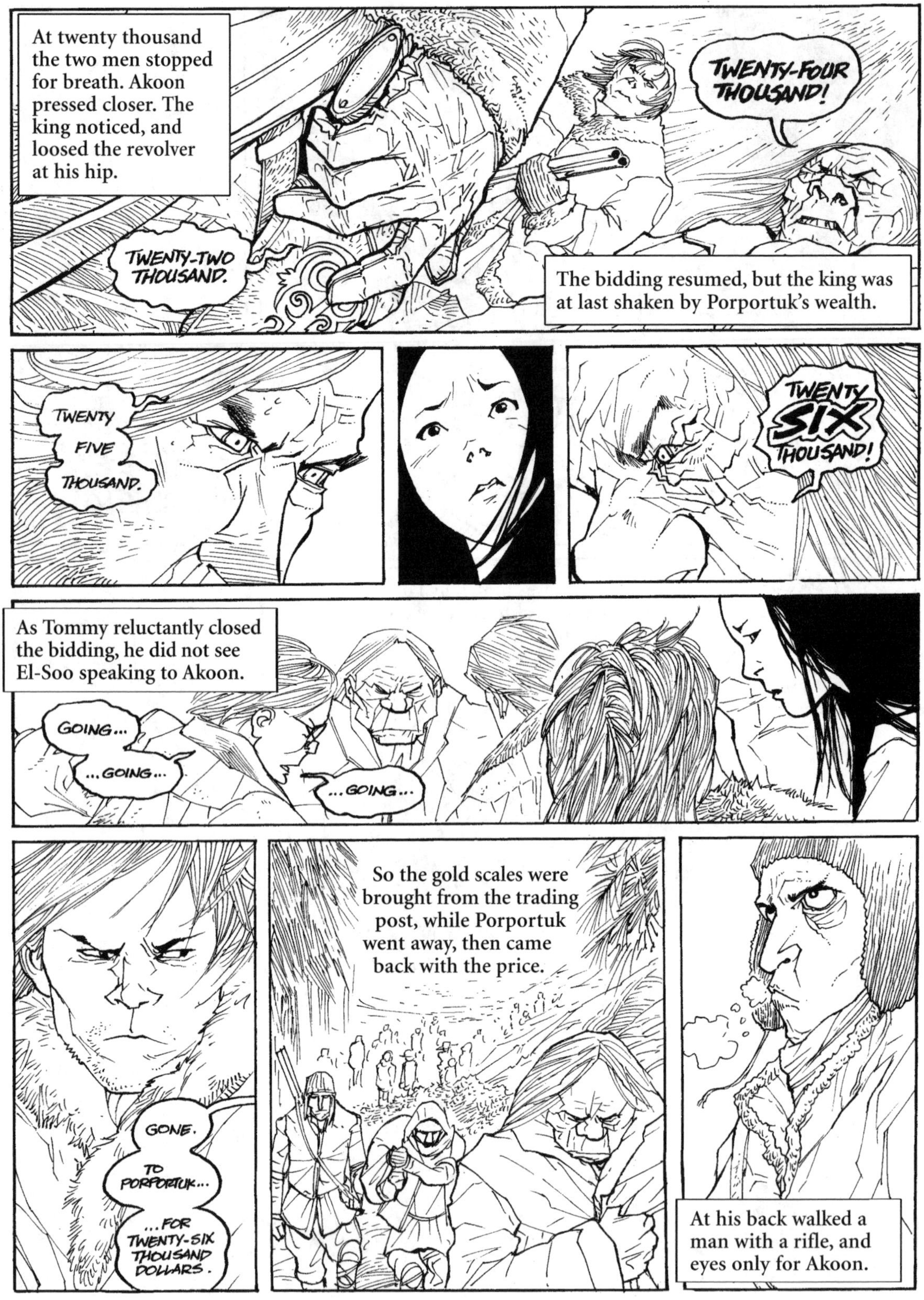
At twenty thousand the two men stopped for breath. Akoon pressed closer. The king noticed, and loosed the revolver at his hip.
TWENTY-TWO THOUSAND.
TWENTY-FOUR THOUSAND!
The bidding resumed, but the king was at last shaken by Porportuk's wealth.
TWENTY FIVE THOUSAND.
TWENTY SIX THOUSAND!
As Tommy reluctantly closed the bidding, he did not see El-Soo speaking to Akoon.
GOING...
...GOING...
...GOING...
GONE.
TO PORPORTUK...
...FOR TWENTY-SIX THOUSAND DOLLARS.
So the gold scales were brought from the trading post, while Porportuk went away, then came back with the price.
At his back walked a man with a rifle, and eyes only for Akoon.

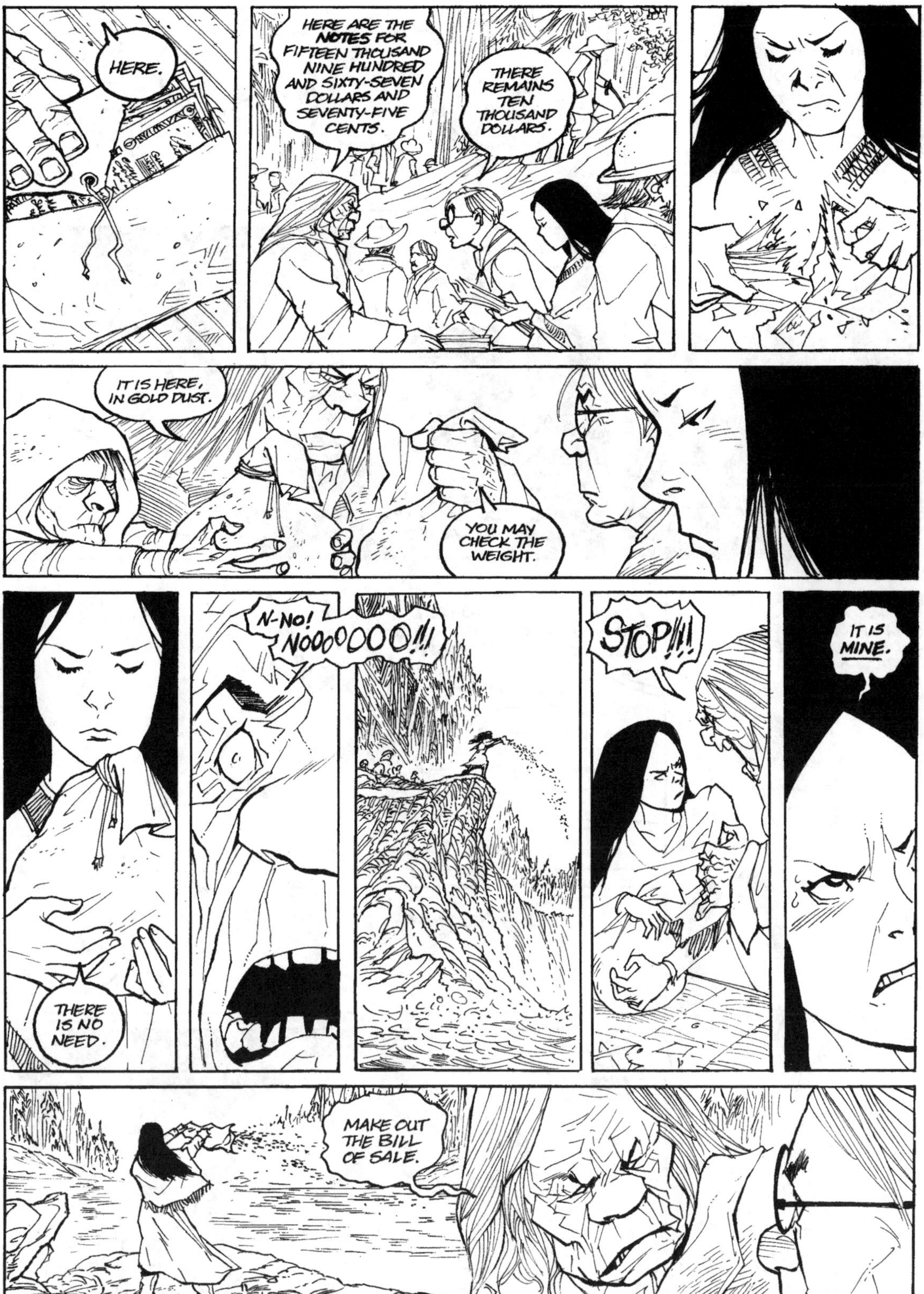
HERE.
HERE ARE THE NOTES FOR FIFTEEN THOUSAND NINE HUNDRED AND SIXTY-SEVEN DOLLARS AND SEVENTY-FIVE CENTS.
THERE REMAINS TEN THOUSAND DOLLARS.
IT IS HERE, IN GOLD DUST.
YOU MAY CHECK THE WEIGHT.
THERE IS NO NEED.
N-NO! NOOOOOOO!!!
STOP!!!!
IT IS MINE.
MAKE OUT THE BILL OF SALE.

And so Tommy made out the bill of sale, wherein all right and title in the woman El-Soo was vested in the man Porportuk.

COME.

WE GO TO MY HOUSE.

DO YOU FORGET THE TWO THINGS I TOLD YOU IN THE SPRING?

MY HEAD WOULD BE *FULL* WITH THE THINGS *WOMEN* SAY, DID I HEED THEM.

I TOLD YOU THAT YOU WOULD BE PAID.

AND I TOLD YOU THAT I WOULD *NEVER* BE YOUR WIFE.

BUT *NOW* I HAVE BOUGHT YOU. AS A *DOG* I OWN YOU.

HAD ANY OTHER MAN BOUGHT ME, I SHOULD HAVE BEEN A GOOD WIFE TO THAT MAN.

SUCH WAS MY WILL. BUT I WILL *NEVER* BE YOUR WIFE.

WHEREFORE, I AM YOUR *DOG*.

THEN I SPEAK TO YOU NOT AS *EL-SOO*, BUT A *DOG*. AND I TELL YOU TO COME WITH ME.

NOT SO FAST, PORPORTUK. YOU BUY A *DOG*. THE DOG RUNS AWAY. IT IS YOUR *LOSS*.

WHAT IF I RUN AWAY?

AS THE OWNER OF THE DOG, I SHALL *BEAT* YOU.

WHEN YOU CATCH ME?

WHEN I CATCH YOU.

THEN CATCH ME.

STOP HER!!!

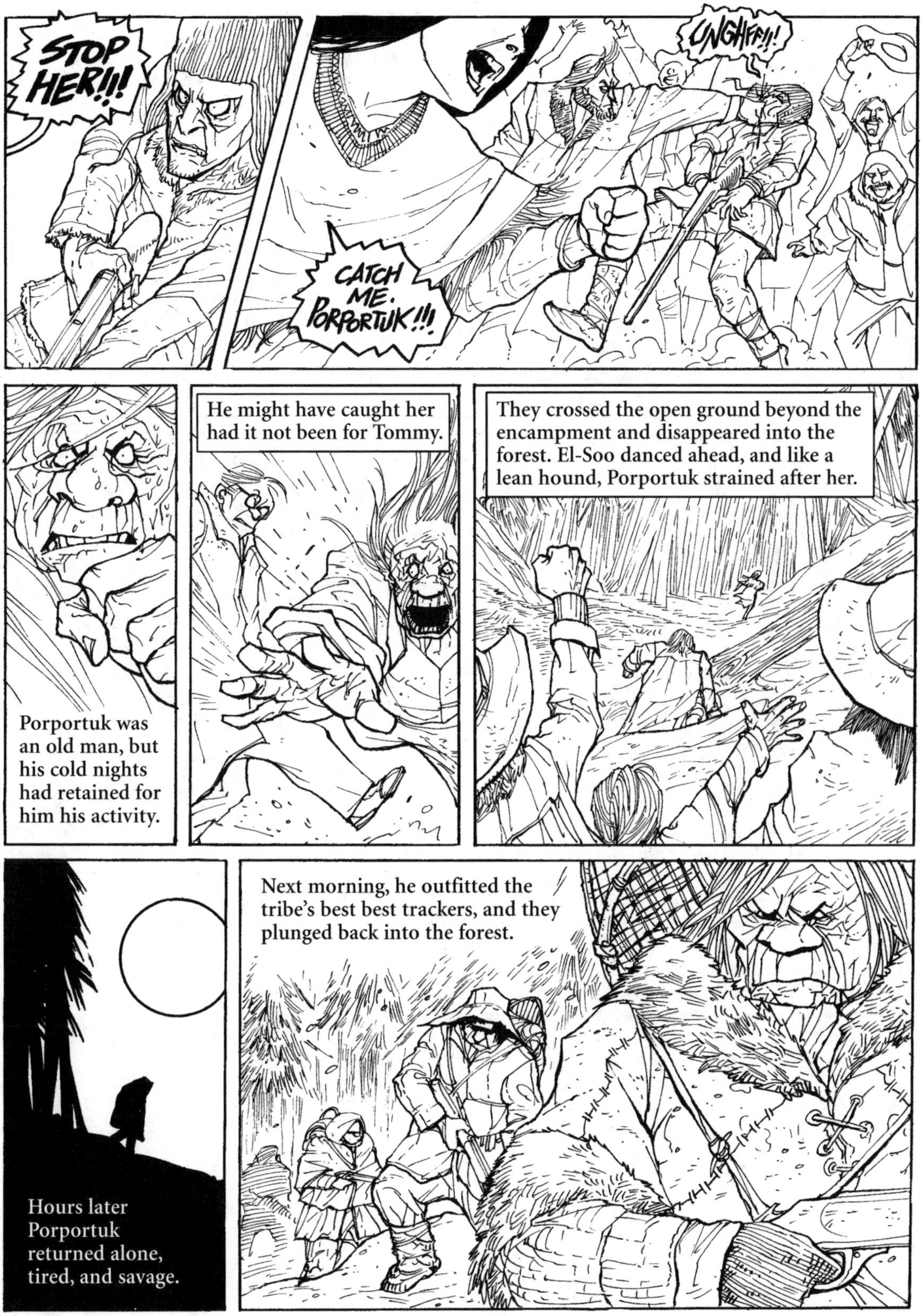
STOP HER!!!
UNGHFF!!!
CATCH ME, PORPORTUK!!!
He might have caught her had it not been for Tommy.
They crossed the open ground beyond the encampment and disappeared into the forest. El-Soo danced ahead, and like a lean hound, Porportuk strained after her.
Porportuk was an old man, but his cold nights had retained for him his activity.
Hours later Porportuk returned alone, tired, and savage.
Next morning, he outfitted the tribe's best best trackers, and they plunged back into the forest.

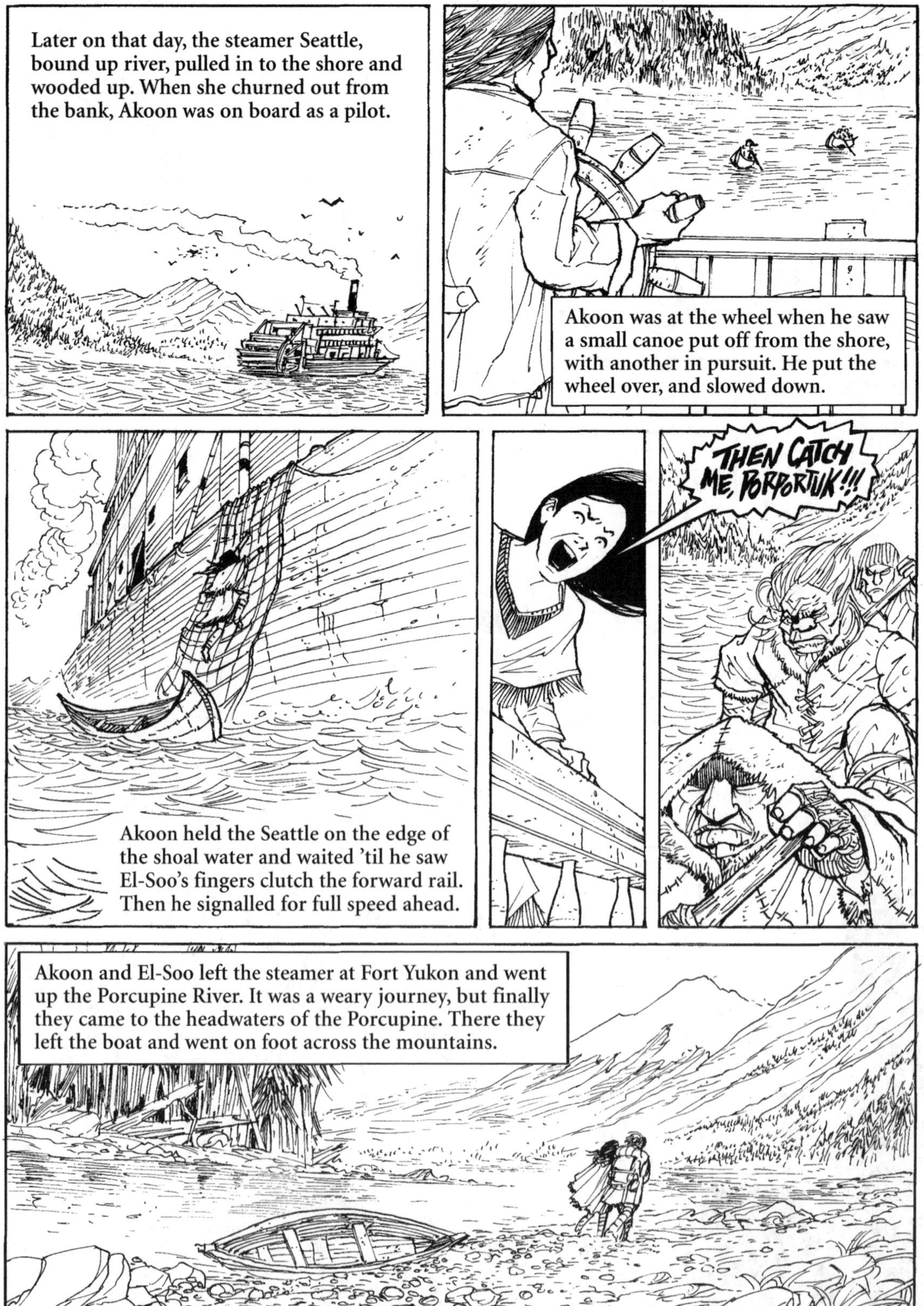
Later on that day, the steamer Seattle, bound up river, pulled in to the shore and wooded up. When she churned out from the bank, Akoon was on board as a pilot.
Akoon was at the wheel when he saw a small canoe put off from the shore, with another in pursuit. He put the wheel over, and slowed down.
Akoon held the Seattle on the edge of the shoal water and waited 'til he saw El-Soo's fingers clutch the forward rail. Then he signalled for full speed ahead.
THEN CATCH ME, PORPORTUK!!!
Akoon and El-Soo left the steamer at Fort Yukon and went up the Porcupine River. It was a weary journey, but finally they came to the headwaters of the Porcupine. There they left the boat and went on foot across the mountains.

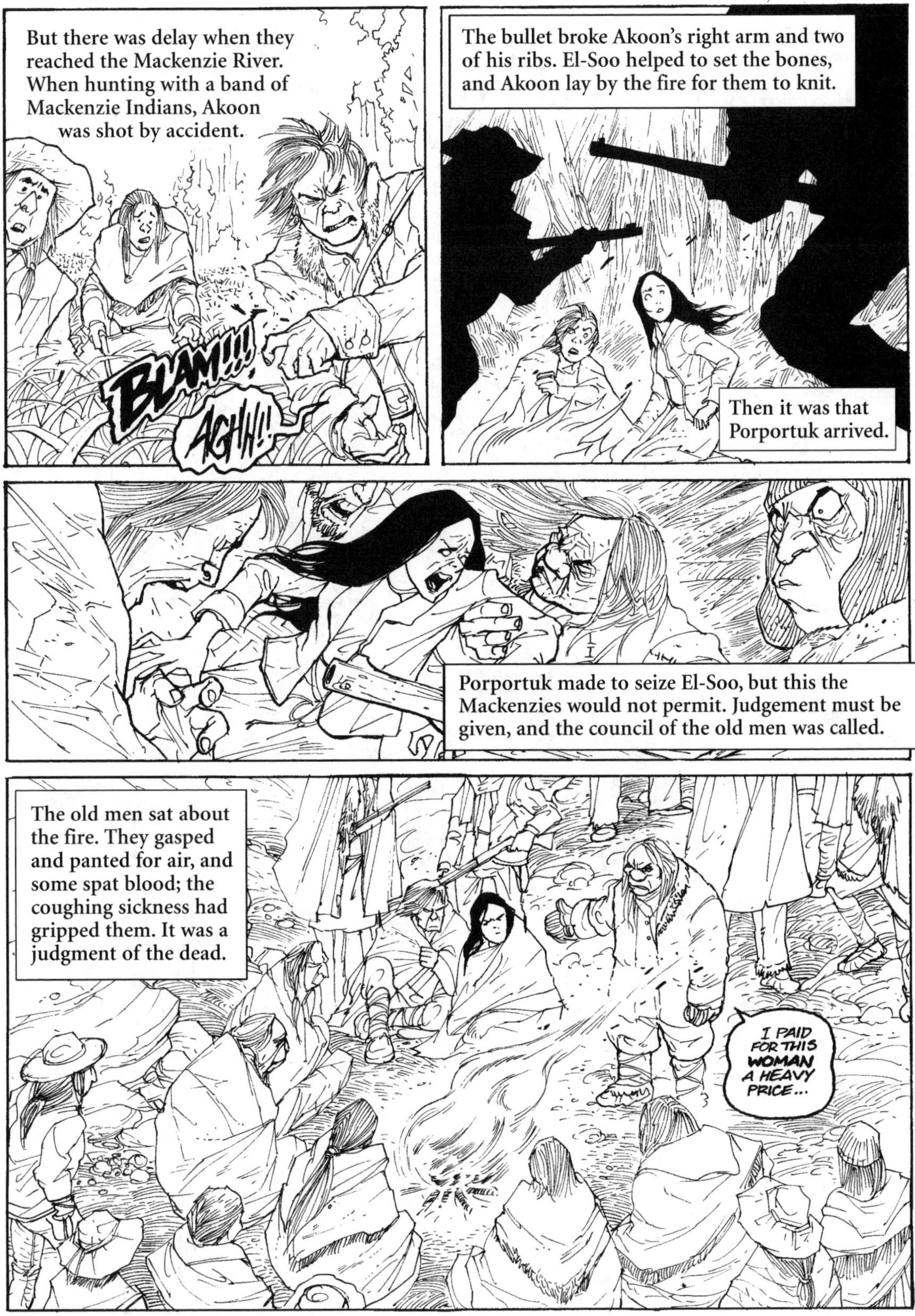
But there was delay when they reached the Mackenzie River. When hunting with a band of Mackenzie Indians, Akoon was shot by accident.
BLAM!!!
AGHH!!
The bullet broke Akoon's right arm and two of his ribs. El-Soo helped to set the bones, and Akoon lay by the fire for them to knit.
Then it was that Porportuk arrived.
Porportuk made to seize El-Soo, but this the Mackenzies would not permit. Judgement must be given, and the council of the old men was called.
The old men sat about the fire. They gasped and panted for air, and some spat blood; the coughing sickness had gripped them. It was a judgment of the dead.
I PAID FOR THIS WOMAN A HEAVY PRICE...

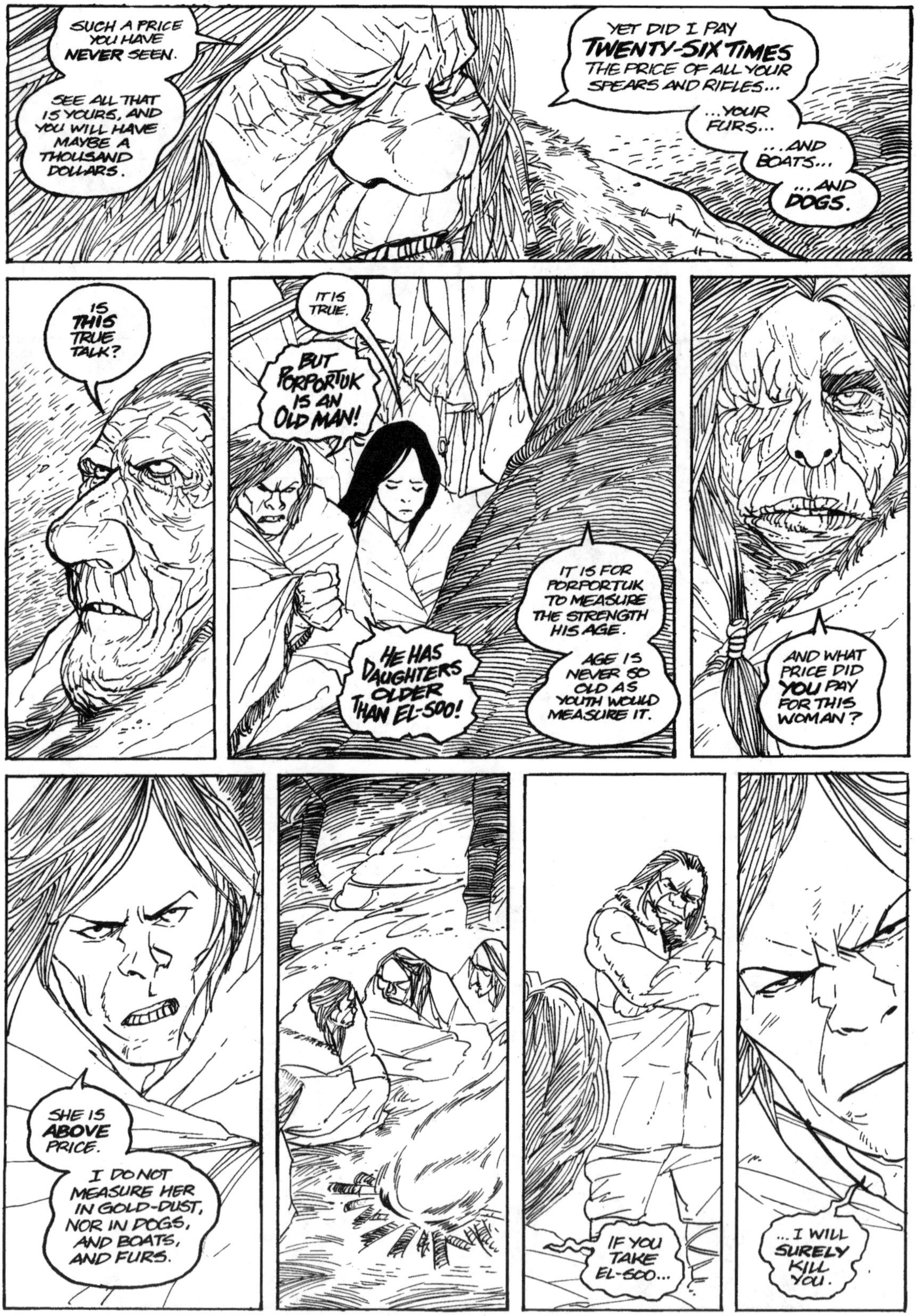
SUCH A PRICE YOU HAVE NEVER SEEN.
SEE ALL THAT IS YOURS, AND YOU WILL HAVE MAYBE A THOUSAND DOLLARS.
YET DID I PAY TWENTY-SIX TIMES THE PRICE OF ALL YOUR SPEARS AND RIFLES...
...YOUR FURS...
...AND BOATS...
...AND DOGS.
IS THIS TRUE TALK?
IT IS TRUE.
BUT PORPORTUK IS AN OLD MAN!
HE HAS DAUGHTERS OLDER THAN EL-SOO!
IT IS FOR PORPORTUK TO MEASURE THE STRENGTH HIS AGE.
AGE IS NEVER SO OLD AS YOUTH WOULD MEASURE IT.
AND WHAT PRICE DID YOU PAY FOR THIS WOMAN?
SHE IS ABOVE PRICE.
I DO NOT MEASURE HER IN GOLD-DUST, NOR IN DOGS, AND BOATS, AND FURS.
IF YOU TAKE EL-SOO...
...I WILL SURELY KILL YOU.

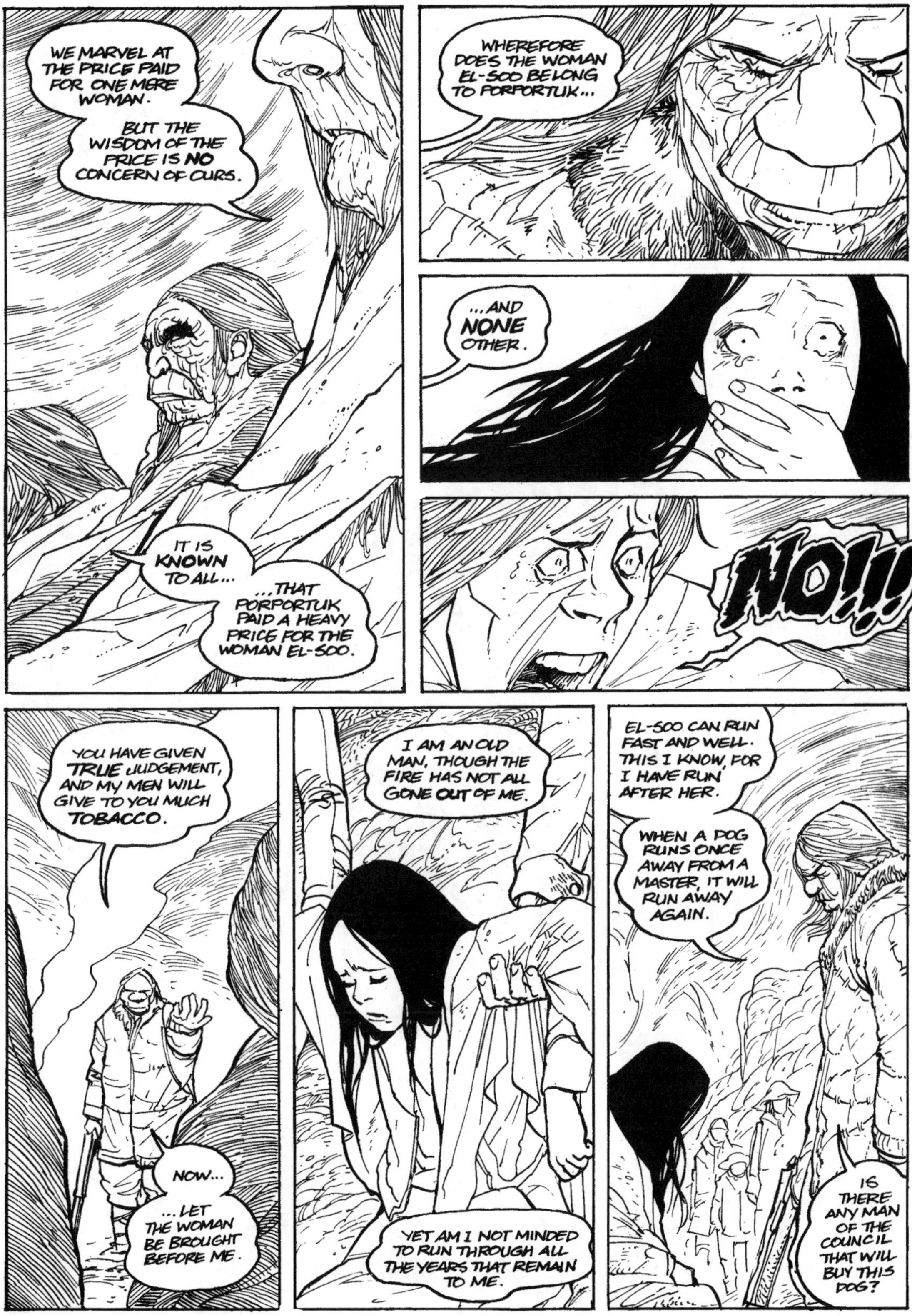
WE MARVEL AT THE PRICE PAID FOR ONE MERE WOMAN.
BUT THE WISDOM OF THE PRICE IS NO CONCERN OF OURS.
IT IS KNOWN TO ALL...
...THAT PORPORTUK PAID A HEAVY PRICE FOR THE WOMAN EL-SOO.
WHEREFORE DOES THE WOMAN EL-SOO BELONG TO PORPORTUK...
...AND NONE OTHER.
NO!!!
YOU HAVE GIVEN TRUE JUDGEMENT, AND MY MEN WILL GIVE TO YOU MUCH TOBACCO.
NOW...
...LET THE WOMAN BE BROUGHT BEFORE ME.
I AM AN OLD MAN, THOUGH THE FIRE HAS NOT ALL GONE OUT OF ME.
YET AM I NOT MINDED TO RUN THROUGH ALL THE YEARS THAT REMAIN TO ME.
EL-SOO CAN RUN FAST AND WELL. THIS I KNOW, FOR I HAVE RUN AFTER HER.
WHEN A DOG RUNS ONCE AWAY FROM A MASTER, IT WILL RUN AWAY AGAIN.
IS THERE ANY MAN OF THE COUNCIL THAT WILL BUY THIS DOG?

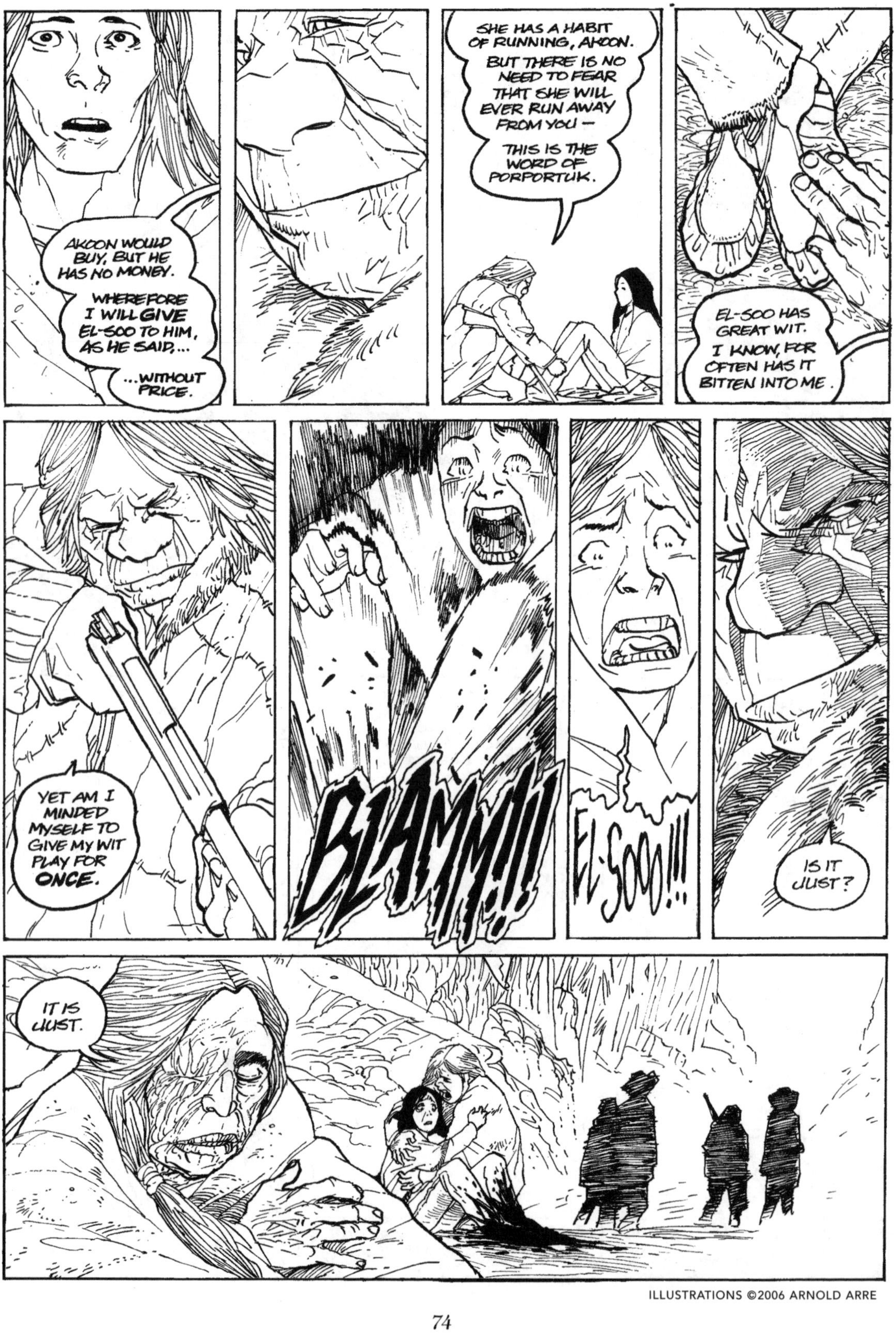
AKOON WOULD BUY, BUT HE HAS NO MONEY.
WHEREFORE I WILL **GIVE** EL-SOO TO HIM, AS HE SAID,...
...WITHOUT PRICE.
SHE HAS A HABIT OF RUNNING, AKOON.
BUT THERE IS NO NEED TO FEAR THAT SHE WILL EVER RUN AWAY FROM YOU —
THIS IS THE WORD OF PORPORTUK.
EL-SOO HAS GREAT WIT.
I KNOW, FOR OFTEN HAS IT BITTEN INTO ME.
YET AM I MINDED MYSELF TO GIVE MY WIT PLAY FOR **ONCE**.
BLAMM!!
EL-SOOO!!!
IS IT JUST?
IT IS JUST.

The Handsome Cabin Boy

story by
JACK LONDON

adapted by
TRINA ROBBINS

illustrated by
ANNE TIMMONS

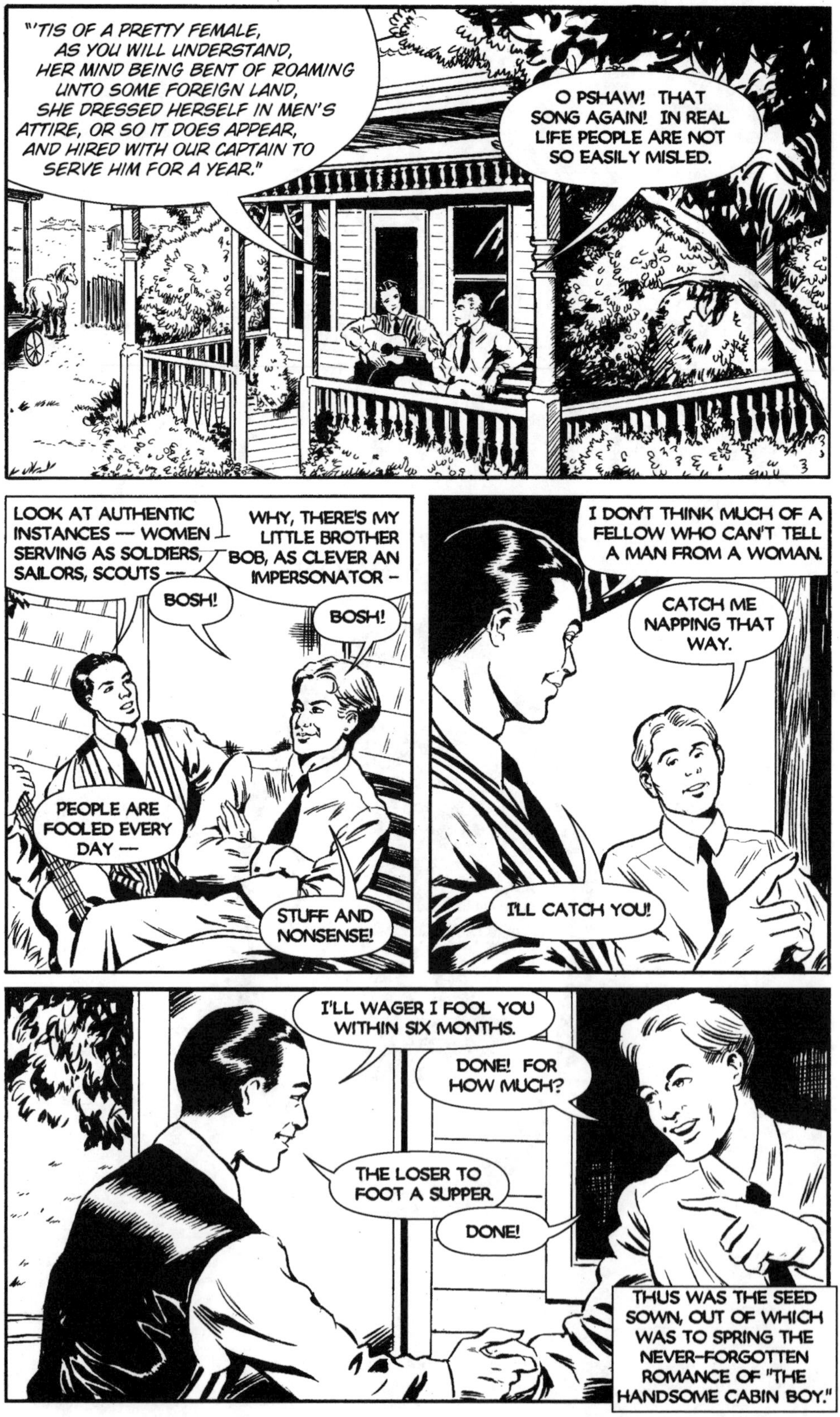
"'TIS OF A PRETTY FEMALE, AS YOU WILL UNDERSTAND, HER MIND BEING BENT OF ROAMING UNTO SOME FOREIGN LAND, SHE DRESSED HERSELF IN MEN'S ATTIRE, OR SO IT DOES APPEAR, AND HIRED WITH OUR CAPTAIN TO SERVE HIM FOR A YEAR."
O PSHAW! THAT SONG AGAIN! IN REAL LIFE PEOPLE ARE NOT SO EASILY MISLED.
LOOK AT AUTHENTIC INSTANCES — WOMEN SERVING AS SOLDIERS, SAILORS, SCOUTS —
BOSH!
WHY, THERE'S MY LITTLE BROTHER BOB, AS CLEVER AN IMPERSONATOR –
BOSH!
PEOPLE ARE FOOLED EVERY DAY —
STUFF AND NONSENSE!
I DON'T THINK MUCH OF A FELLOW WHO CAN'T TELL A MAN FROM A WOMAN.
CATCH ME NAPPING THAT WAY.
I'LL CATCH YOU!
I'LL WAGER I FOOL YOU WITHIN SIX MONTHS.
DONE! FOR HOW MUCH?
THE LOSER TO FOOT A SUPPER.
DONE!
THUS WAS THE SEED SOWN, OUT OF WHICH WAS TO SPRING THE NEVER-FORGOTTEN ROMANCE OF "THE HANDSOME CABIN BOY."

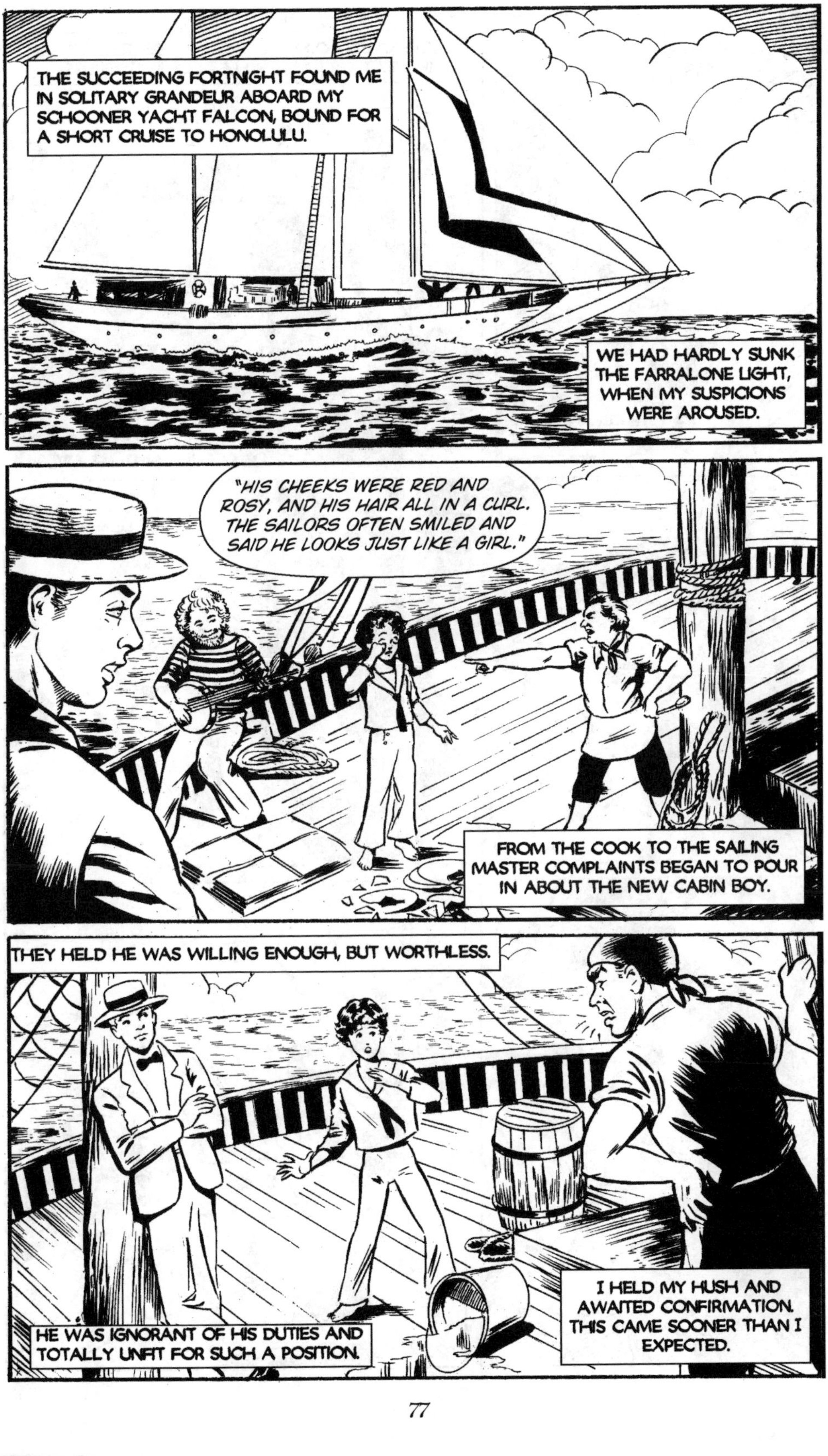
THE SUCCEEDING FORTNIGHT FOUND ME IN SOLITARY GRANDEUR ABOARD MY SCHOONER YACHT FALCON, BOUND FOR A SHORT CRUISE TO HONOLULU.
WE HAD HARDLY SUNK THE FARRALONE LIGHT, WHEN MY SUSPICIONS WERE AROUSED.
"HIS CHEEKS WERE RED AND ROSY, AND HIS HAIR ALL IN A CURL. THE SAILORS OFTEN SMILED AND SAID HE LOOKS JUST LIKE A GIRL."
FROM THE COOK TO THE SAILING MASTER COMPLAINTS BEGAN TO POUR IN ABOUT THE NEW CABIN BOY.
THEY HELD HE WAS WILLING ENOUGH, BUT WORTHLESS.
HE WAS IGNORANT OF HIS DUTIES AND TOTALLY UNFIT FOR SUCH A POSITION.
I HELD MY HUSH AND AWAITED CONFIRMATION. THIS CAME SOONER THAN I EXPECTED.

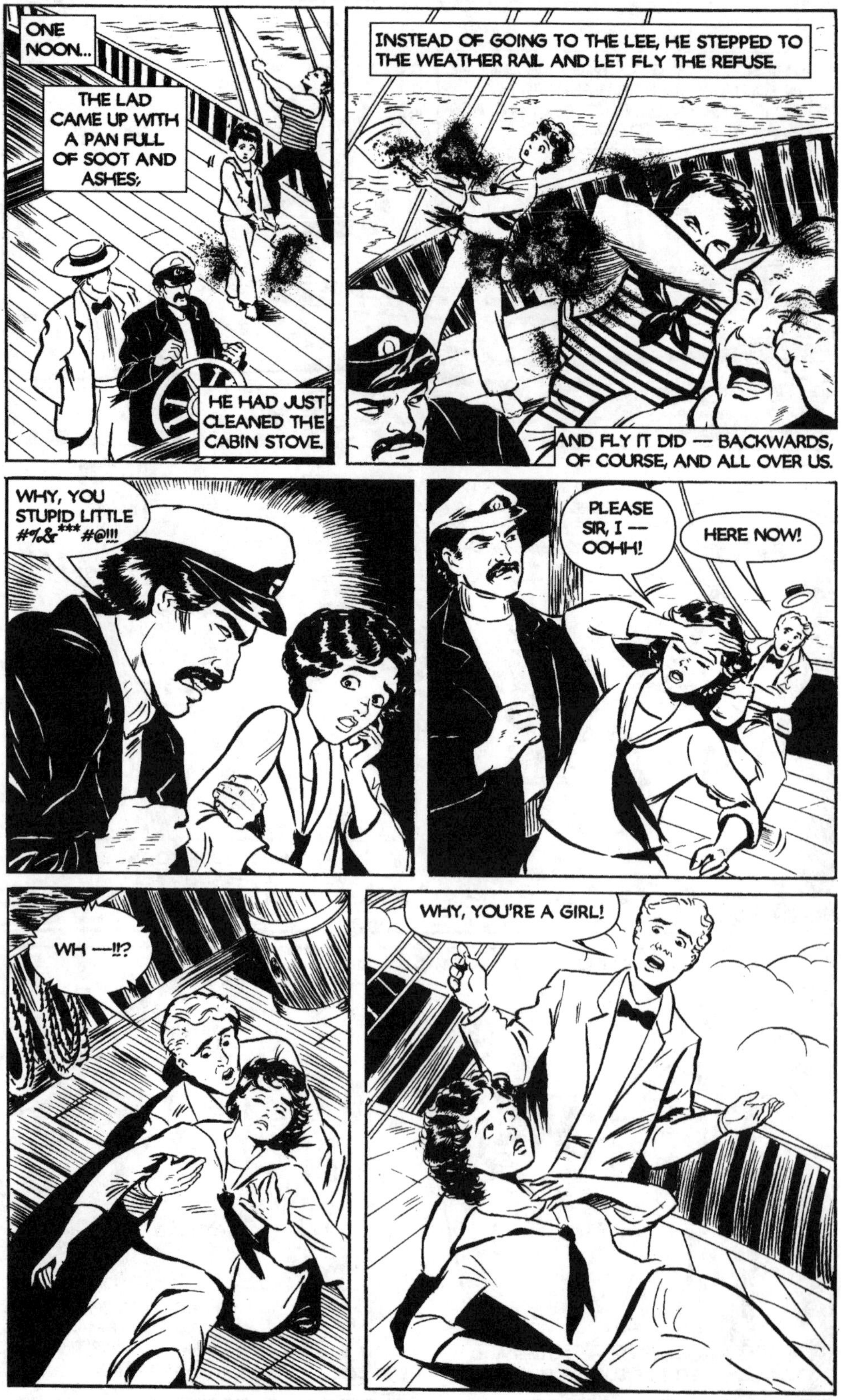
ONE NOON...
THE LAD CAME UP WITH A PAN FULL OF SOOT AND ASHES;
HE HAD JUST CLEANED THE CABIN STOVE.
INSTEAD OF GOING TO THE LEE, HE STEPPED TO THE WEATHER RAIL AND LET FLY THE REFUSE.
AND FLY IT DID — BACKWARDS, OF COURSE, AND ALL OVER US.
WHY, YOU STUPID LITTLE #%&*** #@!!!
PLEASE SIR, I — OOHH!
HERE NOW!
WH —!!?
WHY, YOU'RE A GIRL!

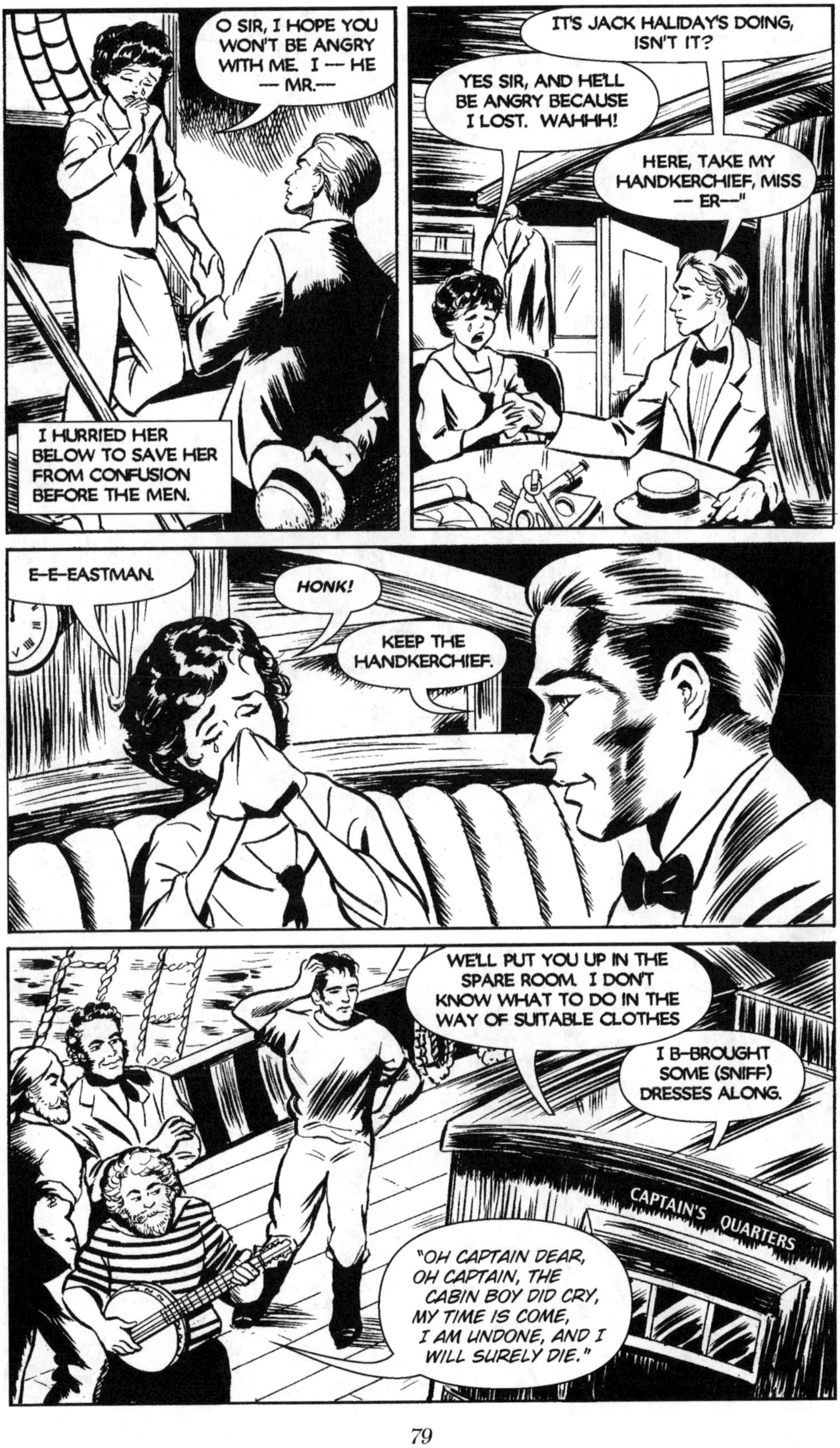
O SIR, I HOPE YOU WON'T BE ANGRY WITH ME. I -- HE -- MR.--
I HURRIED HER BELOW TO SAVE HER FROM CONFUSION BEFORE THE MEN.
IT'S JACK HALIDAY'S DOING, ISN'T IT?
YES SIR, AND HE'LL BE ANGRY BECAUSE I LOST. WAHHH!
HERE, TAKE MY HANDKERCHIEF, MISS -- ER--"
E-E-EASTMAN.
HONK!
KEEP THE HANDKERCHIEF.
WE'LL PUT YOU UP IN THE SPARE ROOM. I DON'T KNOW WHAT TO DO IN THE WAY OF SUITABLE CLOTHES
I B-BROUGHT SOME (SNIFF) DRESSES ALONG.
CAPTAIN'S QUARTERS
"OH CAPTAIN DEAR, OH CAPTAIN, THE CABIN BOY DID CRY, MY TIME IS COME, I AM UNDONE, AND I WILL SURELY DIE."

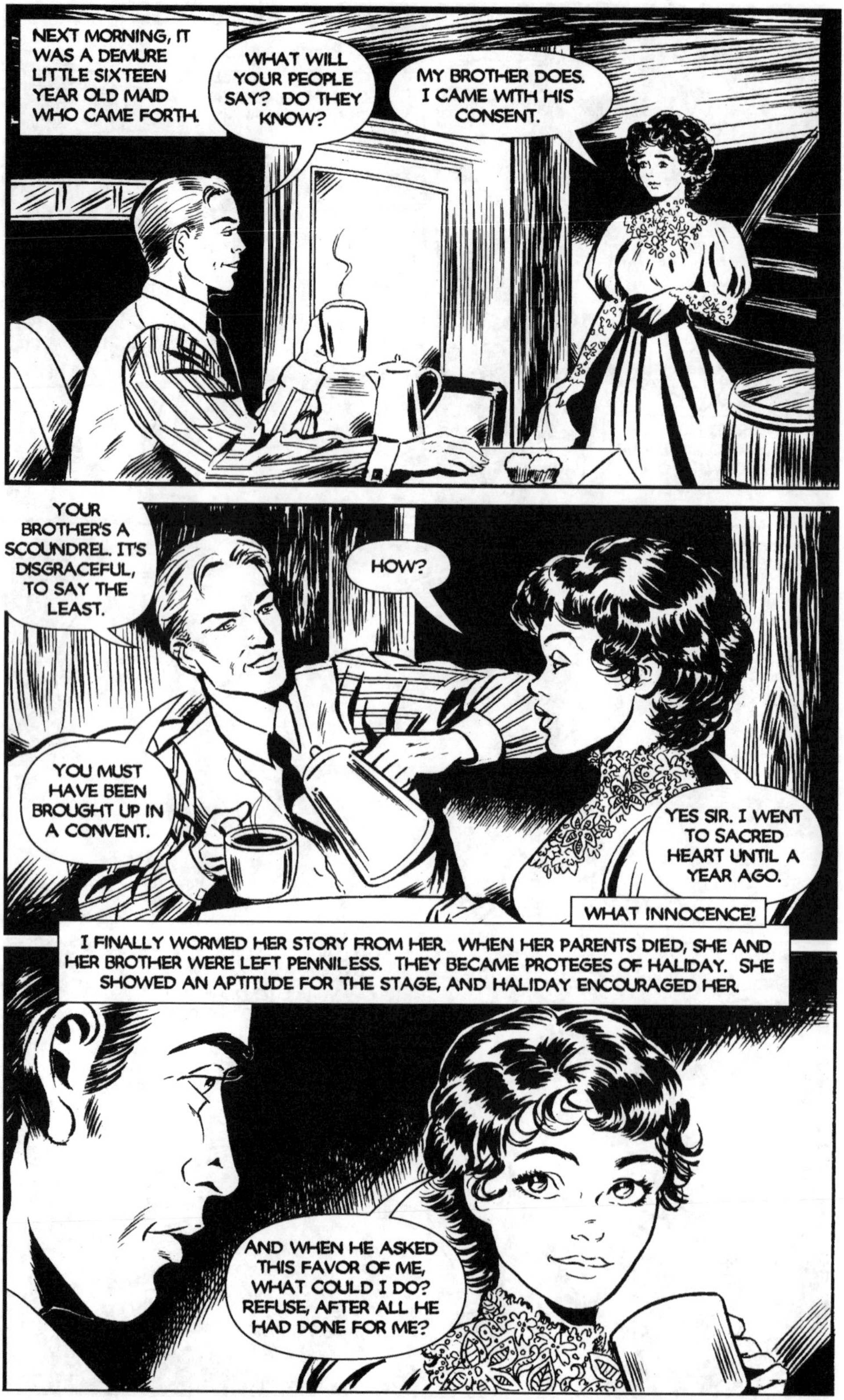
NEXT MORNING, IT WAS A DEMURE LITTLE SIXTEEN YEAR OLD MAID WHO CAME FORTH.
WHAT WILL YOUR PEOPLE SAY? DO THEY KNOW?
MY BROTHER DOES. I CAME WITH HIS CONSENT.
YOUR BROTHER'S A SCOUNDREL. IT'S DISGRACEFUL, TO SAY THE LEAST.
HOW?
YOU MUST HAVE BEEN BROUGHT UP IN A CONVENT.
YES SIR. I WENT TO SACRED HEART UNTIL A YEAR AGO.
WHAT INNOCENCE!
I FINALLY WORMED HER STORY FROM HER. WHEN HER PARENTS DIED, SHE AND HER BROTHER WERE LEFT PENNILESS. THEY BECAME PROTEGES OF HALIDAY. SHE SHOWED AN APTITUDE FOR THE STAGE, AND HALIDAY ENCOURAGED HER.
AND WHEN HE ASKED THIS FAVOR OF ME, WHAT COULD I DO? REFUSE, AFTER ALL HE HAD DONE FOR ME?

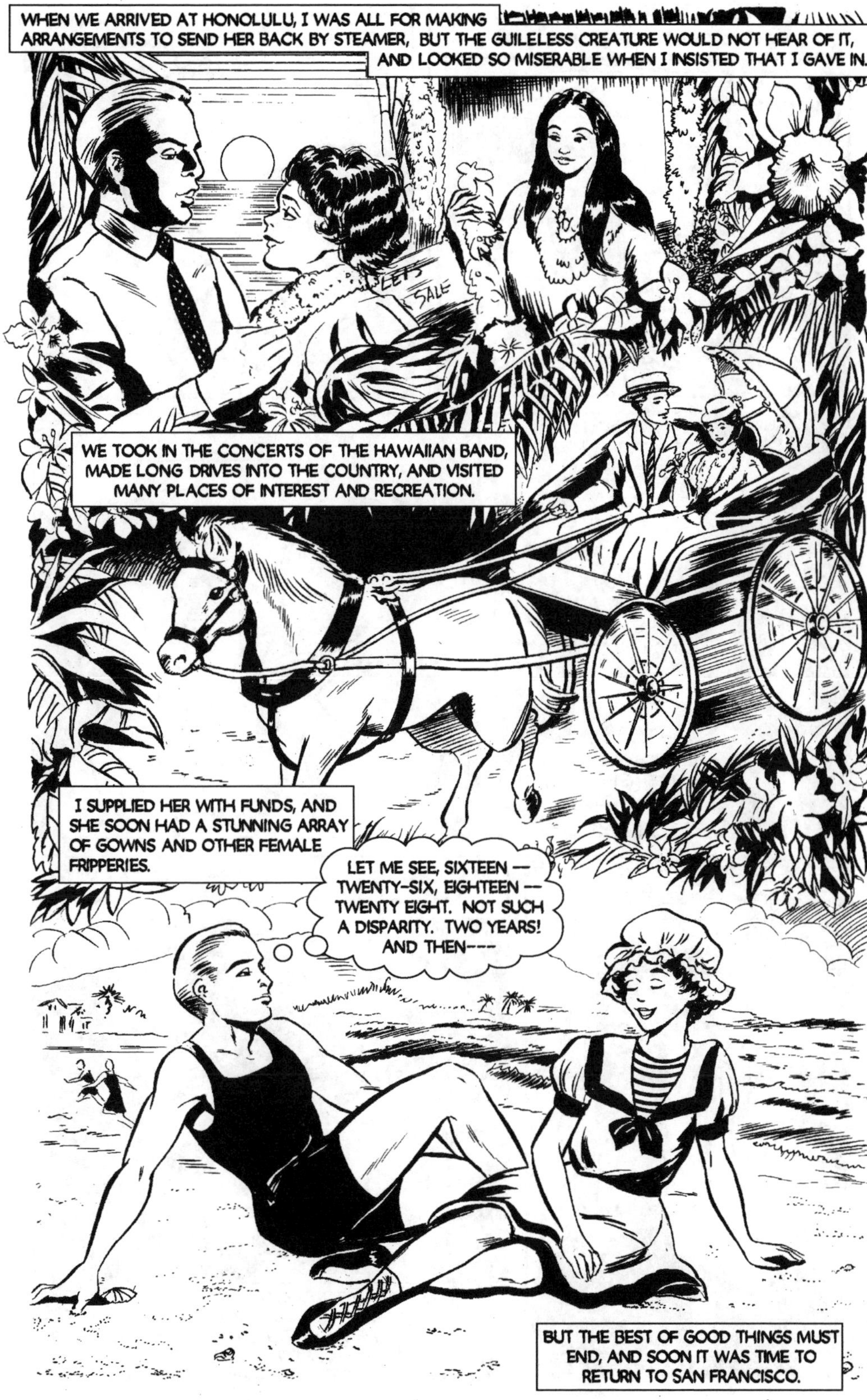
WHEN WE ARRIVED AT HONOLULU, I WAS ALL FOR MAKING ARRANGEMENTS TO SEND HER BACK BY STEAMER, BUT THE GUILELESS CREATURE WOULD NOT HEAR OF IT, AND LOOKED SO MISERABLE WHEN I INSISTED THAT I GAVE IN.
SALE
WE TOOK IN THE CONCERTS OF THE HAWAIIAN BAND, MADE LONG DRIVES INTO THE COUNTRY, AND VISITED MANY PLACES OF INTEREST AND RECREATION.
I SUPPLIED HER WITH FUNDS, AND SHE SOON HAD A STUNNING ARRAY OF GOWNS AND OTHER FEMALE FRIPPERIES.
LET ME SEE, SIXTEEN — TWENTY-SIX, EIGHTEEN -- TWENTY EIGHT. NOT SUCH A DISPARITY. TWO YEARS! AND THEN---
BUT THE BEST OF GOOD THINGS MUST END, AND SOON IT WAS TIME TO RETURN TO SAN FRANCISCO.

BACK IN SAN FRANCISCO, JACK HALIDAY AND THE WHOLE CROWD WERE AT THE CLUB-HOUSE TO MEET US.

HOPE YOU HAD A PLEASANT TRIP, MISS EASTMAN.

O, I DID.

WAS HE ANGRY?

NO, HE WAS REAL NICE. WE HAD A GORGEOUS TIME.

HOW DID YOU DISCOVER IT?

WHY, SHE FAINTED IN MY ARMS, AND ---

OHO! HOO HOO!

WHY, YOU NINNY! THAT'S MY BROTHER, BOB!

IMPOSSIBLE! WHY, WHEN SHE FAINTED IN MY ARMS, I ---

NEEDLESS TO TELL HOW SUPPER CAME OFF, WITH BOB HALIDAY AT THE HEAD OF THE TABLE.

"SO EACH MAN TOOK HIS CUP OF RUM AND DRANK SUCCESS TO TRADE,"

"AND ALSO TO THE CABIN BOY WHO WAS NEITHER MAN NOR MAID. AND HERE'S HOPING FOR A JOLLY LOT MORE LIKE THE HANDSOME CABIN BOY."

The Handsome Cabin Boy

Traditional Sea Chantey

'Tis of a pretty fe— male, as you will un- der stand, Her mind being bent of
ro- a- ming un- to some for- eign land, She dressed her- self in men's at- tire or
so it does ap- pear, And hi- red with our cap- tain to serve him for a year.

The captain's wife, she being on board, she seemed in great joy,
To think her husband had engaged such a handsome cabin boy.
And now and then she'd slip him a kiss, and she would 'a liked to toy,
But was the captain found out the secret of the handsome cabin boy.

His cheeks were red and rosy, and his hair all in a curl.
The sailors often smiled and said, "He looks just like a girl."
But eating of the captain's biscuit, her color did destroy,
And the waist did swell of pretty Nell, the handsome cabin boy.

It was in the Bay of Biscayne, our gallant ship did plough.
One night among the sailors was a fearful flurry and row.
They tumbled from their hammocks, for sleep it did destroy.
They swore about the groaning of the handsome cabin boy.

"Oh captain dear, oh captain," the cabin boy did cry,
"My time is come, I am undone, and I will surely die."
The doctor came a-runnin', and smilin' at the fun,
To think a sailor lad should have a daughter or a son.

The sailors, when they saw the joke, they all did stand and stare.
The child belonged to none of them, they solemnly did swear.
The captain's wife she says to him, "My dear I wish you joy,
For it's either you or me's betrayed the handsome cabin boy."

So each man took his cup of rum, and drank success to trade,
And also to the cabin boy, who was neither man nor maid.
"Here's hoping wars don't rise again, our sailors to destroy,
And here's hoping for a jolly lot more like the handsome cabin boy."

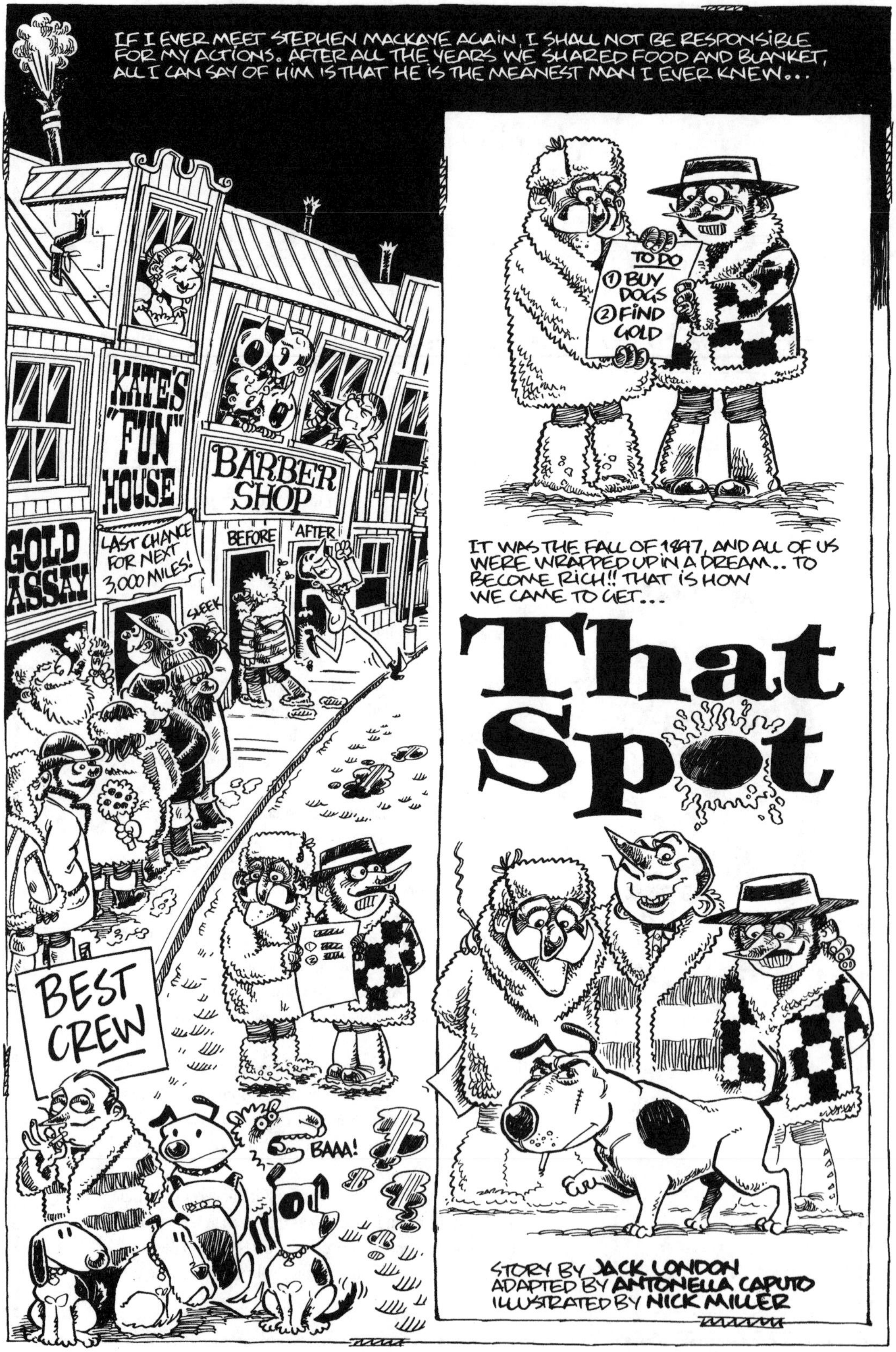
IF I EVER MEET STEPHEN MACKAYE AGAIN, I SHALL NOT BE RESPONSIBLE FOR MY ACTIONS. AFTER ALL THE YEARS WE SHARED FOOD AND BLANKET, ALL I CAN SAY OF HIM IS THAT HE IS THE MEANEST MAN I EVER KNEW...
KATE'S "FUN" HOUSE
BARBER SHOP
GOLD ASSAY
LAST CHANCE FOR NEXT 3,000 MILES!
BEFORE
AFTER
SLEEK
TO DO
1 BUY DOGS
2 FIND GOLD
BEST CREW
BAAA!
IT WAS THE FALL OF 1897, AND ALL OF US WERE WRAPPED UP IN A DREAM... TO BECOME RICH!! THAT IS HOW WE CAME TO GET...
That Spot
STORY BY JACK LONDON
ADAPTED BY ANTONELLA CAPUTO
ILLUSTRATED BY NICK MILLER

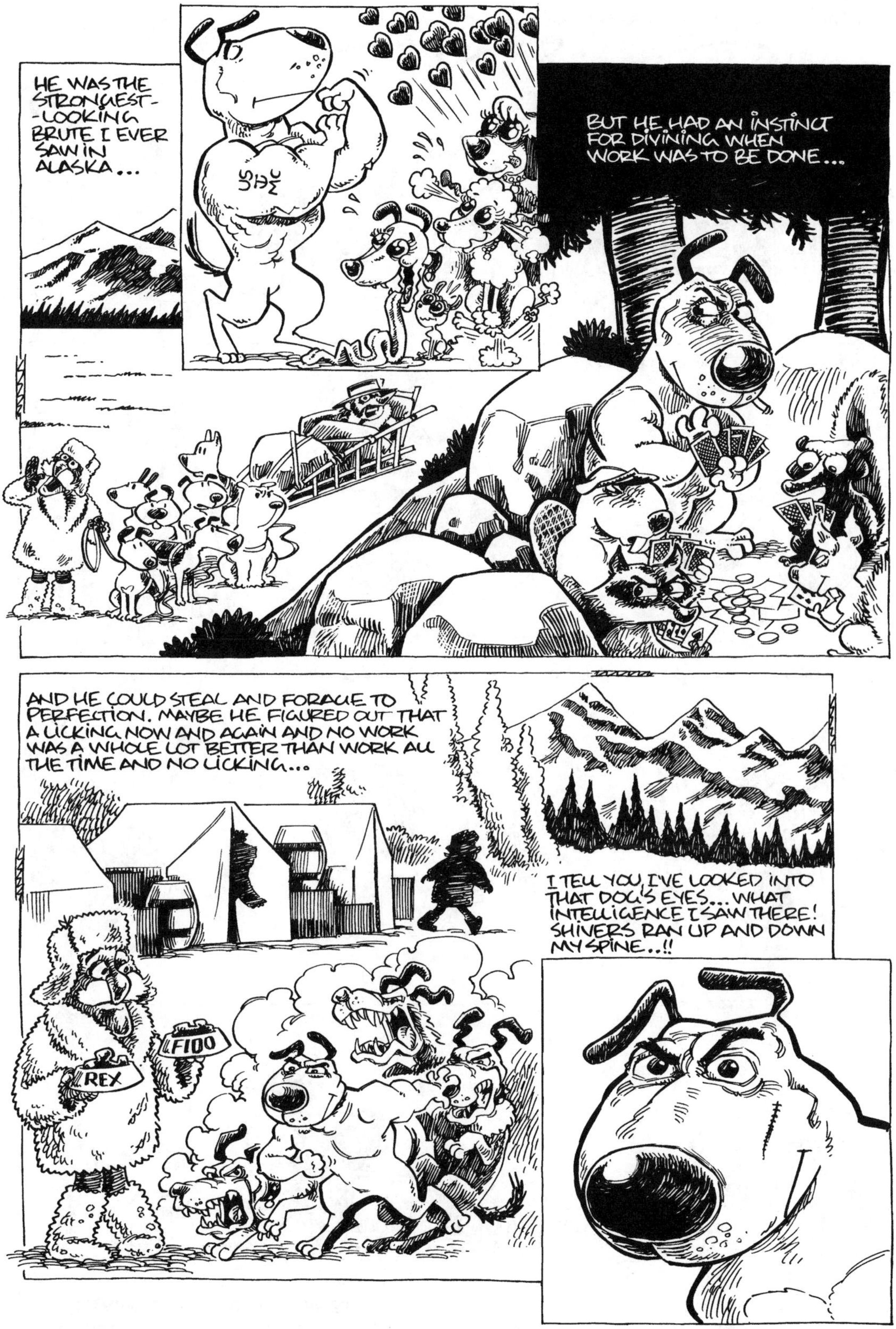
HE WAS THE STRONGEST-LOOKING BRUTE I EVER SAW IN ALASKA...
BUT HE HAD AN INSTINCT FOR DIVINING WHEN WORK WAS TO BE DONE...
AND HE COULD STEAL AND FORAGE TO PERFECTION. MAYBE HE FIGURED OUT THAT A LICKING NOW AND AGAIN AND NO WORK WAS A WHOLE LOT BETTER THAN WORK ALL THE TIME AND NO LICKING...
FIDO
REX
I TELL YOU, I'VE LOOKED INTO THAT DOG'S EYES... WHAT INTELLIGENCE I SAW THERE! SHIVERS RAN UP AND DOWN MY SPINE..!!

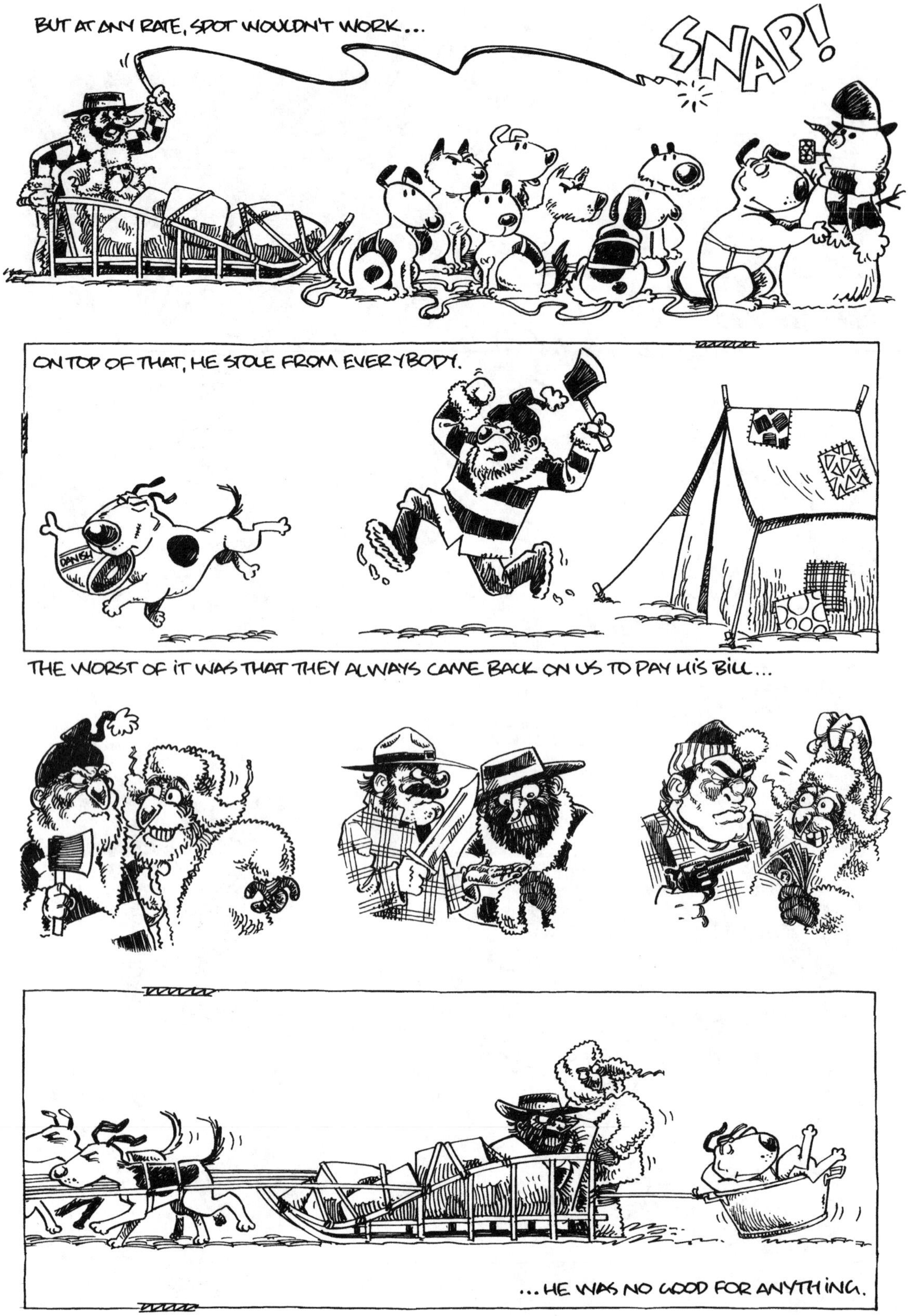
BUT AT ANY RATE, SPOT WOULDN'T WORK...
SNAP!
ON TOP OF THAT, HE STOLE FROM EVERYBODY.
DANISH
THE WORST OF IT WAS THAT THEY ALWAYS CAME BACK ON US TO PAY HIS BILL...
...HE WAS NO GOOD FOR ANYTHING.

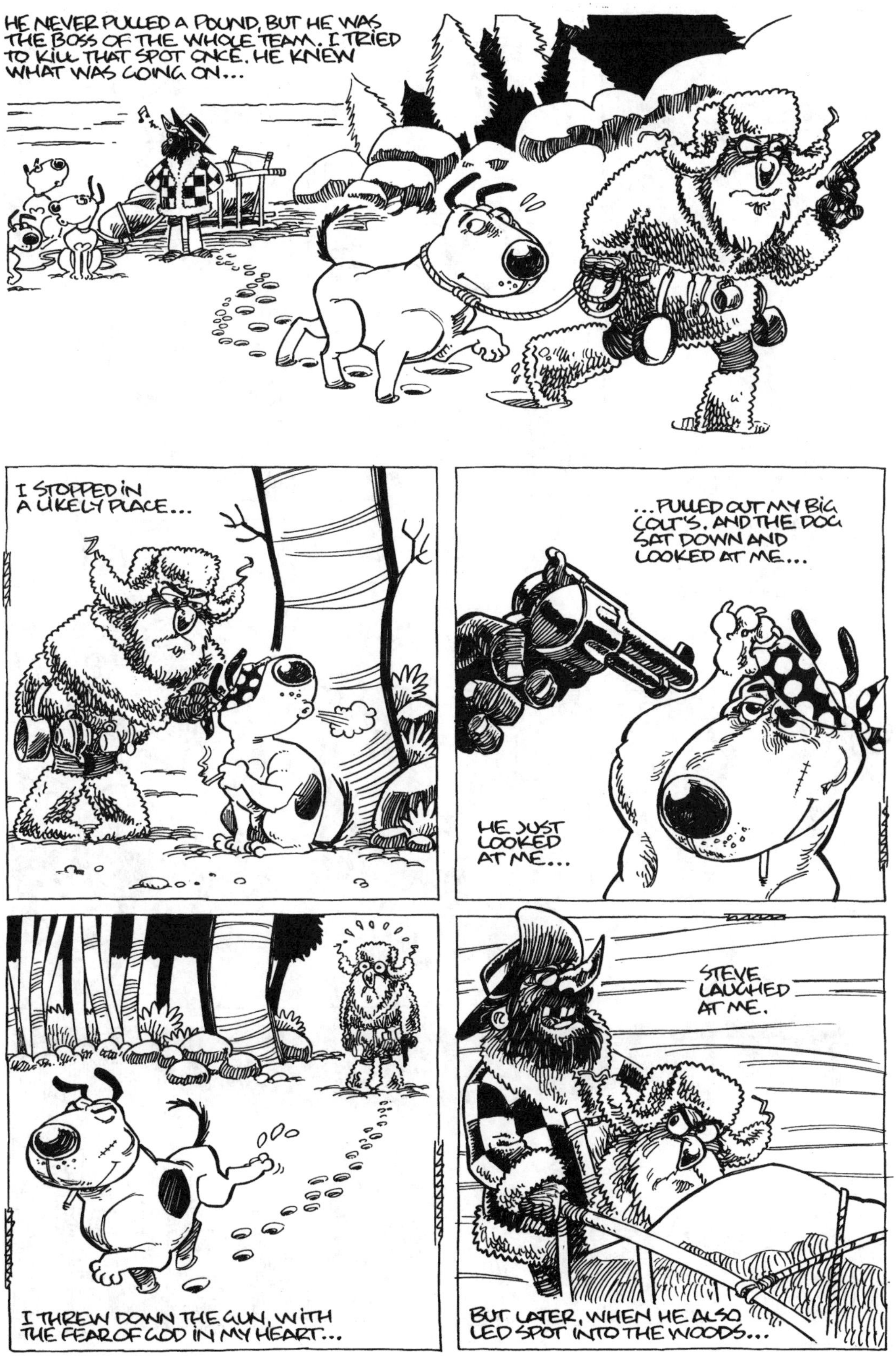
HE NEVER PULLED A POUND, BUT HE WAS THE BOSS OF THE WHOLE TEAM. I TRIED TO KILL THAT SPOT ONCE. HE KNEW WHAT WAS GOING ON...
I STOPPED IN A LIKELY PLACE...
...PULLED OUT MY BIG COLT'S. AND THE DOG SAT DOWN AND LOOKED AT ME...
HE JUST LOOKED AT ME...
I THREW DOWN THE GUN, WITH THE FEAR OF GOD IN MY HEART...
STEVE LAUGHED AT ME.
BUT LATER, WHEN HE ALSO LED SPOT INTO THE WOODS...

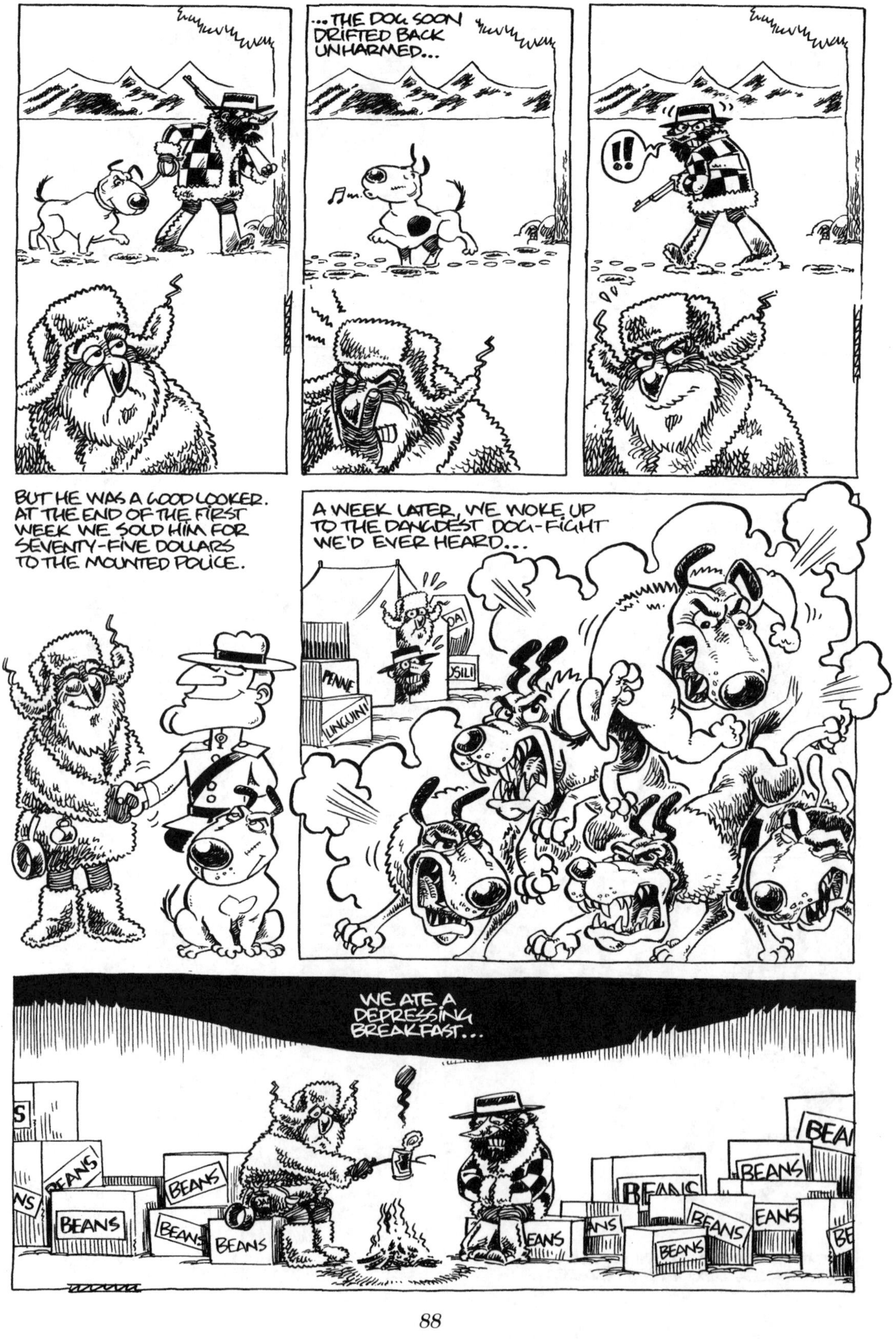
...THE DOG SOON DRIFTED BACK UNHARMED...
!!
BUT HE WAS A GOOD LOOKER. AT THE END OF THE FIRST WEEK WE SOLD HIM FOR SEVENTY-FIVE DOLLARS TO THE MOUNTED POLICE.
A WEEK LATER, WE WOKE UP TO THE DANGDEST DOG-FIGHT WE'D EVER HEARD...
PENNE
LINGUINI
WE ATE A DEPRESSING BREAKFAST...
BEANS
BEANS
BEANS
BEANS
BEANS
BEANS
BEANS
BEANS

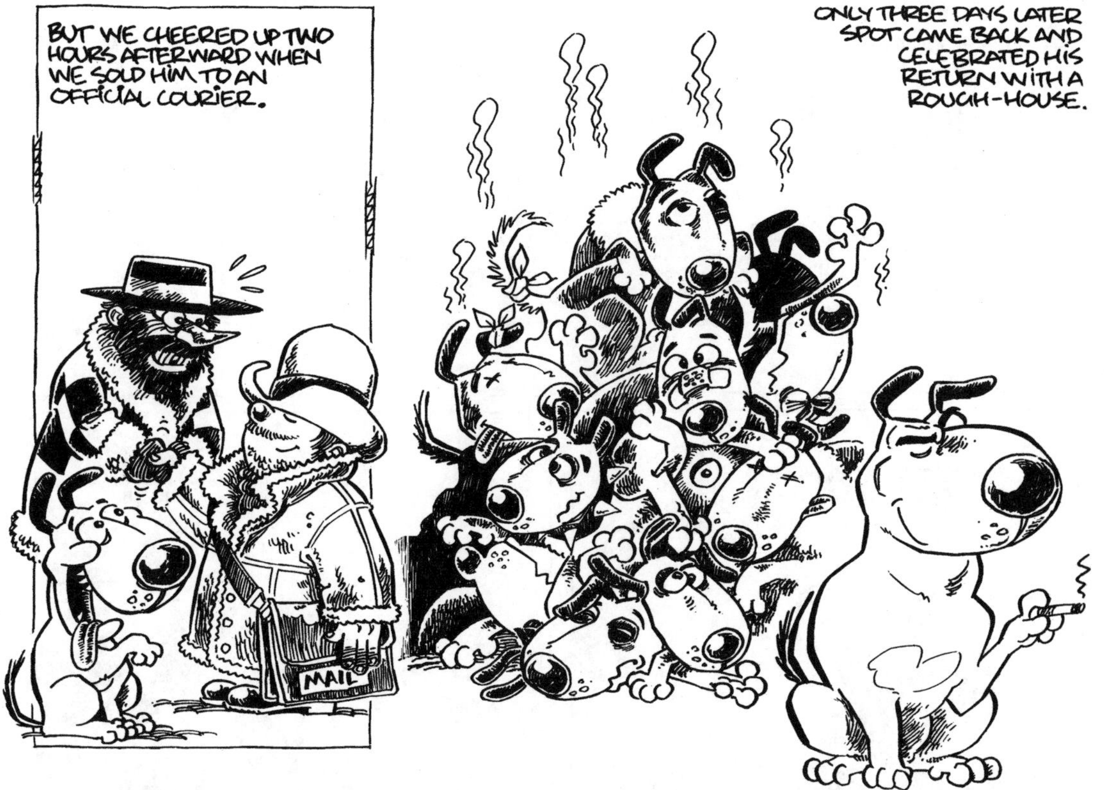
BUT WE CHEERED UP TWO HOURS AFTERWARD WHEN WE SOLD HIM TO AN OFFICIAL COURIER.
MAIL
ONLY THREE DAYS LATER SPOT CAME BACK AND CELEBRATED HIS RETURN WITH A ROUGH-HOUSE.

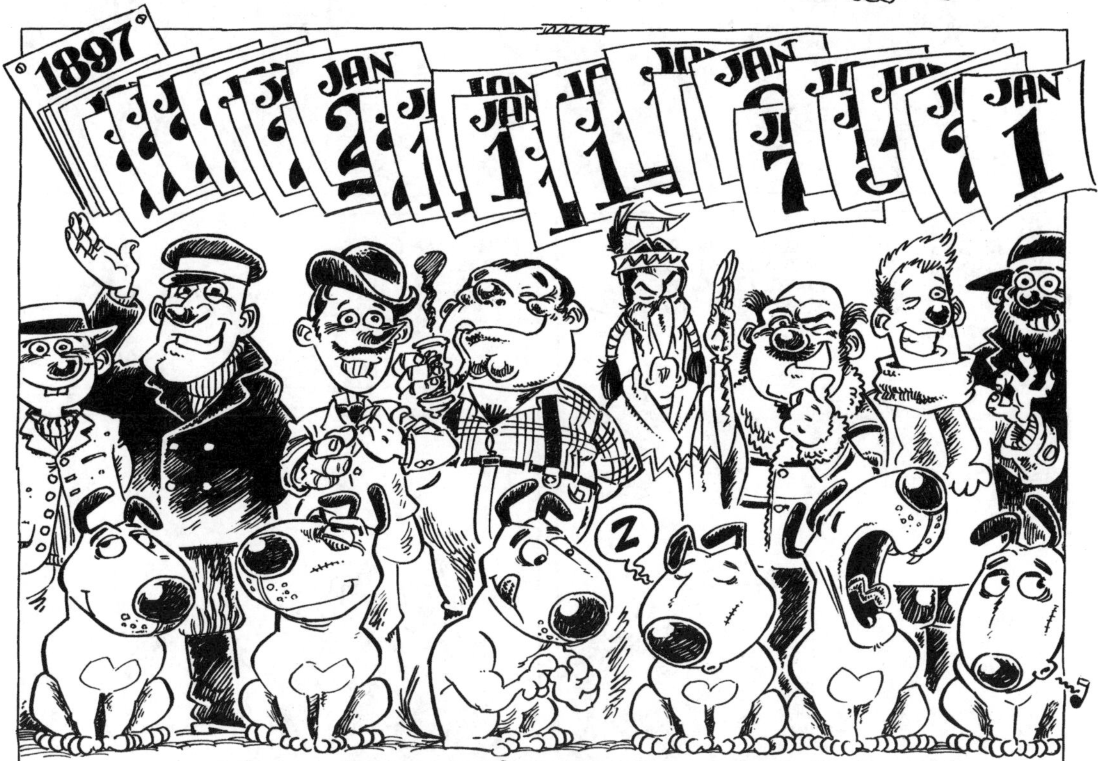
1897
JAN
1
Z
WE SOLD HIM TWENTY TIMES AND HE ALWAYS RETURNED, AND NO ONE ASKED FOR THEIR MONEY BACK.

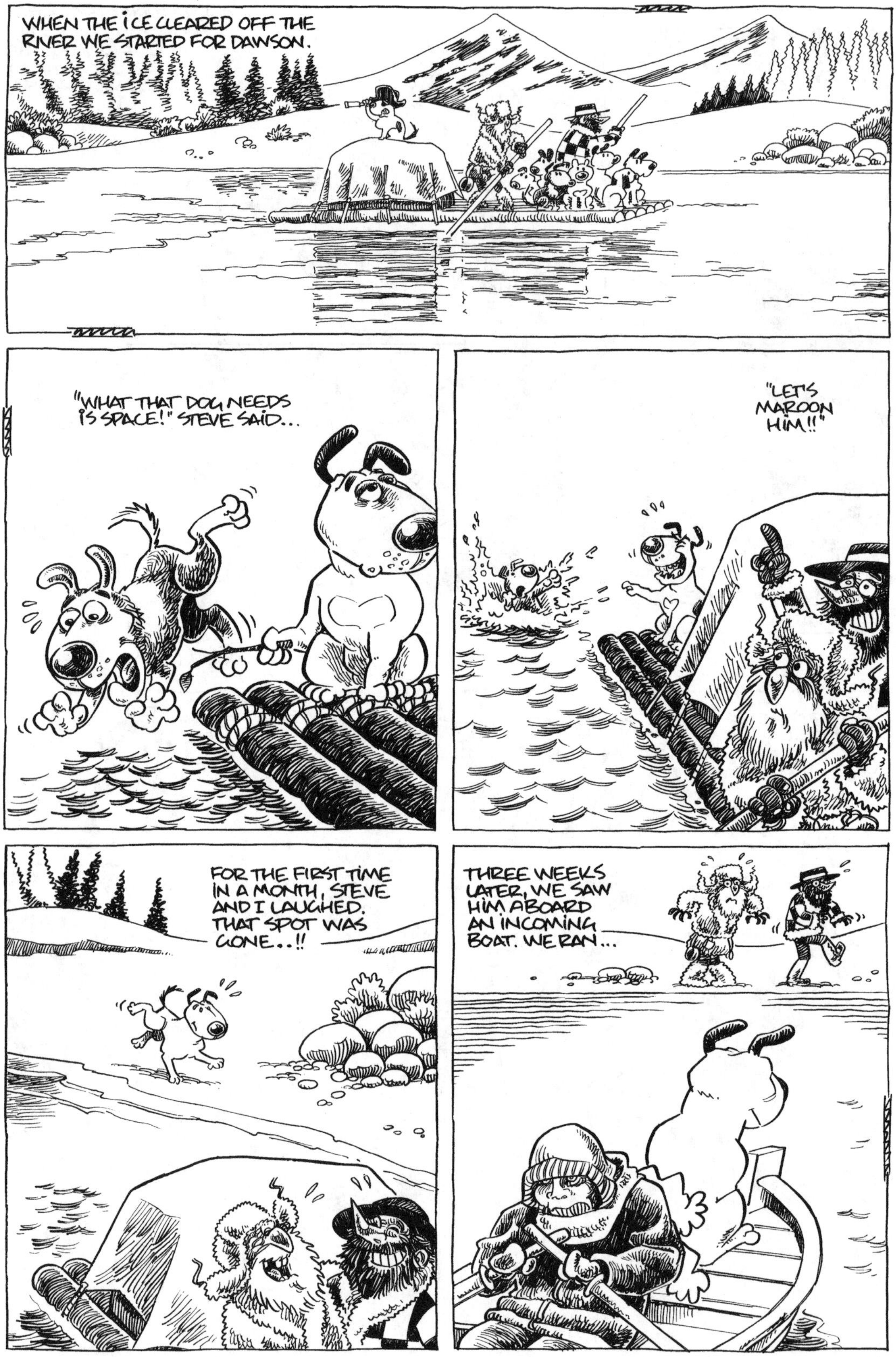
WHEN THE ICE CLEARED OFF THE RIVER WE STARTED FOR DAWSON.
"WHAT THAT DOG NEEDS IS SPACE!" STEVE SAID...
"LET'S MAROON HIM!!"
FOR THE FIRST TIME IN A MONTH, STEVE AND I LAUGHED. THAT SPOT WAS GONE..!!
THREE WEEKS LATER, WE SAW HIM ABOARD AN INCOMING BOAT. WE RAN...

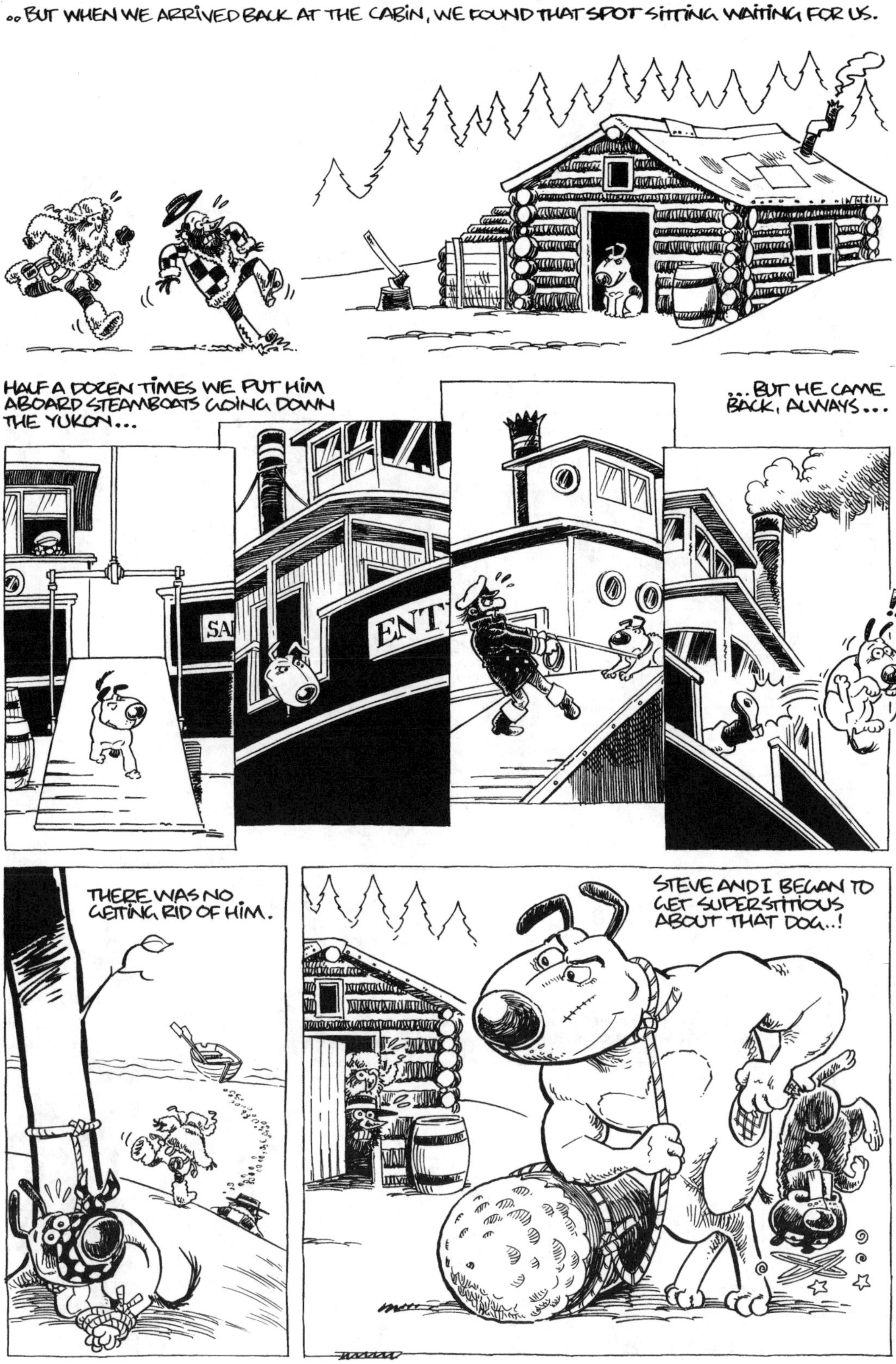
..BUT WHEN WE ARRIVED BACK AT THE CABIN, WE FOUND THAT SPOT SITTING WAITING FOR US.
HALF A DOZEN TIMES WE PUT HIM ABOARD STEAMBOATS GOING DOWN THE YUKON...
...BUT HE CAME BACK, ALWAYS...
SA
ENT
!!
THERE WAS NO GETTING RID OF HIM.
STEVE AND I BEGAN TO GET SUPERSTITIOUS ABOUT THAT DOG..!

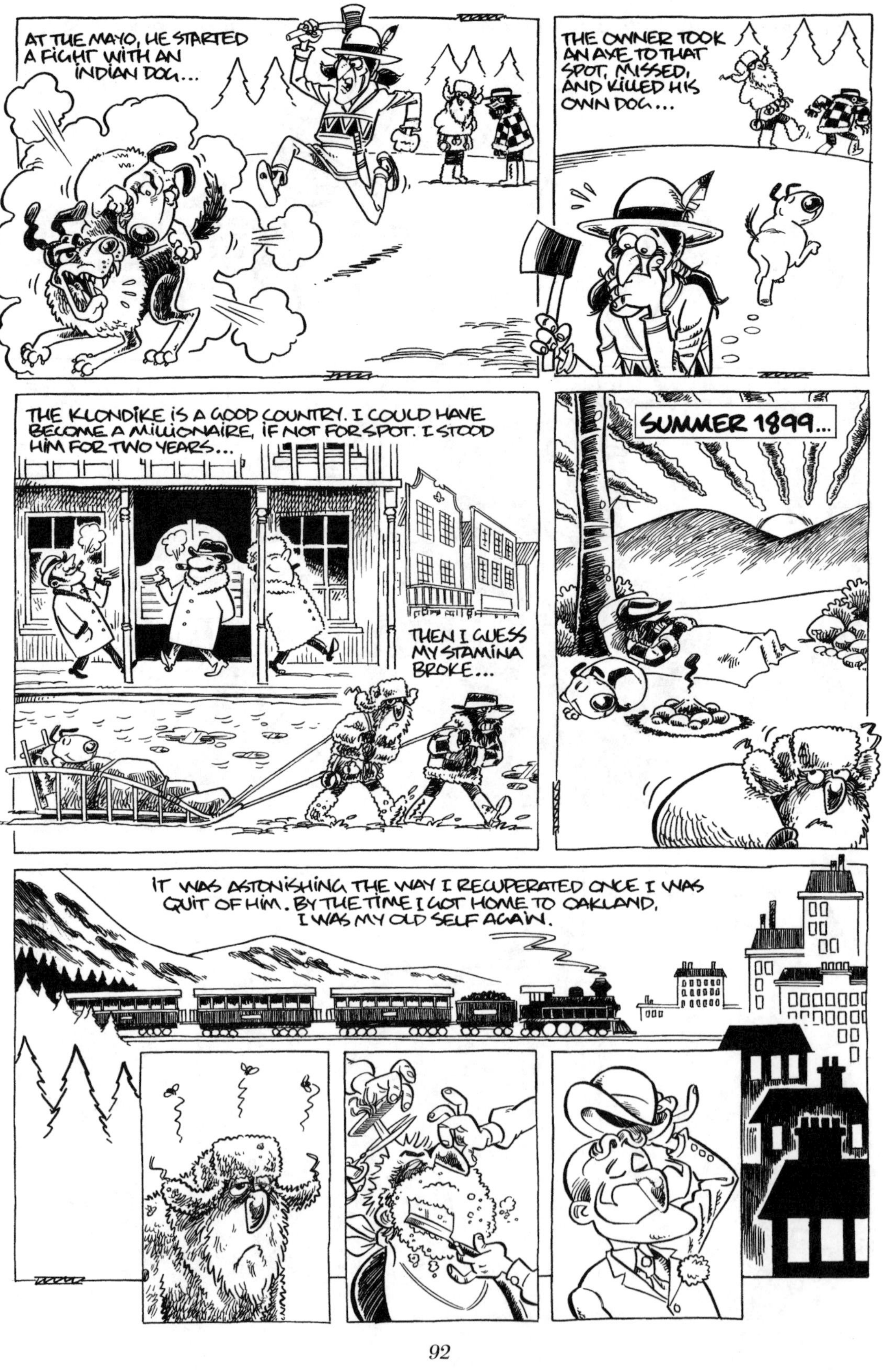
AT THE MAYO, HE STARTED A FIGHT WITH AN INDIAN DOG...
THE OWNER TOOK AN AXE TO THAT SPOT, MISSED, AND KILLED HIS OWN DOG...
THE KLONDIKE IS A GOOD COUNTRY. I COULD HAVE BECOME A MILLIONAIRE, IF NOT FOR SPOT. I STOOD HIM FOR TWO YEARS...
THEN I GUESS MY STAMINA BROKE...
SUMMER 1899...
IT WAS ASTONISHING THE WAY I RECUPERATED ONCE I WAS QUIT OF HIM. BY THE TIME I GOT HOME TO OAKLAND, I WAS MY OLD SELF AGAIN.

ONE YEAR LATER, I WAS BACK IN MY OFFICE AND PROSPERING. THEN A MESSAGE FROM STEVE ARRIVED...

THAT SPOT WAS BACK AGAIN.

SEAT...

ALL-A BOARD!

MY WIFE MADE ME BUY HIM A COLLAR AND TAG.

AN HOUR LATER, HE SHOWED HIS GRATITUDE BY KILLING HER PET PERSIAN CAT.

LAST NIGHT THAT SPOT KILLED NINETEEN OF MY NEIGHBOR'S CHICKENS.

I SHALL HAVE TO PAY FOR THEM.

MY NEIGHBORS HAVE MOVED OUT.

SPOT WAS THE CAUSE OF IT.

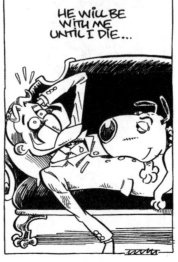

HE WILL BE WITH ME UNTIL I DIE...

...THAT IS WHY I AM SO DISAPPOINTED IN STEPHEN MACKAYE...

...I HAD NO IDEA HE WAS SO MEAN A MAN..!!

The End

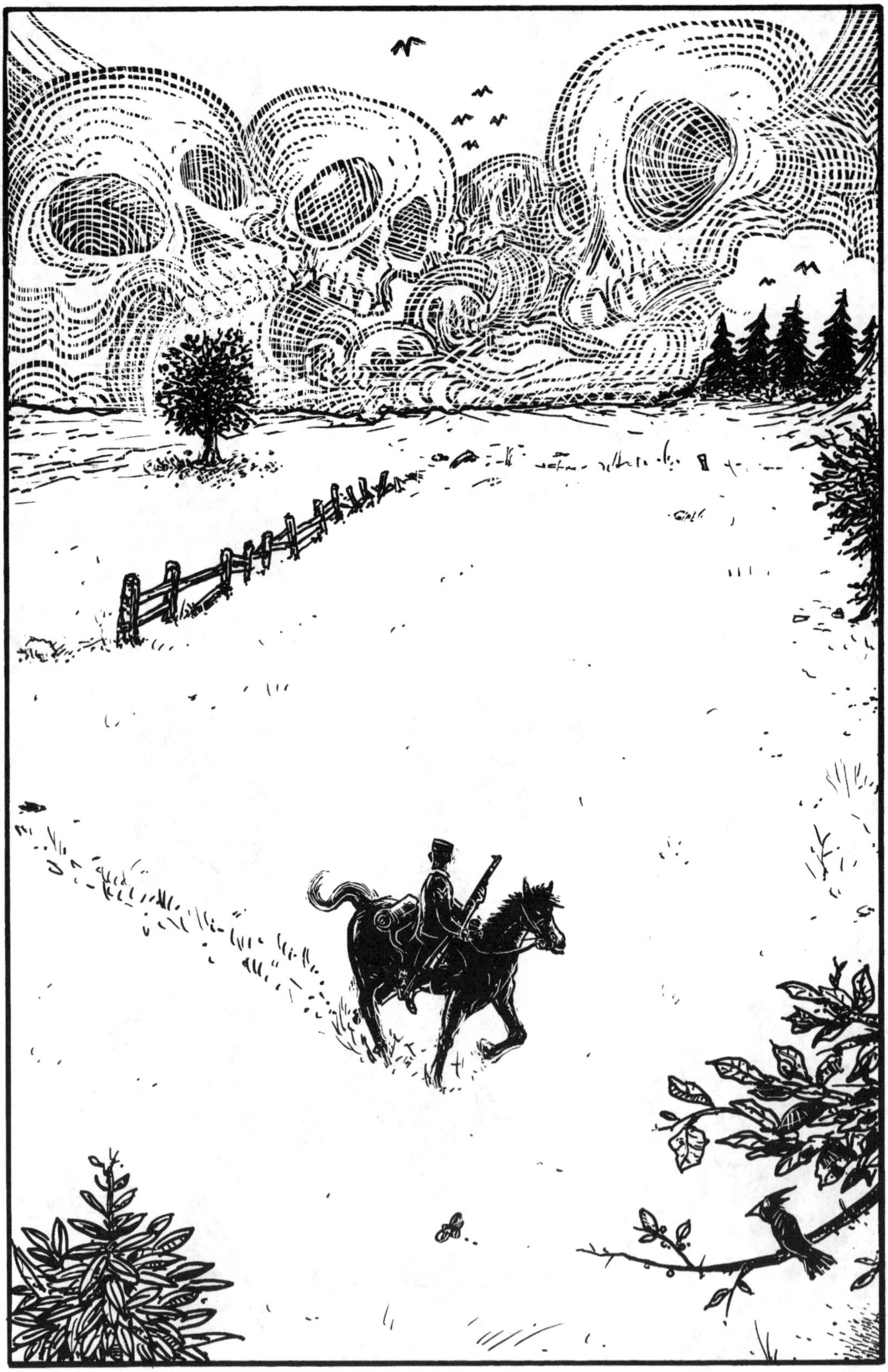

WAR

story by **JACK LONDON**

illustrated by **PETER KUPER**

HE WAS A YOUNG MAN, not more than twenty-four or five, and he might have sat his horse with the careless grace of his youth had he not been so catlike and tense. His black eyes roved everywhere, catching the movements of twigs and branches where small birds hopped, questing ever onward through the changing vistas of trees and brush, and returning always to the clumps of undergrowth on either side. And as he watched, so did he listen, though he rode on in silence, save for the boom of heavy guns from far to the west. This had been sounding monotonously in his ears for hours, and only its cessation could have aroused his notice. For he had business closer to hand. Across his saddle-bow was balanced a carbine.

So tensely was he strung, that a bunch of quail, exploding into flight from under his horse's nose, startled him to such an extent that automatically, instantly, he had reined in and fetched the carbine halfway to his shoulder. He grinned sheepishly, recovered himself, and rode on. So tense was he, so bent upon the work he had to do, that the sweat stung his eyes unwiped, and unheeded rolled down his nose and spattered his saddle pommel. The band of his cavalryman's hat was fresh-stained with

sweat. The roan horse under him was likewise wet. It was high noon of a breathless day of heat. Even the birds and squirrels did not dare the sun, but sheltered in shady hiding places among the trees.

Man and horse were littered with leaves and dusted with yellow pollen, for the open was ventured no more than was compulsory. They kept to the brush and trees, and invariably the man halted and peered out before crossing a dry glade or naked stretch of upland pasturage. He worked always to the north, though his way was devious, and it was from the north that he seemed most to apprehend that for which he was looking. He was no coward, but his courage was only that of the average civilized man, and he was looking to live, not die.

Up a small hillside he followed a cow-path through such dense scrub that he was forced to dismount and lead his horse. But when the path swung around to the west, he abandoned it and headed to the north again along the oak-covered top of the ridge.

The ridge ended in a steep descent—so steep that he zigzagged back and forth across the face of the slope, sliding and stumbling among the dead leaves and matted vines and keeping a watchful eye on the horse above that threatened to fall down upon him. The sweat ran from him, and the pollen-dust, settling pungently in mouth and nostrils, increased his thirst. Try as he would, nevertheless the descent was noisy, and frequently he stopped, panting in the dry heat and listening for any warning from beneath.

At the bottom he came out on a flat, so densely forested that he could not make out its extent. Here the character of the woods changed, and he was able to remount. Instead of the twisted hillside oaks, tall straight trees, big-trunked and prosperous, rose from the damp fat soil. Only here and there were thickets, easily avoided, while he encountered winding, park-like glades where the cattle had pastured in the days before war had run them off.

His progress was more rapid now, as he came down into the valley, and at the end of half an hour he halted at an ancient rail fence on the edge of a clearing. He did not like the openness of it, yet his path lay across to the fringe of trees that marked the banks of the stream. It was a mere quarter of a mile across that open, but the thought of venturing out in it was repugnant. A rifle, a score of them, a thousand, might lurk in that fringe by the stream.

Twice he essayed to start, and twice he paused. He was appalled by his own loneliness. The pulse of war that beat from the West suggested the companionship of battling thousands; here was naught but silence, and himself, and possible death-dealing bullets from a myriad ambushes. And yet his task was to find what he feared to find. He must on, and on, till somewhere, some time, he encountered another man, or other men, from the other side, scouting, as he was scouting, to make report, as he must make report, of having come in touch.

Changing his mind, he skirted inside the woods for a distance, and again

peeped forth. This time, in the middle of the clearing, he saw a small farmhouse. There were no signs of life. No smoke curled from the chimney, not a barnyard fowl clucked and strutted. The kitchen door stood open, and he gazed so long and hard into the black aperture that it seemed almost that a farmer's wife must emerge at any moment.

He licked the pollen and dust from his dry lips, stiffened himself, mind and body, and rode out into the blazing sunshine. Nothing stirred. He went on past the house, and approached the wall of trees and bushes by the river's bank. One thought persisted maddeningly. It was of the crash into his body of a high-velocity bullet. It made him feel very fragile and defenseless, and he crouched lower in the saddle.

Tethering his horse in the edge of the wood, he continued a hundred yards on foot till he came to the stream. Twenty feet wide it was, without perceptible current, cool and inviting, and he was very thirsty. But he waited inside his screen of leafage, his eyes fixed on the screen on the opposite side. To make the wait endurable, he sat down, his carbine resting on his knees. The minutes passed, and slowly his tenseness relaxed. At last he decided there was no danger; but just as he prepared to part the bushes and bend down to the water, a movement among the opposite bushes caught his eye.

It might be a bird. But he waited. Again there was an agitation of the bushes, and then, so suddenly that it almost startled a cry from him, the bushes parted and a face peered out. It was a face covered with several weeks' growth of ginger-colored beard. The eyes were blue and wide apart, with laughter-wrinkles in the corners that showed despite the tired and anxious expression of the whole face.

All this he could see with microscopic clearness, for the distance was no more than twenty feet. And all this he saw in

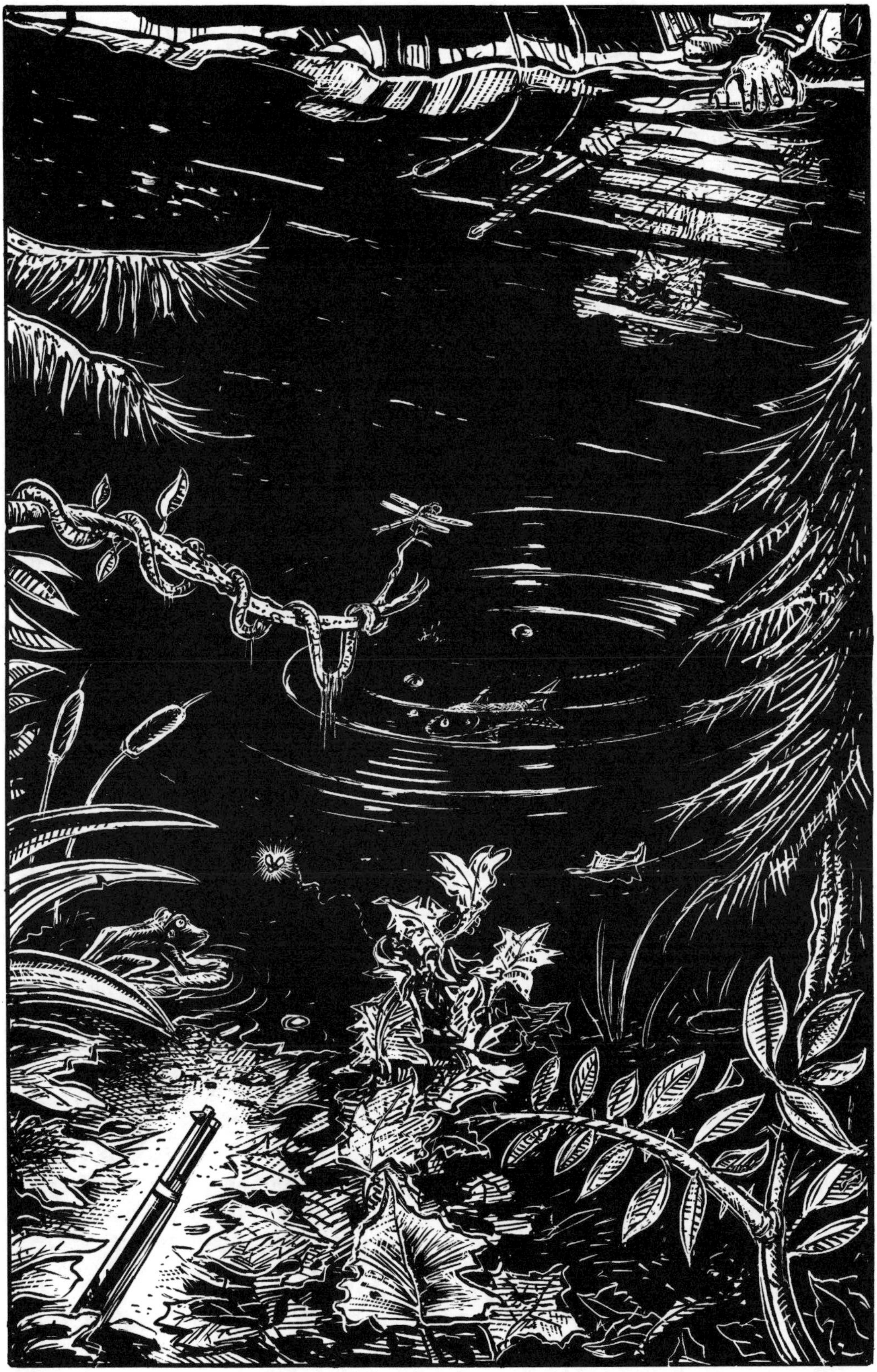

such brief time, that he saw it as he lifted his carbine to his shoulder. He glanced along the sights, and knew that he was gazing upon a man who was as good as dead. It was impossible to miss at such point-blank range.

But he did not shoot. Slowly he lowered the carbine and watched. A hand, clutching a water-bottle, became visible and the ginger beard bent downward to fill the bottle. He could hear the gurgle of the water. Then arm and bottle and ginger beard disappeared behind the closing bushes. A long time he waited, when, with thirst unslaked, he crept back to his horse, rode slowly across the sun-washed clearing, and passed into the shelter of the woods beyond.

TWO

ANOTHER DAY, HOT AND BREATHLESS. A deserted farmhouse, large, with many out-buildings and an orchard, standing in a clearing. From the woods, on a roan horse, carbine across pommel, rode the young man with the quick black eyes. He breathed with relief as he gained the house. That a fight had taken place here earlier in the season was evident. Clips and empty cartridges, tarnished with verdigris, lay on the ground, which, while wet, had been torn up by the hoofs of horses. Hard by the kitchen garden were graves, tagged and numbered. From the oak tree by the kitchen door, in tattered, weatherbeaten garments, hung the bodies of two men. The faces, shriveled and defaced, bore no likeness to the faces of men. The roan horse snorted beneath them, and the rider caressed and soothed it and tied it farther away.

Entering the house, he found the interior a wreck. He trod on empty cartridges as he walked from room to room to reconnoiter from the windows. Men had camped and slept everywhere, and on the floor of one room he came upon stains unmistakable where the wounded had been laid down.

Again outside, he led the horse around behind the barn and invaded the orchard. A dozen trees were burdened with ripe apples. He filled his pockets, eating while he picked. Then a thought came to him, and he glanced at the sun, calculating the time of his return to camp. He pulled off his shirt, tying the sleeves and making a bag. This he proceeded to fill with apples.

As he was about to mount his horse, the animal suddenly pricked up its ears. The man, too, listened, and heard, faintly, the thud of hoofs on soft earth. He crept to the corner of the barn and peered out. A dozen mounted men, strung out loosely, approaching from the opposite side of the clearing, were only a matter of a hundred yards or so away. They rode on to the house. Some dismounted, while others remained in the saddle as an earnest that their stay would be short. They seemed to be holding a council, for he could hear them talking excitedly in the detested tongue of the alien invader. The time passed, but they seemed unable to reach a decision. He put the carbine away in its boot, mounted, and waited impatiently, balancing the shirt of apples on the pommel.

He heard footsteps approaching, and drove his spurs so fiercely into the roan as to force a surprised groan from the animal as it leaped forward. At the corner of the barn he saw the intruder, a mere boy of nineteen or twenty, jump back to escape being run down. At the same moment the roan swerved and its rider caught a glimpse of the aroused men by the house. Some were springing from their horses, and he could see the rifles going to their shoulders. He passed the kitchen door and the corpses swinging in the shade, compelling his foes to run around the front of the house. A rifle cracked, and a second, but he was going fast, leaning forward, low in the saddle, one hand clutching the shirt of apples, the other guiding the horse.

The top bar of the fence was four feet high, but he knew his roan and leaped it at full career to the accompaniment of several scattered shots. Eight hundred yards straight away were the woods, and the roan was covering the distance with mighty strides. Every man was now firing. pumping their guns so rapidly that he no longer heard individual shots. A bullet went through his hat, but he was unaware, though he did know when another tore through the apples on the pommel. And he winced and ducked even lower when a third bullet, fired low, struck a stone between his horse's legs and ricocheted off through the air, buzzing and humming like some incredible insect.

The shots died down as the magazines were emptied, until, quickly, there was no more shooting. The young man was elated. Through that astonishing fusillade he had come unscathed. He glanced back. Yes, they had emptied their magazines. He could see several reloading. Others were running back behind the house for their horses. As he looked, two already mounted, came back into view around the corner, riding hard. And at the same moment, he saw the man with the unmistakable ginger beard kneel down on the ground, level his gun, and coolly take his time for the long shot.

The young man threw his spurs into the horse, crouched very low, and swerved in his flight in order to distract the other's aim. And still the shot did not come. With each jump of the horse, the woods sprang nearer. They were only two hundred yards away and still the shot was delayed.

And then he heard it, the last thing he was to hear, for he was dead ere he hit the ground in the long crashing fall from the saddle. And they, watching at the house, saw him fall, saw his body bounce when it struck the earth, and saw the burst of red-cheeked apples that rolled about him. They laughed at the unexpected eruption of apples, and clapped their hands in applause of the long shot by the man with the ginger beard.

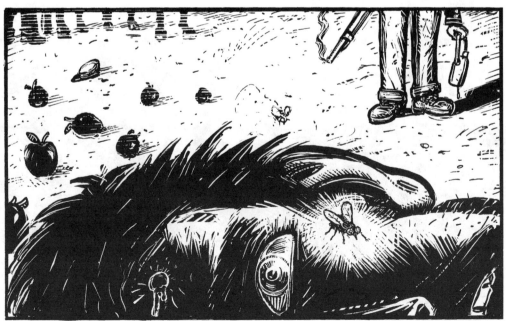

The Francis Spaight

A True Tale Retold by JACK LONDON

illustrated by JOHN W. PIERARD

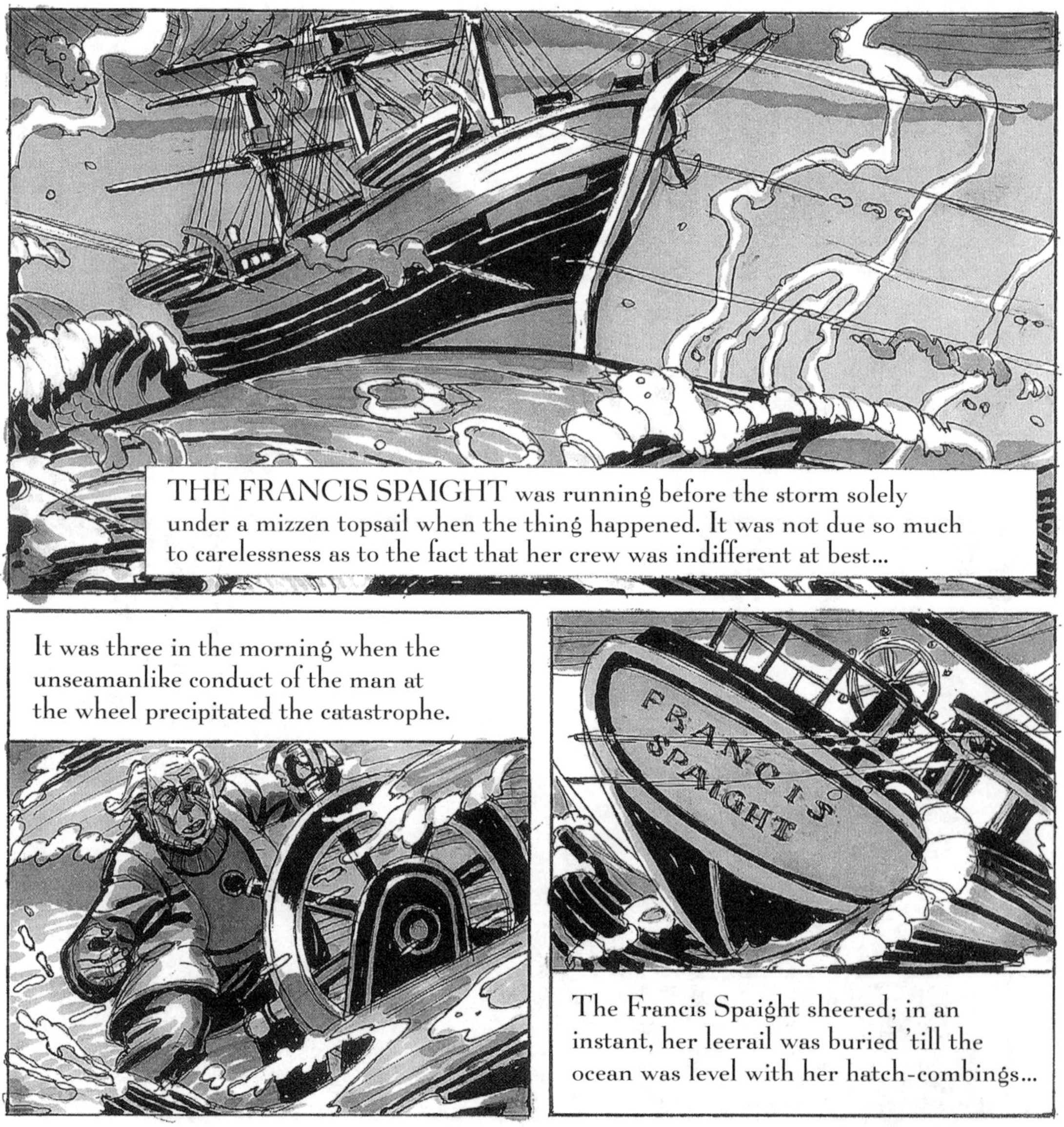
THE FRANCIS SPAIGHT was running before the storm solely under a mizzen topsail when the thing happened. It was not due so much to carelessness as to the fact that her crew was indifferent at best...
It was three in the morning when the unseamanlike conduct of the man at the wheel precipitated the catastrophe.
FRANCIS SPAIGHT
The Francis Spaight sheered; in an instant, her leerail was buried 'till the ocean was level with her hatch-combings...

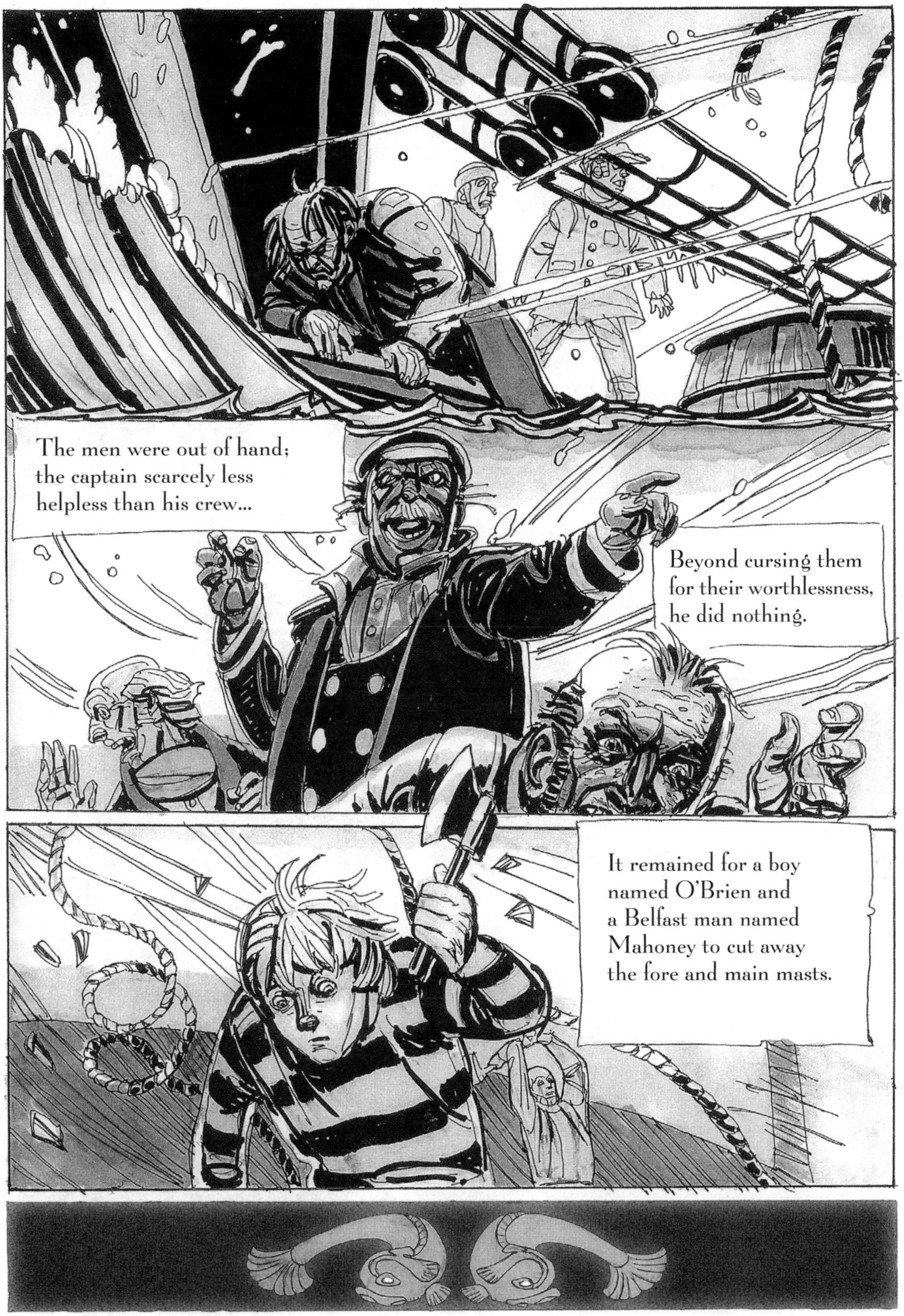
The men were out of hand; the captain scarcely less helpless than his crew...
Beyond cursing them for their worthlessness, he did nothing.
It remained for a boy named O'Brien and a Belfast man named Mahoney to cut away the fore and main masts.

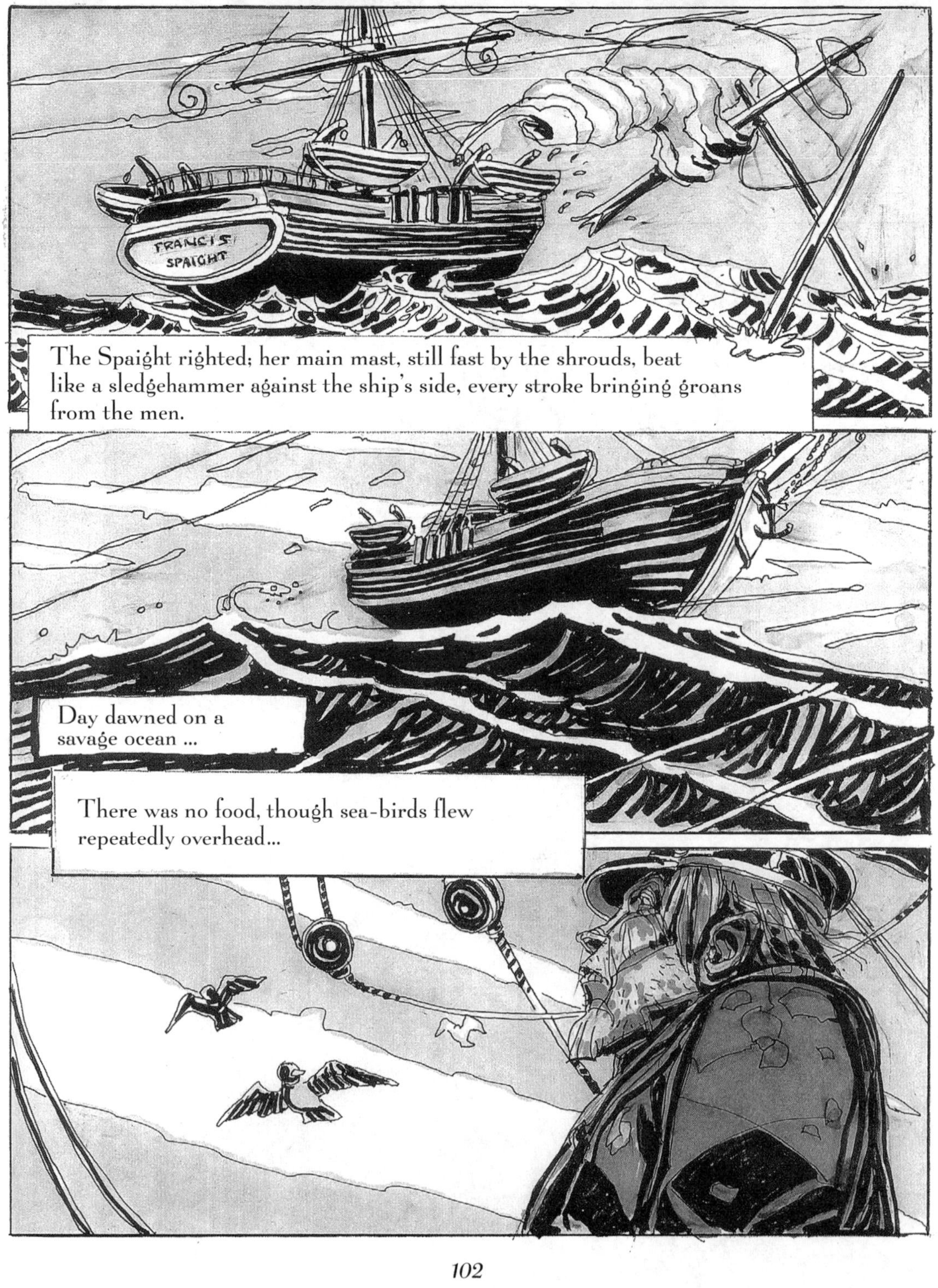
FRANCIS SPAIGHT
The Spaight righted; her main mast, still fast by the shrouds, beat like a sledgehammer against the ship's side, every stroke bringing groans from the men.
Day dawned on a savage ocean ...
There was no food, though sea-birds flew repeatedly overhead...

Long hours of standing in salt-water caused sores to form on their legs...

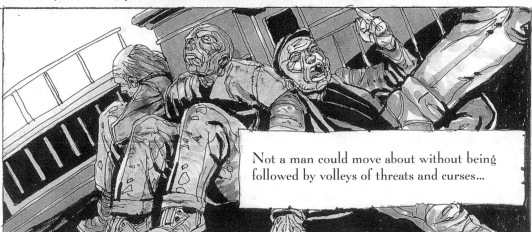

Not a man could move about without being followed by volleys of threats and curses...

Young O'Brien became a favorite target of their abuse...

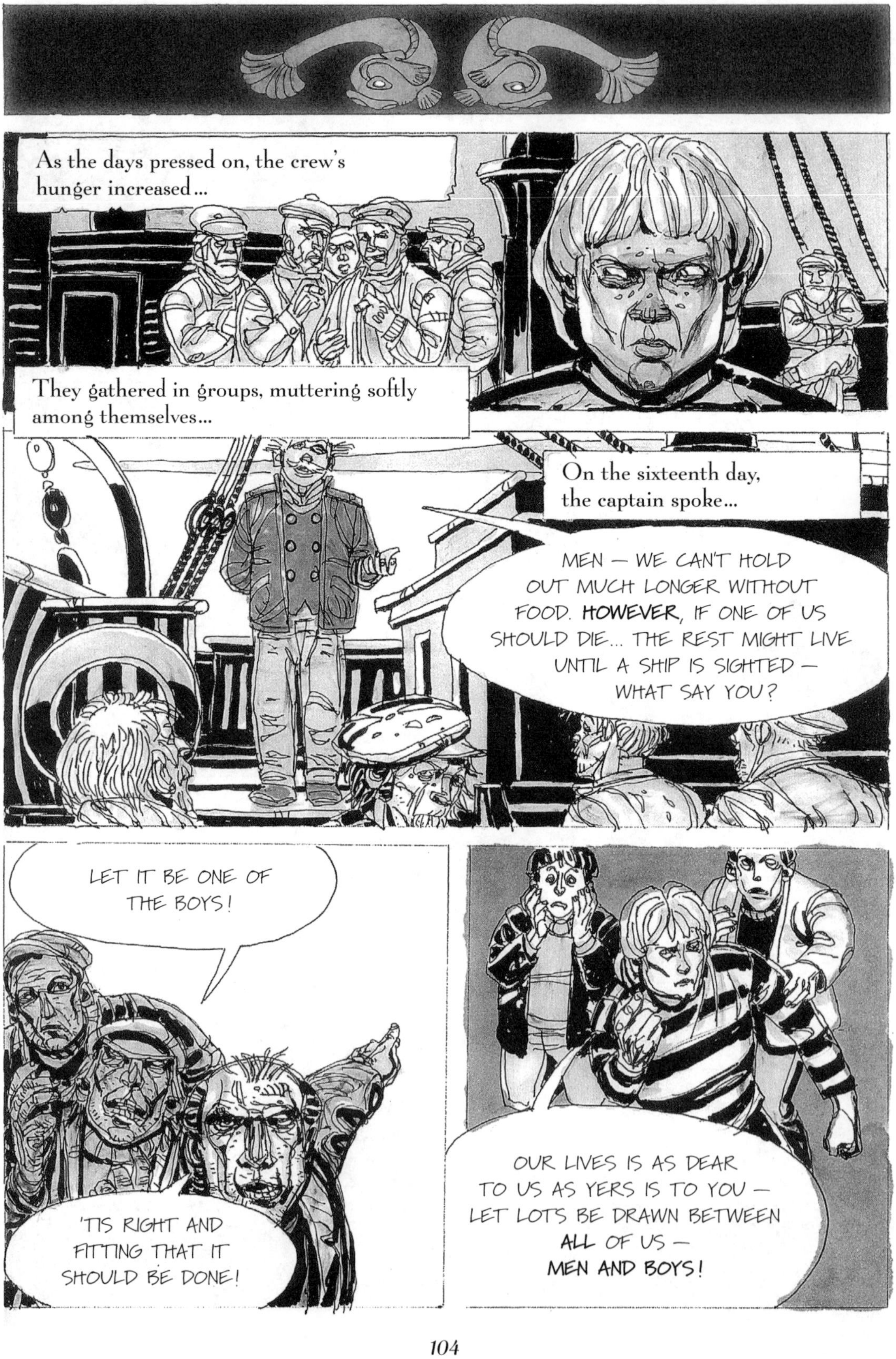
As the days pressed on, the crew's hunger increased...
They gathered in groups, muttering softly among themselves...
On the sixteenth day, the captain spoke...
MEN — WE CAN'T HOLD OUT MUCH LONGER WITHOUT FOOD. HOWEVER, IF ONE OF US SHOULD DIE... THE REST MIGHT LIVE UNTIL A SHIP IS SIGHTED — WHAT SAY YOU?
LET IT BE ONE OF THE BOYS!
'TIS RIGHT AND FITTING THAT IT SHOULD BE DONE!
OUR LIVES IS AS DEAR TO US AS YERS IS TO YOU — LET LOTS BE DRAWN BETWEEN ALL OF US — MEN AND BOYS!

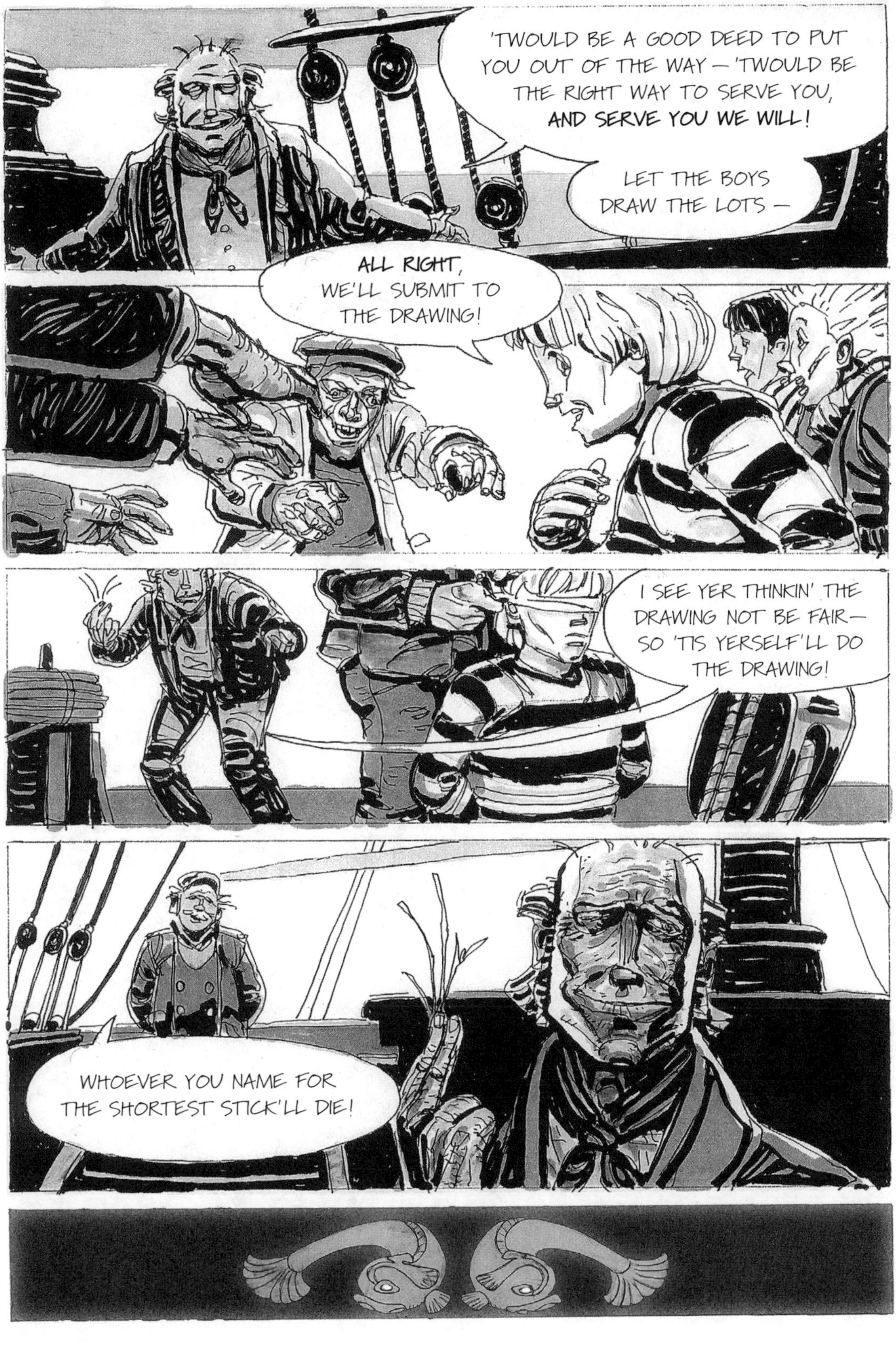
'TWOULD BE A GOOD DEED TO PUT YOU OUT OF THE WAY — 'TWOULD BE THE RIGHT WAY TO SERVE YOU, **AND SERVE YOU WE WILL!**
LET THE BOYS DRAW THE LOTS —
ALL RIGHT, WE'LL SUBMIT TO THE DRAWING!
I SEE YER THINKIN' THE DRAWING NOT BE FAIR— SO 'TIS YERSELF'LL DO THE DRAWING!
WHOEVER YOU NAME FOR THE SHORTEST STICK'LL DIE!

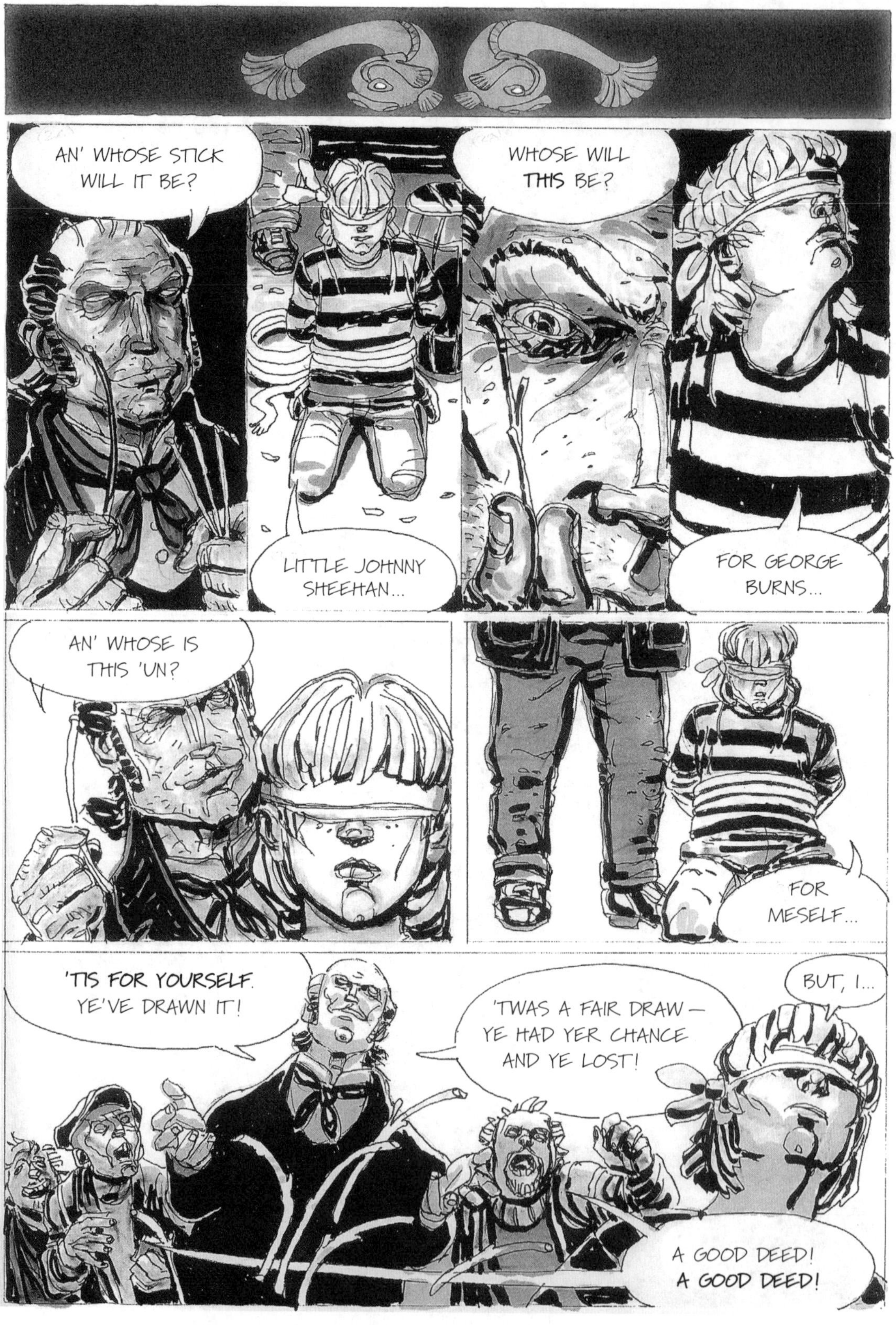
AN' WHOSE STICK WILL IT BE?
LITTLE JOHNNY SHEEHAN...
WHOSE WILL THIS BE?
FOR GEORGE BURNS...
AN' WHOSE IS THIS 'UN?
FOR MESELF...
'TIS FOR YOURSELF. YE'VE DRAWN IT!
'TWAS A FAIR DRAW— YE HAD YER CHANCE AND YE LOST!
BUT, I...
A GOOD DEED! A GOOD DEED!

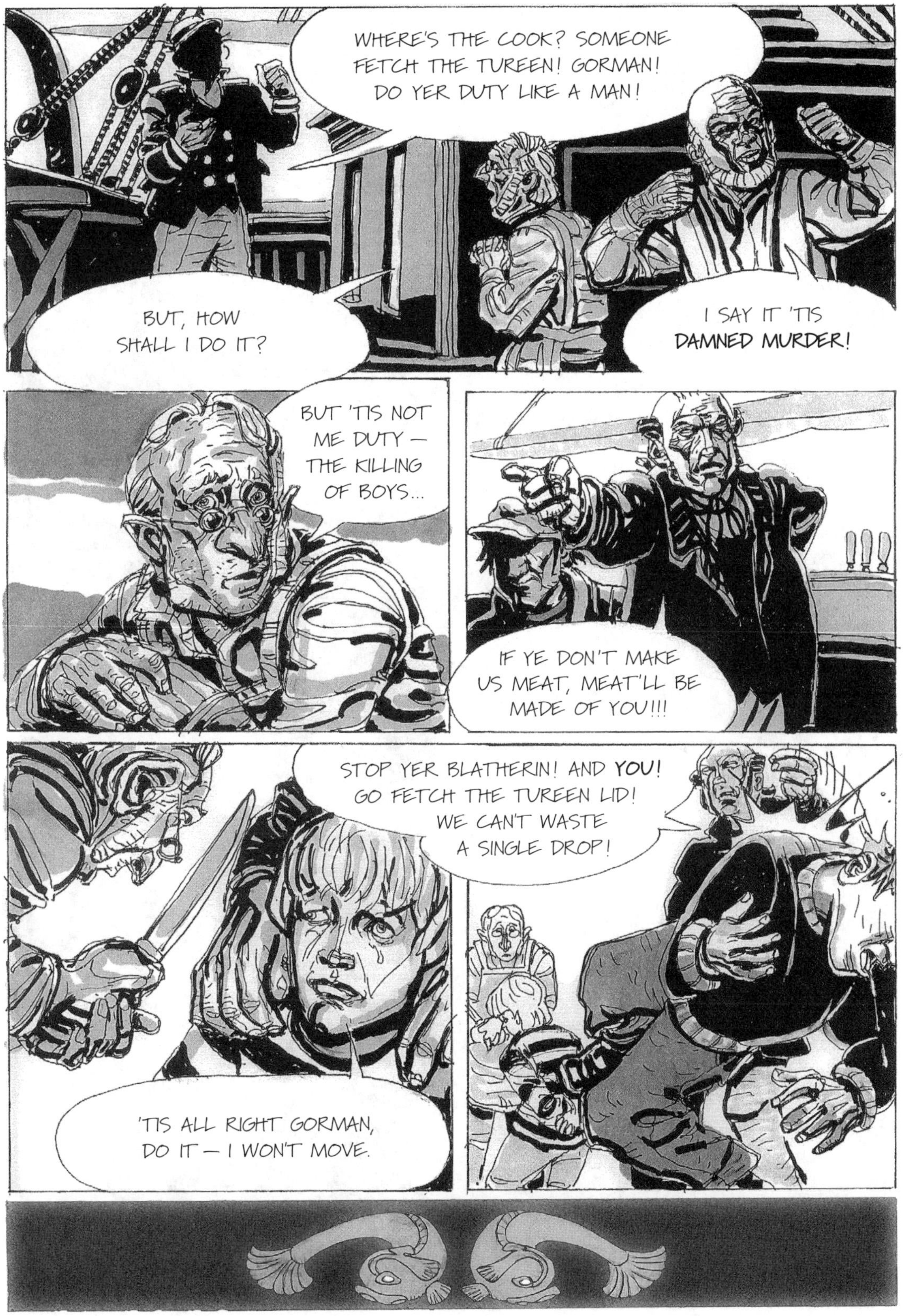
WHERE'S THE COOK? SOMEONE FETCH THE TUREEN! GORMAN! DO YER DUTY LIKE A MAN!
BUT, HOW SHALL I DO IT?
I SAY IT 'TIS DAMNED MURDER!
BUT 'TIS NOT ME DUTY — THE KILLING OF BOYS...
IF YE DON'T MAKE US MEAT, MEAT'LL BE MADE OF YOU!!!
STOP YER BLATHERIN! AND YOU! GO FETCH THE TUREEN LID! WE CAN'T WASTE A SINGLE DROP!
'TIS ALL RIGHT GORMAN, DO IT — I WON'T MOVE.

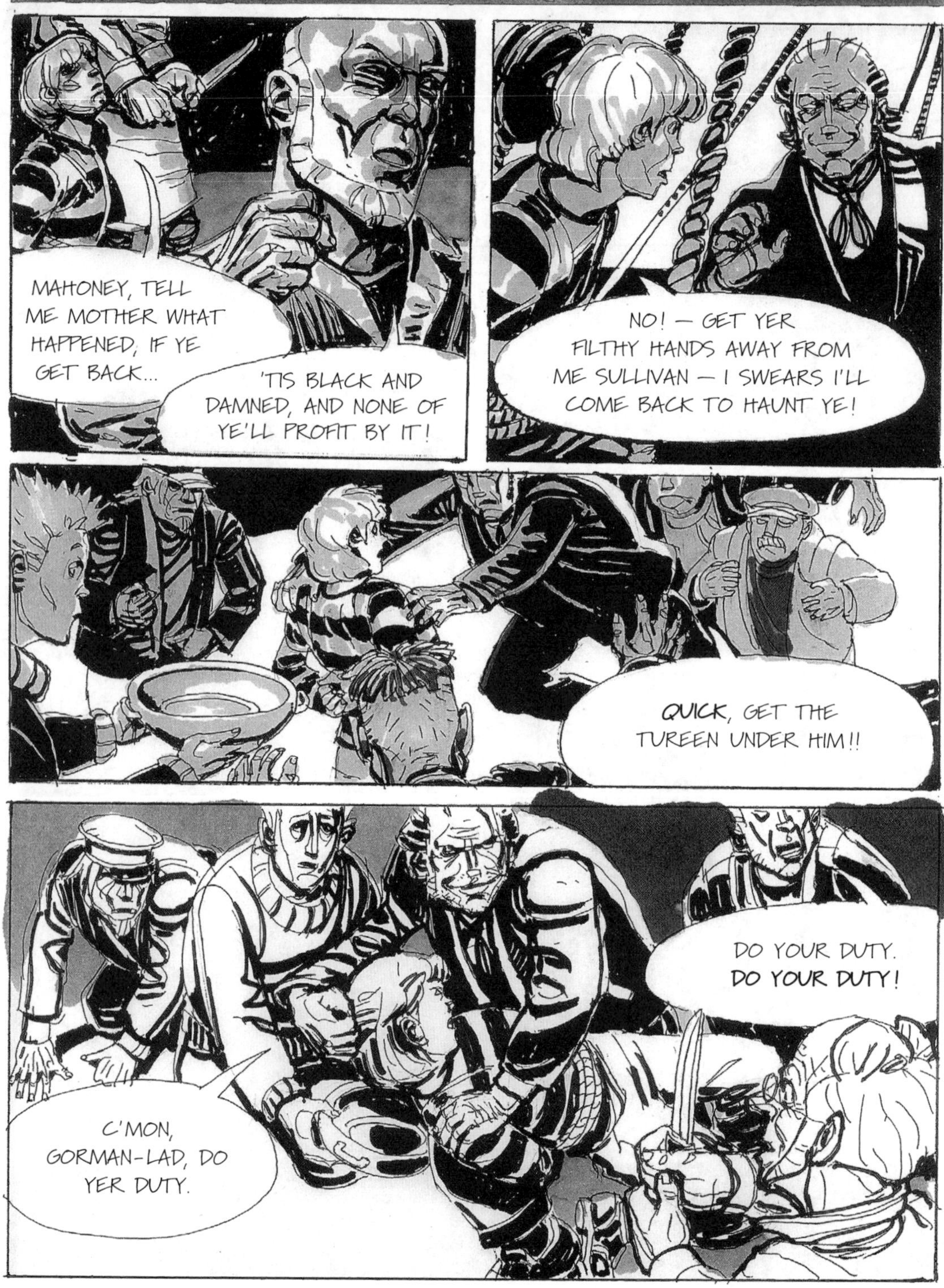
MAHONEY, TELL ME MOTHER WHAT HAPPENED, IF YE GET BACK...
'TIS BLACK AND DAMNED, AND NONE OF YE'LL PROFIT BY IT!
NO! — GET YER FILTHY HANDS AWAY FROM ME SULLIVAN — I SWEARS I'LL COME BACK TO HAUNT YE!
QUICK, GET THE TUREEN UNDER HIM!!
DO YOUR DUTY. DO YOUR DUTY!
C'MON, GORMAN-LAD, DO YER DUTY.

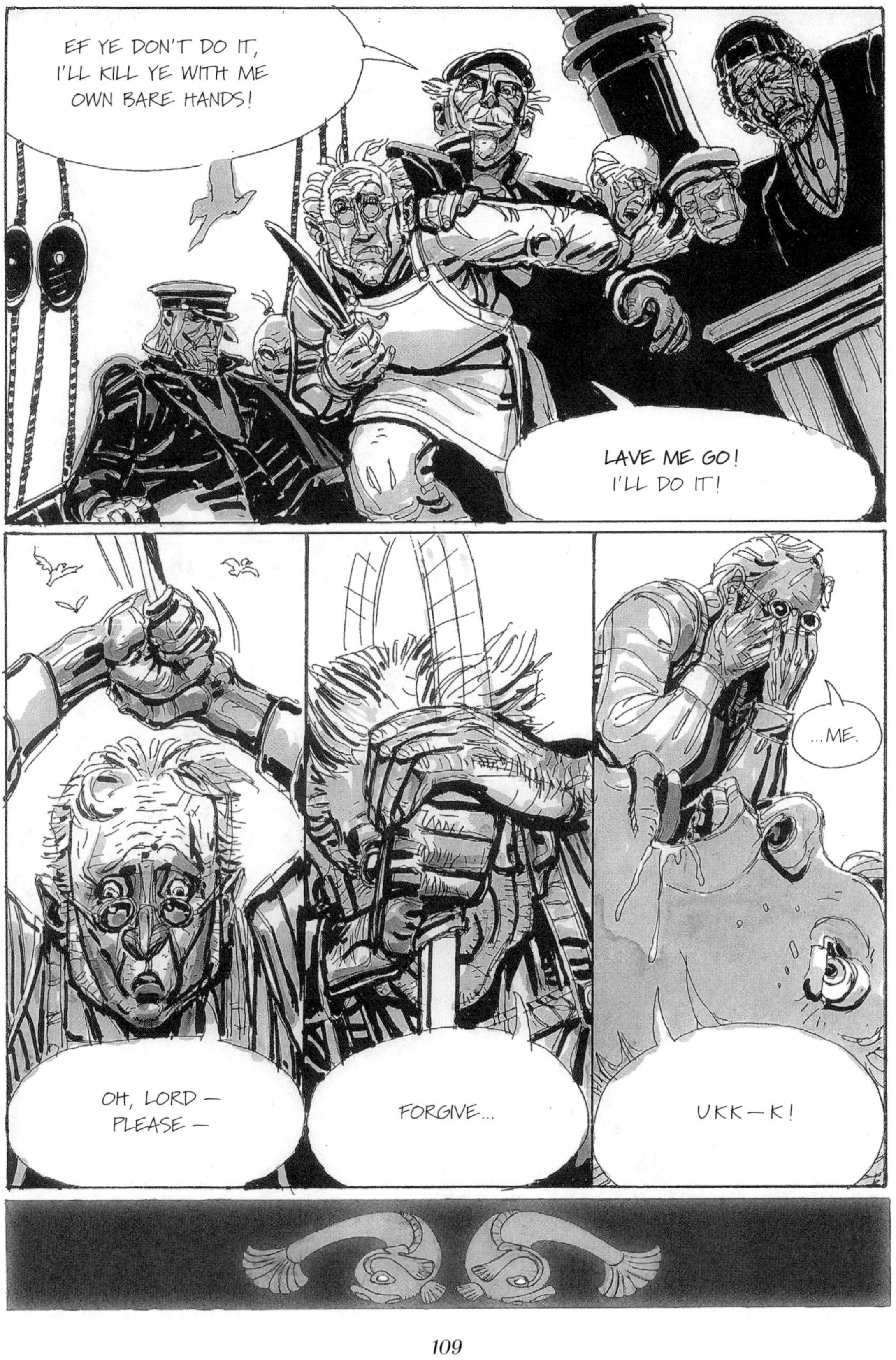
EF YE DON'T DO IT,
I'LL KILL YE WITH ME
OWN BARE HANDS!
LAVE ME GO!
I'LL DO IT!
OH, LORD —
PLEASE —
FORGIVE...
...ME.
UKK—K!

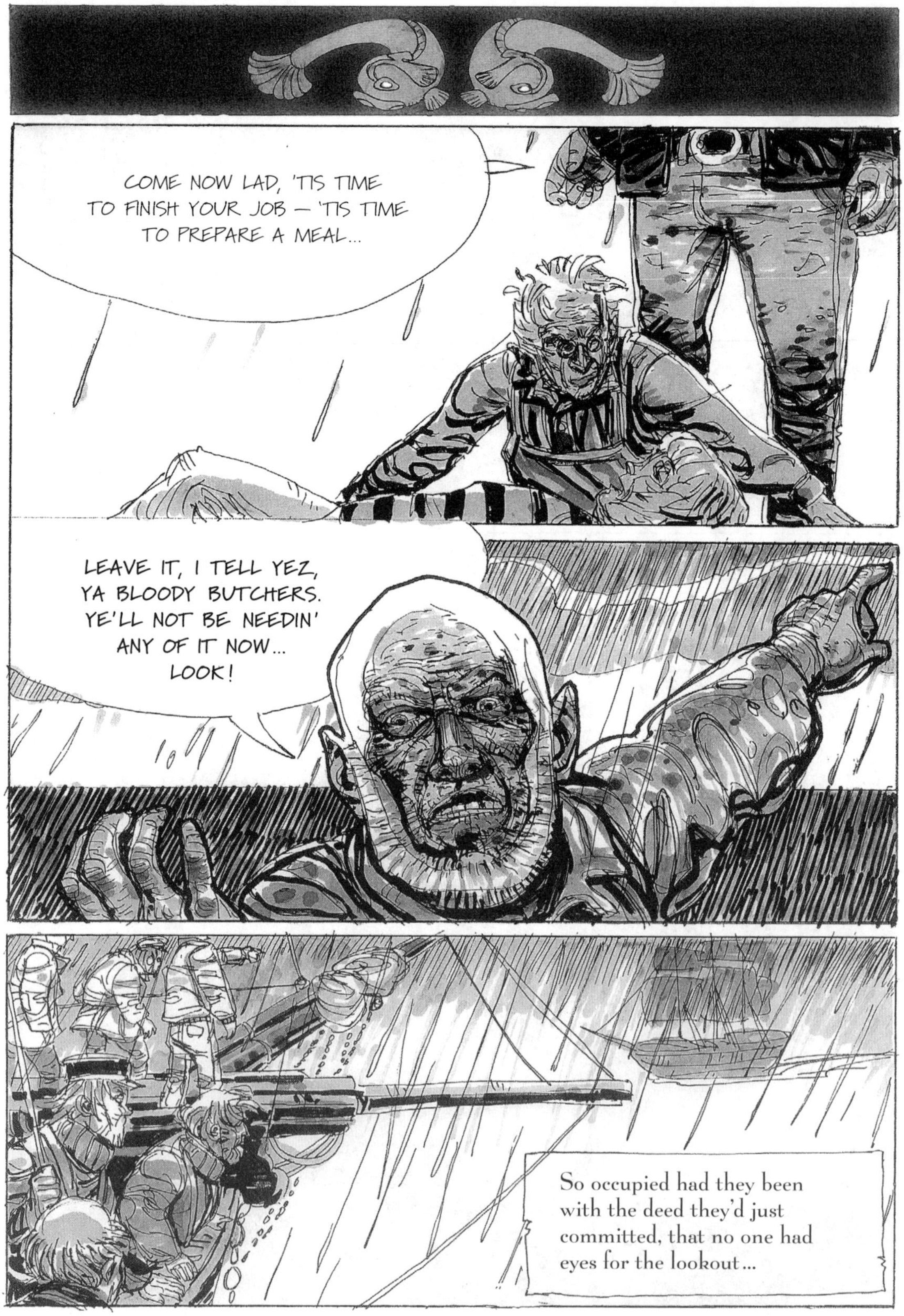
COME NOW LAD, 'TIS TIME TO FINISH YOUR JOB — 'TIS TIME TO PREPARE A MEAL...
LEAVE IT, I TELL YEZ, YA BLOODY BUTCHERS. YE'LL NOT BE NEEDIN' ANY OF IT NOW... LOOK!
So occupied had they been with the deed they'd just committed, that no one had eyes for the lookout...

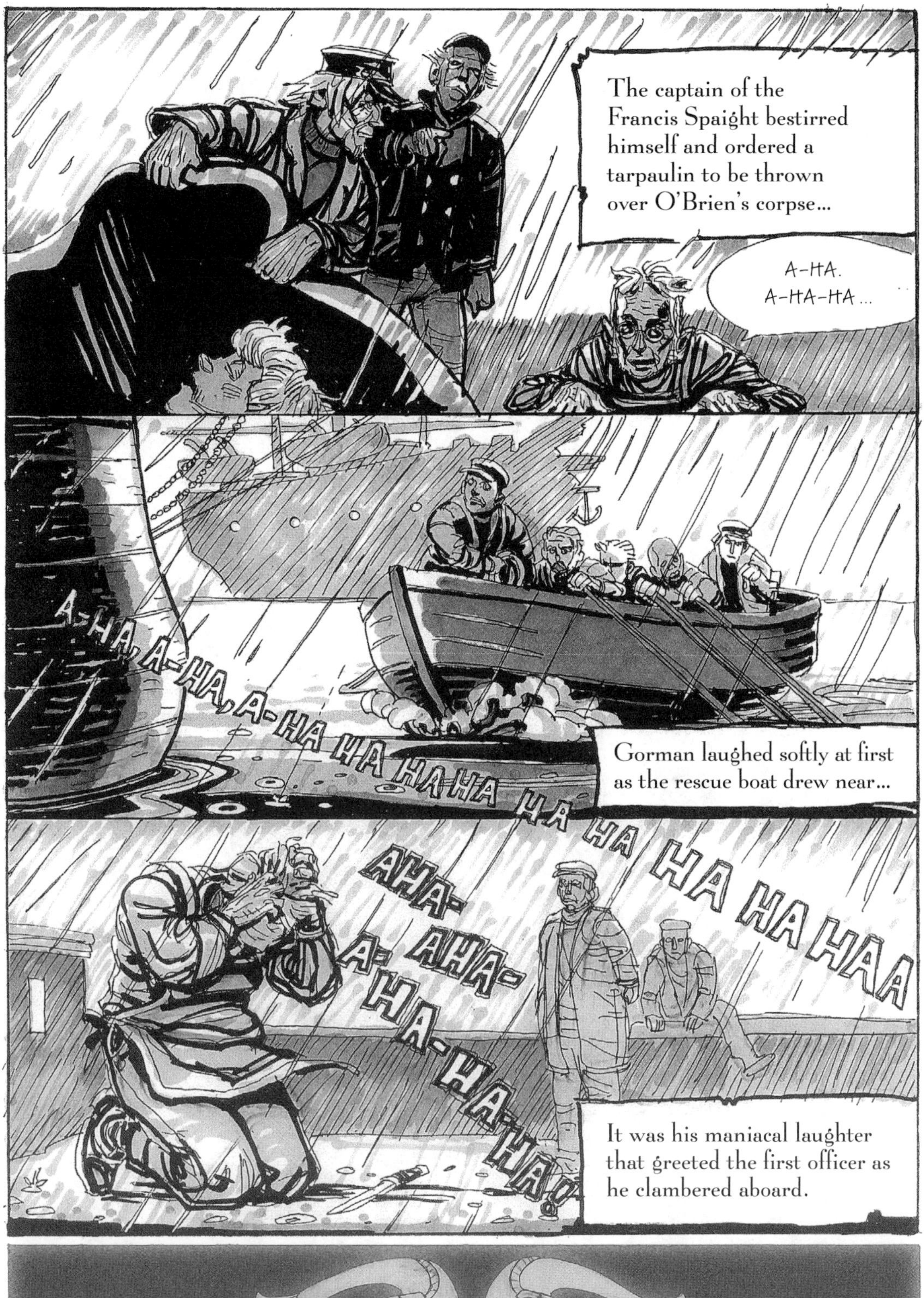
The captain of the Francis Spaight bestirred himself and ordered a tarpaulin to be thrown over O'Brien's corpse...
A-HA. A-HA-HA...
A-HA, A-HA, A-HA HA HA HAHA HA HA
Gorman laughed softly at first as the rescue boat drew near...
HA HA HA HAHAA
AHA- AHA- A- HA- HA- HA- HA- HA!
It was his maniacal laughter that greeted the first officer as he clambered aboard.

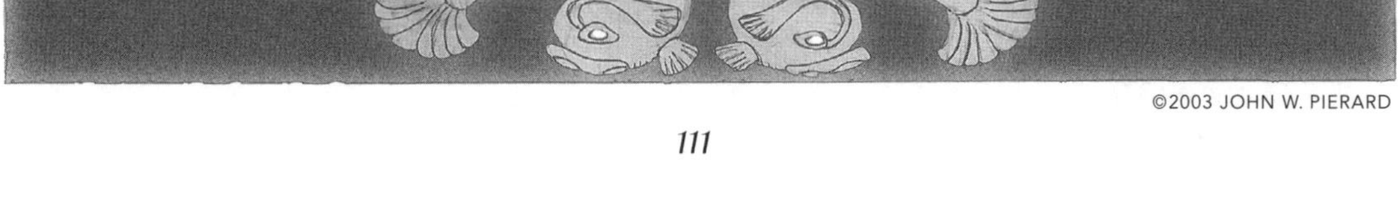

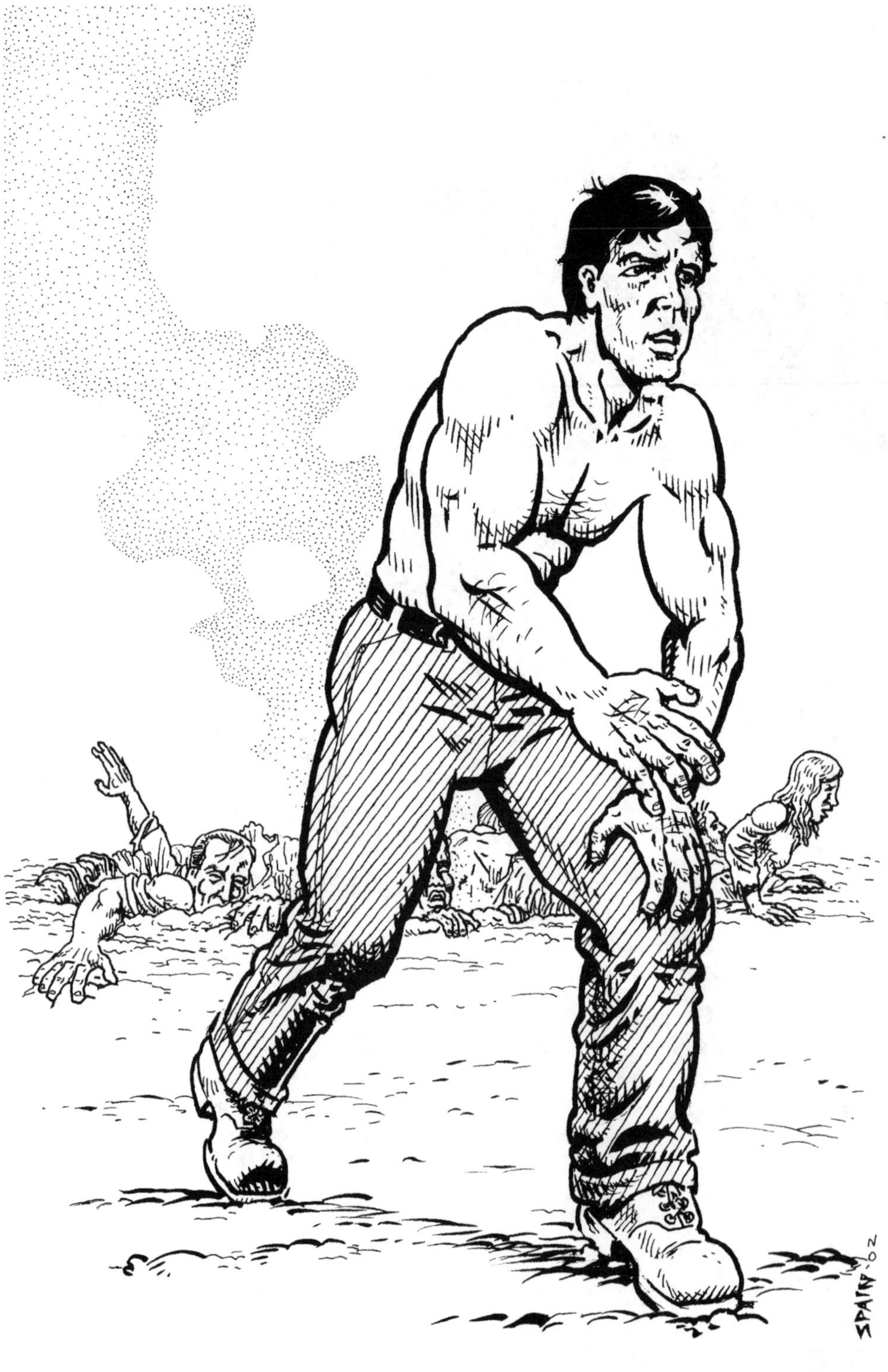
SPAIN '02

HOW I BECAME A SOCIALIST

an essay by **JACK LONDON**
illustrated by **SPAIN RODRIGUEZ**

IT IS QUITE FAIR TO SAY that I became a Socialist in a fashion somewhat similar to the way in which the Teutonic pagans became Christians— it was hammered into me. Not only was I not looking for Socialism at the time of my conversion, but I was fighting it. I was very young and callow, did not know much of anything, and though I had never even heard of a school called "Individualism," I sang the paean of the strong with all my heart.

This was because I was strong myself. By strong I mean that I had good health and hard muscles, both of which possessions are easily accounted for. I had lived my childhood on California ranches, my boyhood hustling newspapers on the streets of a healthy Western city, and my youth on the ozone-laden waters of San Francisco Bay and the Pacific Ocean. I loved life in the open, and I toiled in the open, at the hardest kinds of work. Learning no trade, but drifting along from job to job, I looked on the world and called it good, every bit of it. Let me repeat, this optimism was because I was healthy and strong, bothered with neither aches nor weaknesses, never turned down by the boss because I did not look fit, able always to get a job at shovelling coal, sailorizing, or manual labor of some sort.

And because of all this, exulting in my young life, able to hold my own at work or fight, I was a rampant individualist. It was very natural. I was a winner. Wherefore I called the game, as I saw it played, or thought I saw it played, a very proper game for MEN. To be a MAN was to write man in large capitals on my heart. To adventure like a man, and fight like a man, and do a man's work (even for a boy's pay)—these were things that reached right in and gripped hold of me as no other thing could. And I looked ahead into long vistas of a hazy and interminable future, into which, playing what I conceived to be MAN'S game, I should continue to travel with unfailing

health, without accidents, and with muscles ever vigorous. As I say, this future was interminable. I could see myself only raging through life without end like one of Nietzsche's blond beasts, lustfully roving and conquering by sheer superiority and strength.

As for the unfortunates, the sick, and ailing, and old, and maimed, I must confess I hardly thought of them at all, save that I vaguely felt that they, barring accidents, could be as good as I if they wanted to work real hard, and could work just as well. Accidents? Well, they represented FATE, also spelled out in capitals, and there was no getting around FATE. Napoleon had had an accident at Waterloo, but that did not dampen my desire to be another and later Napoleon. Further, the optimism bred of a stomach which could digest scrap iron and a body which flourished on hardships did not permit me to consider accidents as even remotely related to my glorious personality.

I hope I have made it clear that I was proud to be one of Nature's strong-armed noblemen. The dignity of labor was to me the most impressive thing in the world. Without having read Carlyle, or Kipling, I formulated a gospel of work which put theirs in the shade. Work was everything. It was sanctification and salvation. The pride I took in a hard day's work well done would be inconceivable to you. It is almost inconceivable to me as I look back upon it. I was as faithful a wage slave as ever capitalist exploited. To shirk or malinger on the man who paid me my wages was a sin, first, against myself, and second, against him. I considered it a crime second only to treason and just about as bad.

In short, my joyous individualism was dominated by the orthodox bourgeois ethics. I read the bourgeois papers, listened to the bourgeois preachers, and shouted at the sonorous platitudes of the bourgeois politicians. And I doubt not, if other events had not changed my career, that I should have evolved into a professional strike-breaker, (one of [Harvard] President Eliot's American heroes), and had my head and my earning power irrevocably smashed by a club in the hands of some militant trades-unionist.

Just about this time, returning from a seven months' voyage before the mast, and just turned eighteen, I took it into my head to go tramping. On rods and blind baggages I fought my way from the open West, where men bucked big and the job hunted the man, to the congested labor centers of the East, where men were small potatoes and hunted the job for all they were worth. And on this new blond-beast adventure I found myself looking upon life from a new and totally different angle. I had dropped down from the proletariat into what sociologists love to call the "submerged tenth," and I was startled to discover the way in which that submerged tenth was recruited.

I found there all sorts of men, many of whom had once been as good as myself and just as blond-beastly; sailor-men, soldier-men, labor-men, all wrenched and distorted and twisted out of shape by toil and hardship and accident, and cast adrift by their masters like so many old horses. I battered on the drag and slammed back gates with them, or shivered with them in box cars and city parks, listening the while to life-histories which began under auspices as fair as mine, with digestions and bodies equal to and better than mine, and which ended there before my eyes in the shambles at the bottom of the Social Pit.

And as I listened my brain began to work. The woman of the streets and the man of the gutter drew very close to me. I saw the picture of the Social Pit as vividly as though it were a concrete thing, and at the bottom of the Pit I saw them, myself above them, not far, and hanging on to the slippery wall by main strength and sweat. And I confess a terror seized me. What when my strength failed? When I should be unable to work shoulder to shoulder with the strong men who were as yet babes unborn? And there and then I swore a great oath. It ran something like this: All my days I have worked hard with my body and according to the number of days I have worked, by just that much am I nearer the bottom of the Pit. I shall climb out of the Pit, but

not by the muscles of my body shall I climb out. I shall do no more hard work, and may God strike me dead if I do another day's hard work with my body more than I absolutely have to do. And I have been busy ever since running away from hard work.

Incidentally, while tramping some ten thousand miles through the United States and Canada, I strayed into Niagara Falls, was nabbed by a fee-hunting constable, denied the right to plead guilty or not guilty, sentenced out of hand to thirty days' imprisonment for having no fixed abode and no visible means of support, handcuffed and chained to a bunch of men similarly circumstanced, carted down-country to Buffalo, registered at the Erie County Penitentiary, had my head clipped and my budding mustache shaved, was dressed in convict stripes, compulsorily vaccinated by a medical student who practiced on such as we, made to march the lockstep, and put to work under the eyes of guards armed with Winchester rifles — all for adventuring in blond-beastly fashion. Concerning further details deponent sayeth not, though he may hint that some of his plethoric national patriotism simmered down and leaked out of the bottom of his soul somewhere — at least, since that experience he finds that he cares more for men and women and little children than for imaginary geographical lines.

To return to my conversion. I think it is apparent that my rampant individualism was pretty effectively hammered out of me, and something else as effectively hammered in. But, just as I had been an individualist without knowing it, I was now a Socialist without knowing it, withal, an unscientific one. I had been reborn, but not renamed, and I was running around to find out what manner of thing I was. I ran back to California and opened the books. I do not remember which ones I opened first. It is an unimportant detail anyway. I was already It, whatever It was, and by aid of the books I discovered that It was a Socialist. Since that day I have opened many books, but no economic argument, no lucid demonstration of the logic and inevitableness of Socialism affects me as profoundly and convincingly as I was affected on the day when I first saw the walls of the Social Pit rise around me and felt myself slipping down, down, into the shambles at the bottom.

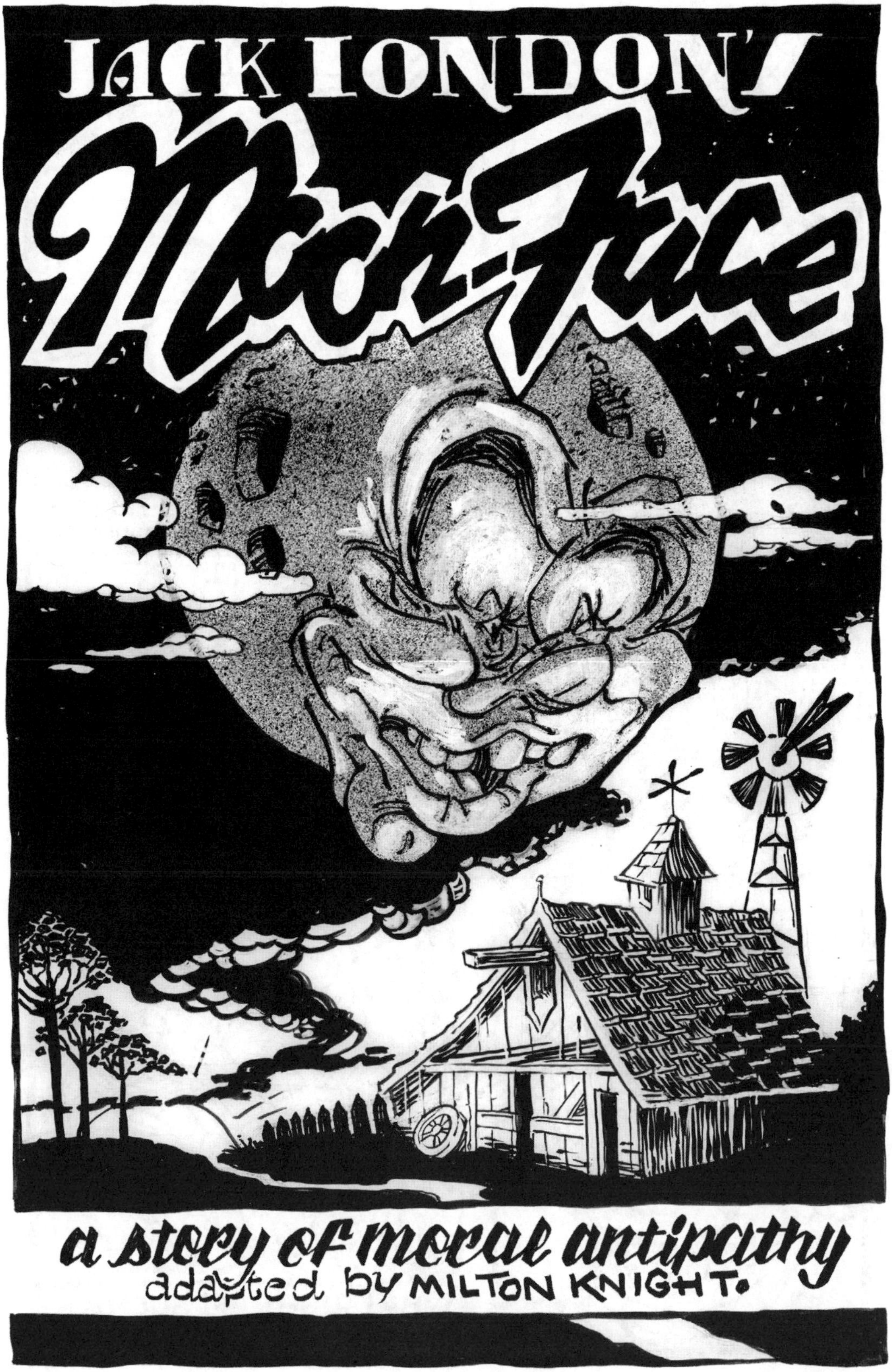
JACK LONDON'S
Moon-Face
a story of moral antipathy
adapted by MILTON KNIGHT.

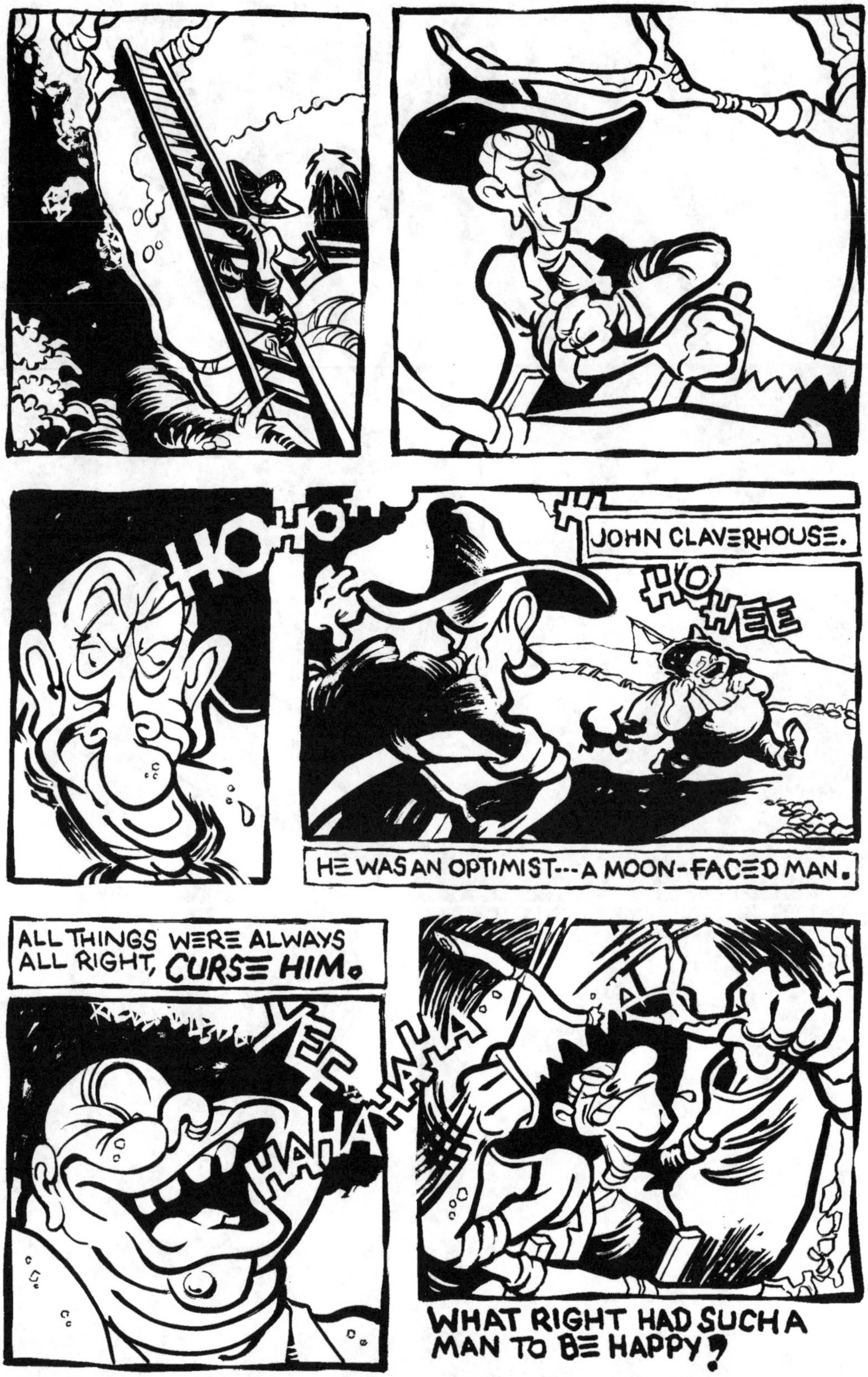
HO HO HO
JOHN CLAVERHOUSE.
HO HEE
HE WAS AN OPTIMIST---A MOON-FACED MAN.
ALL THINGS WERE ALWAYS ALL RIGHT, CURSE HIM.
YEE HAHAHA
HAHA
WHAT RIGHT HAD SUCH A MAN TO BE HAPPY?

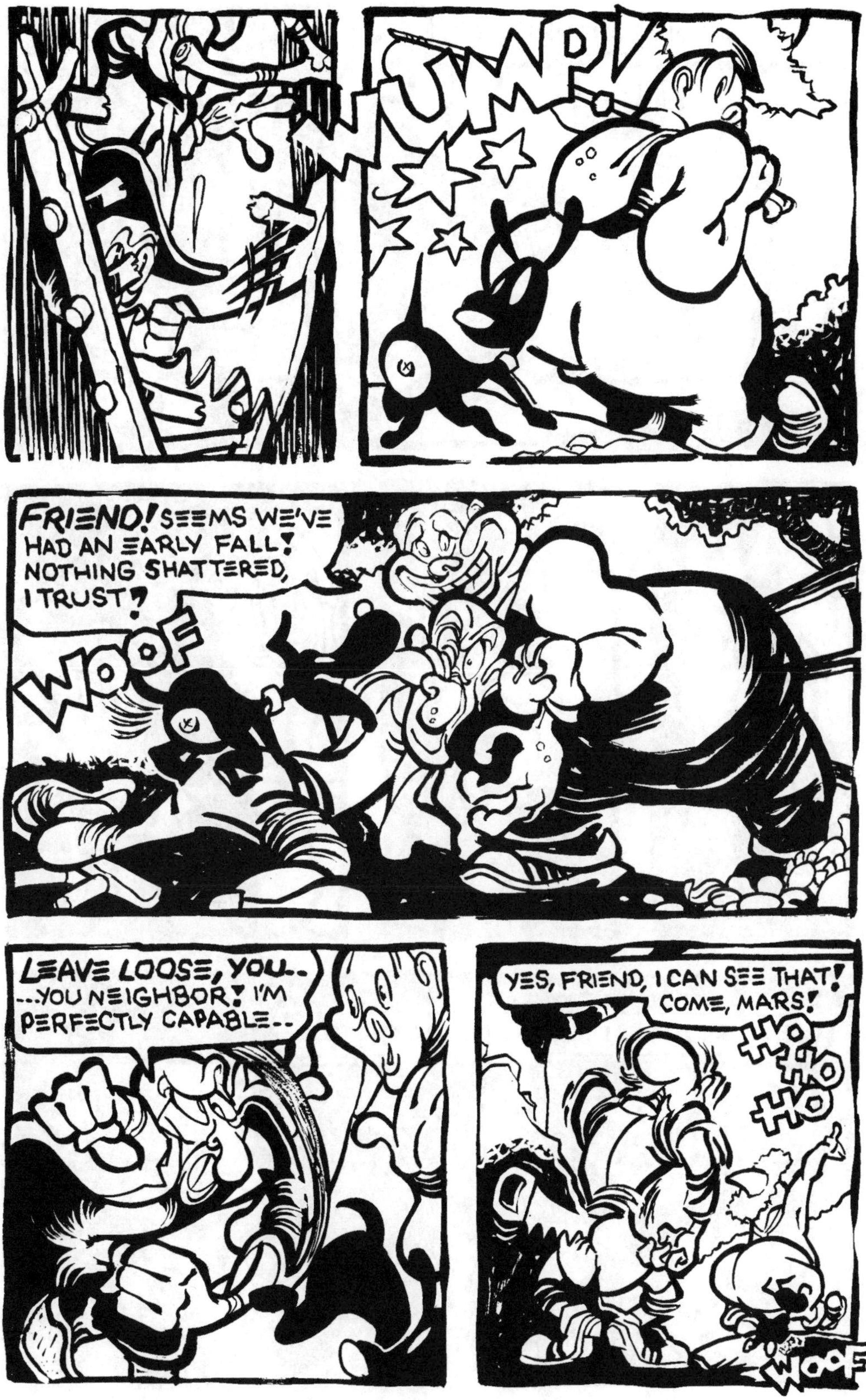
WUMP!
FRIEND! SEEMS WE'VE HAD AN EARLY FALL! NOTHING SHATTERED, I TRUST?
WOOF
LEAVE LOOSE, YOU.. ...YOU NEIGHBOR! I'M PERFECTLY CAPABLE..
YES, FRIEND, I CAN SEE THAT! COME, MARS!
HO HO HO HO
WOOF

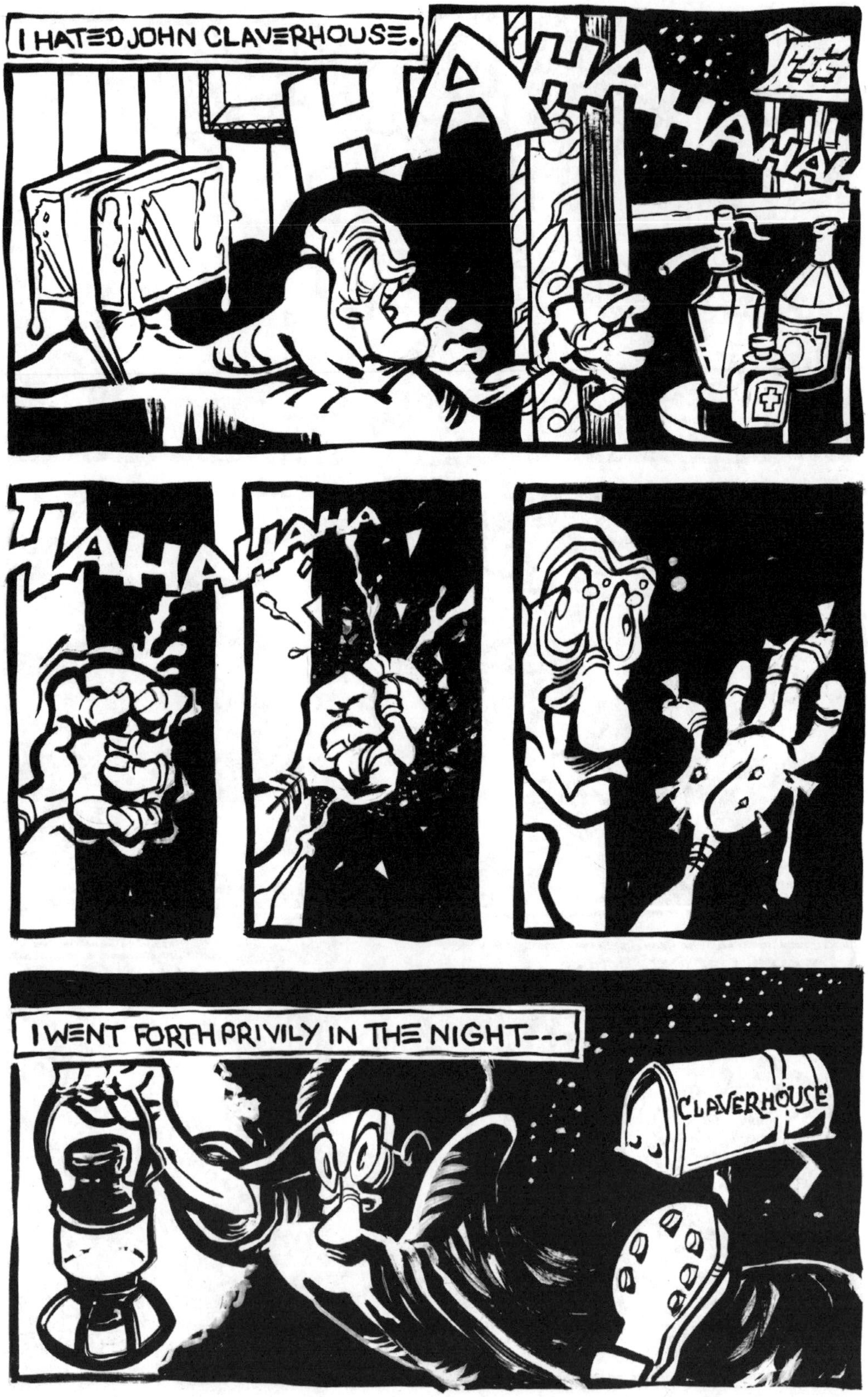
I HATED JOHN CLAVERHOUSE.
HAHAHAHAHA
HAHAHAHAHA
I WENT FORTH PRIVILY IN THE NIGHT---
CLAVERHOUSE

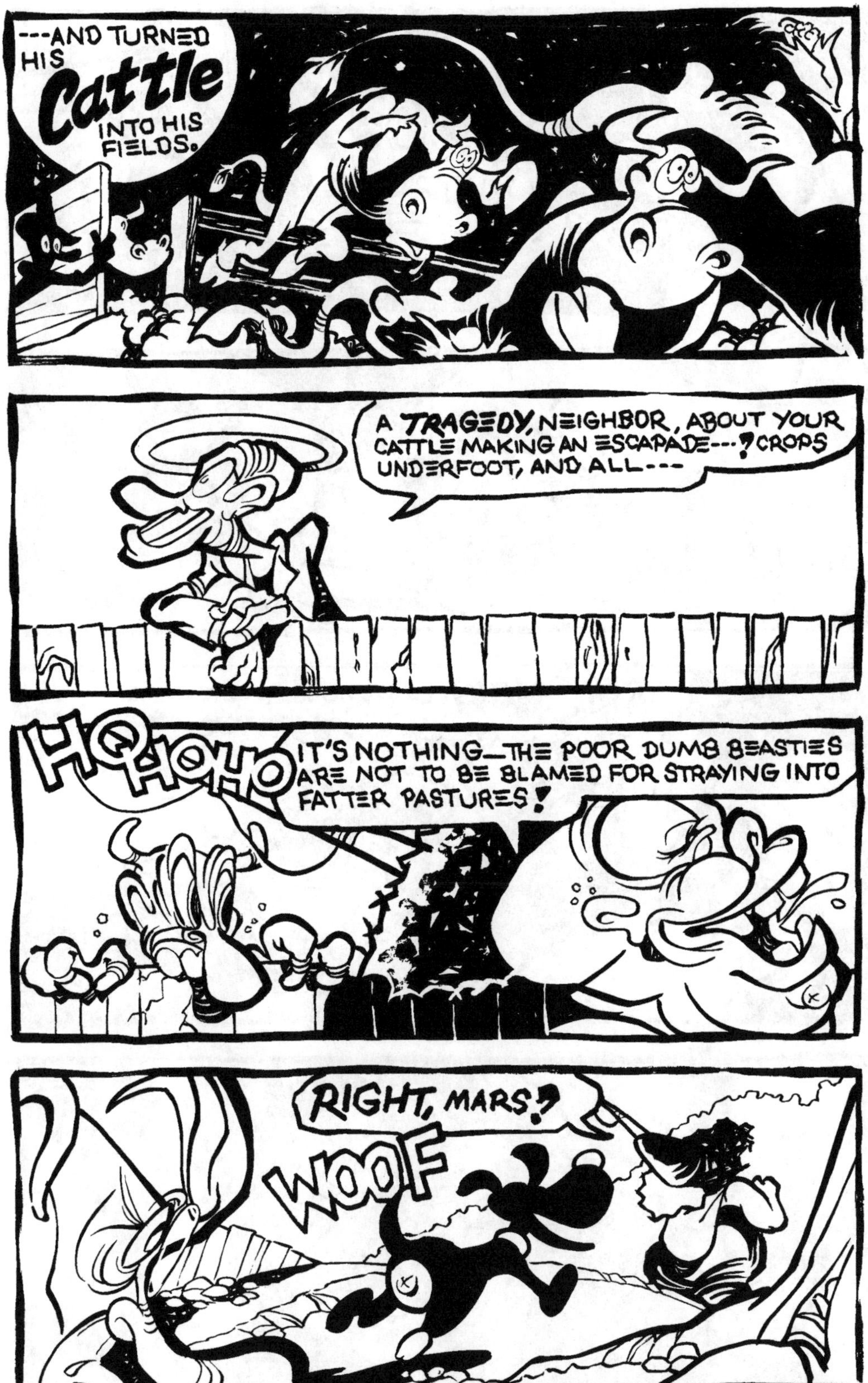
---AND TURNED HIS Cattle INTO HIS FIELDS.
A TRAGEDY, NEIGHBOR, ABOUT YOUR CATTLE MAKING AN ESCAPADE---? CROPS UNDERFOOT, AND ALL---
HOHOHO
IT'S NOTHING—THE POOR DUMB BEASTIES ARE NOT TO BE BLAMED FOR STRAYING INTO FATTER PASTURES!
RIGHT, MARS?
WOOF

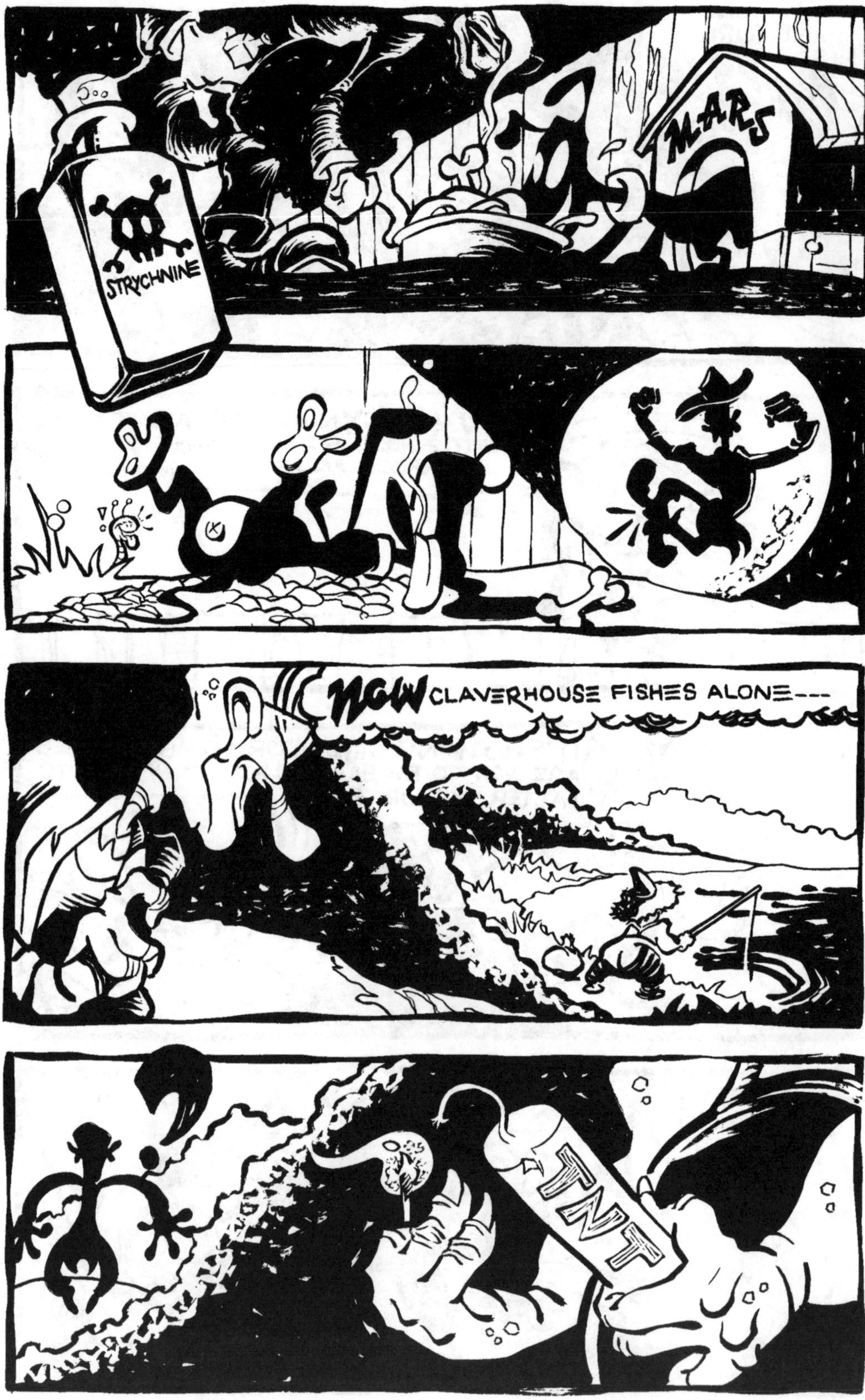
MARS
STRYCHNINE
NOW CLAVERHOUSE FISHES ALONE---
TNT

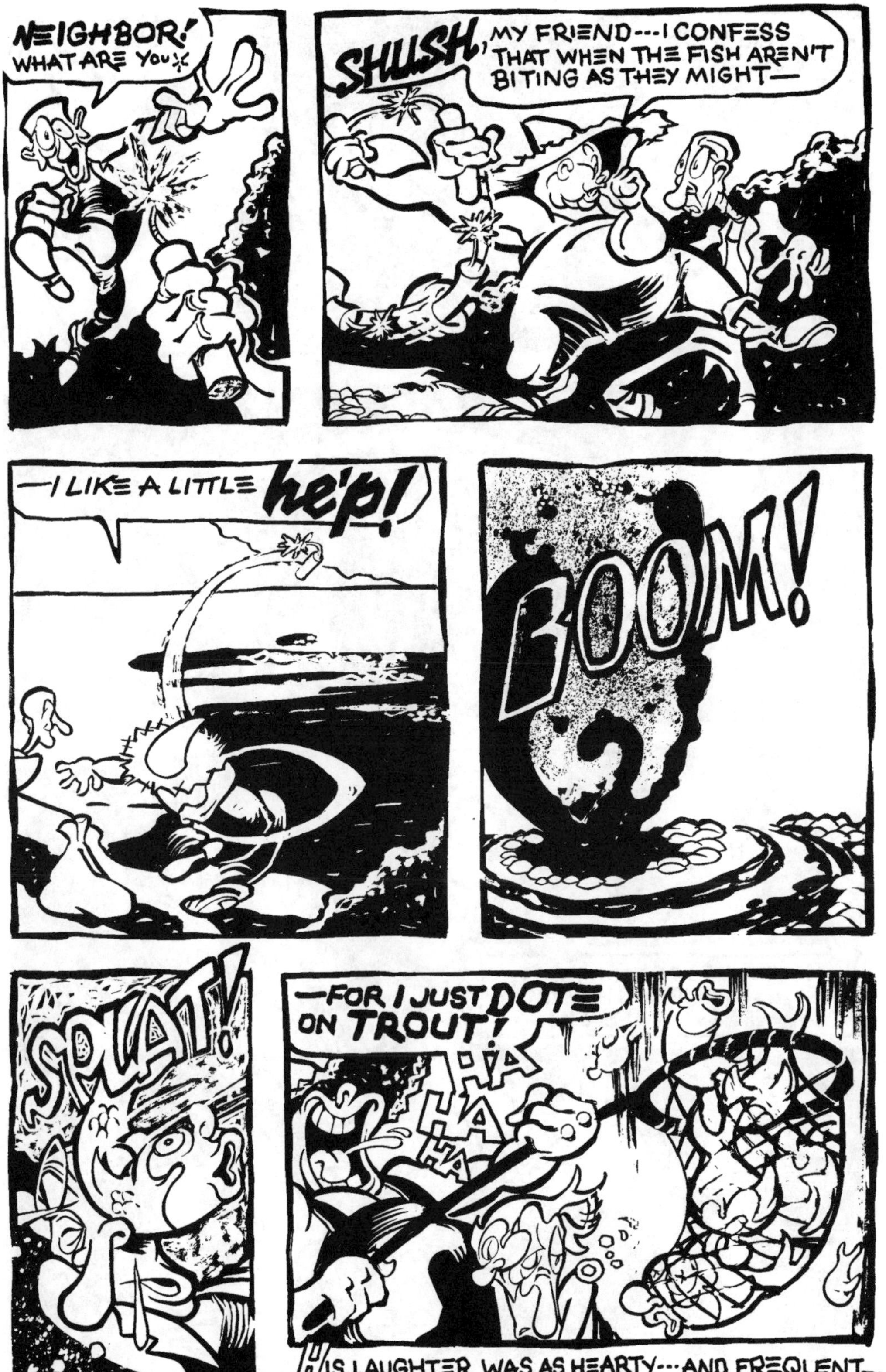
NEIGHBOR! WHAT ARE YOU-!
SHUSH, MY FRIEND---I CONFESS THAT WHEN THE FISH AREN'T BITING AS THEY MIGHT—
—I LIKE A LITTLE he'p!
BOOM!
SPLAT!
—FOR I JUST DOTE ON TROUT!
HA HA HA
HIS LAUGHTER WAS AS HEARTY---AND FREQUENT—.

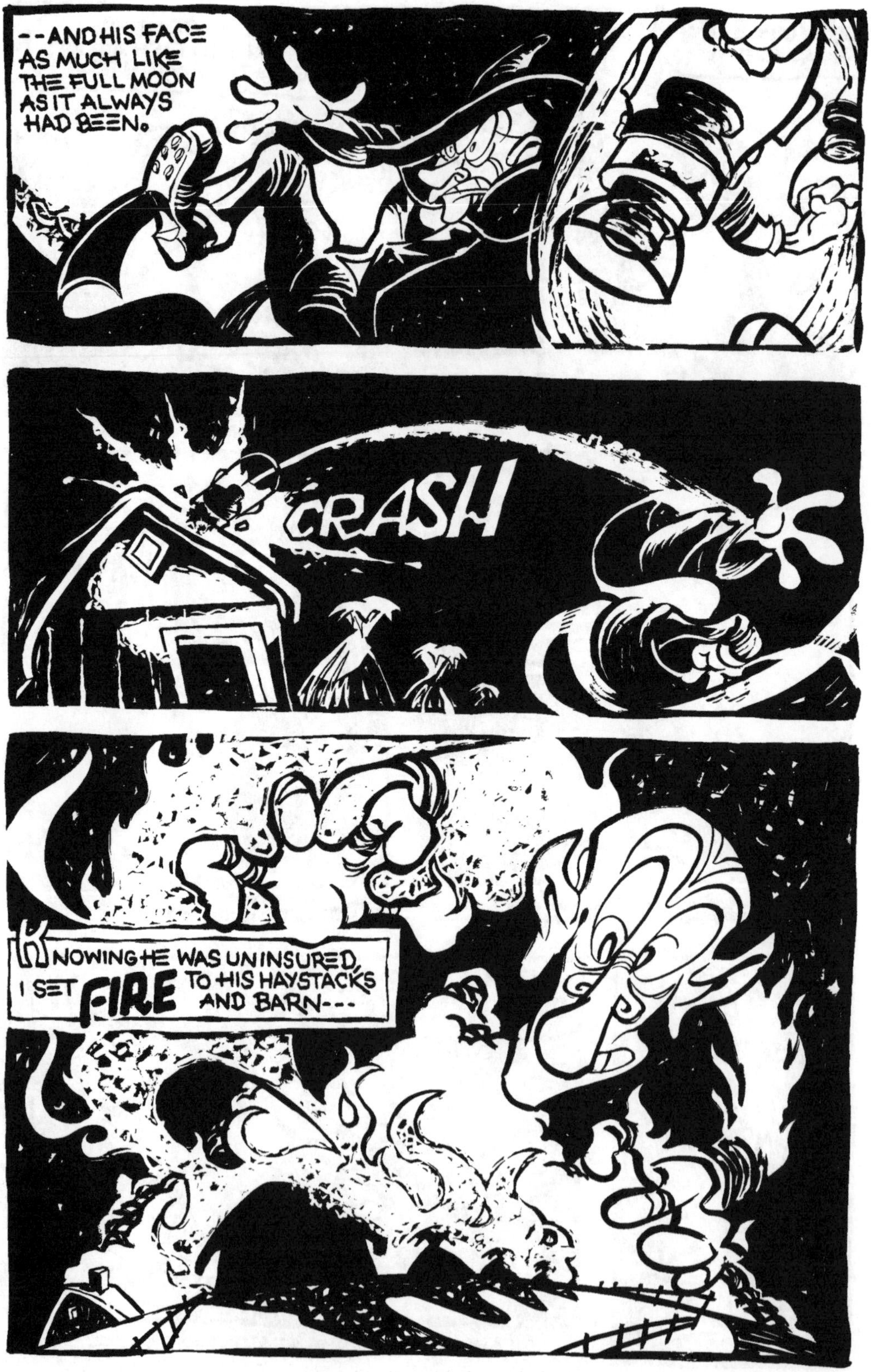
--AND HIS FACE AS MUCH LIKE THE FULL MOON AS IT ALWAYS HAD BEEN.
CRASH
KNOWING HE WAS UNINSURED, I SET FIRE TO HIS HAYSTACKS AND BARN---

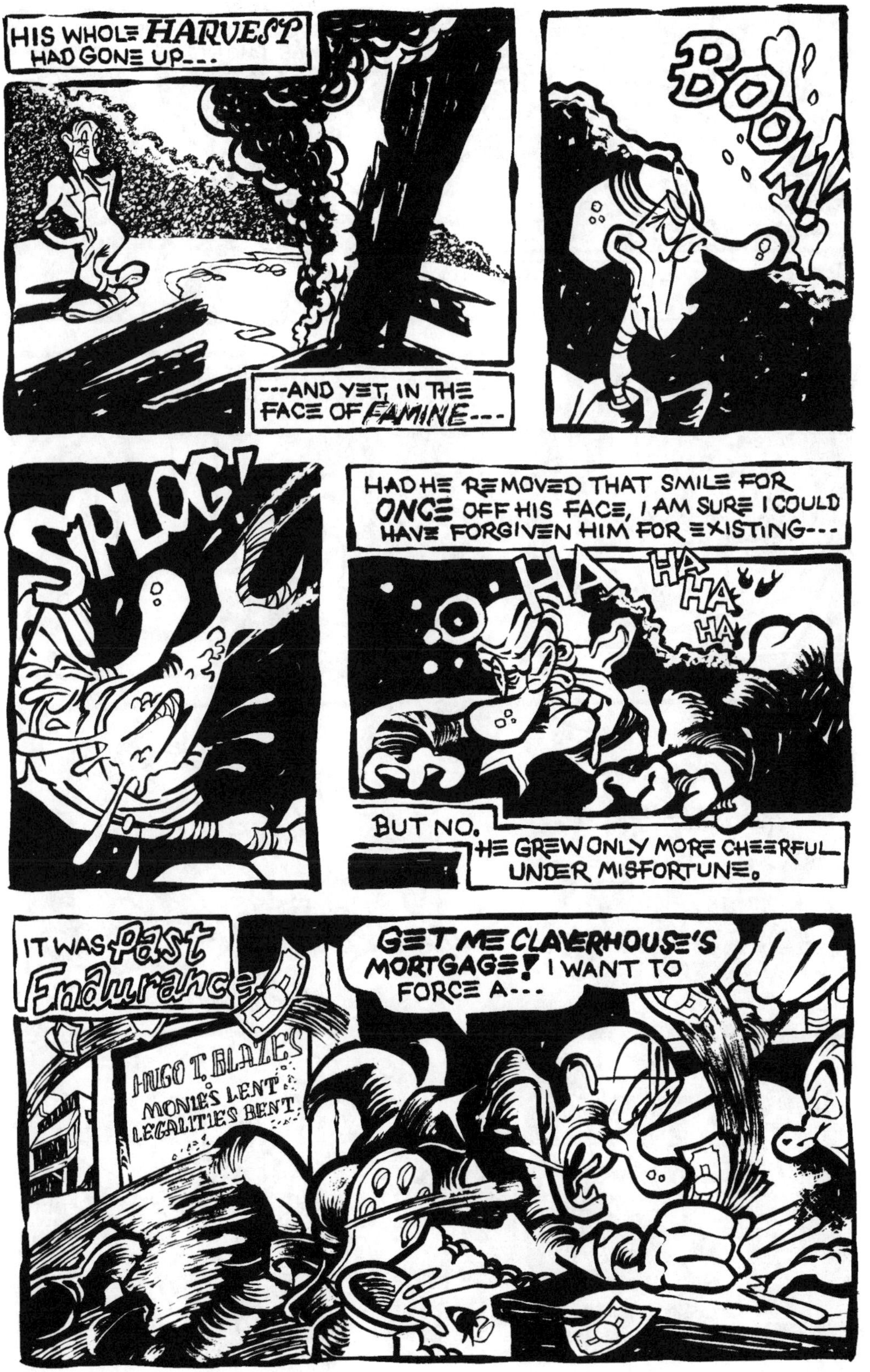
HIS WHOLE HARVEST HAD GONE UP---
---AND YET, IN THE FACE OF FAMINE---
BOOM!
SPLOG!
HAD HE REMOVED THAT SMILE FOR ONCE OFF HIS FACE, I AM SURE I COULD HAVE FORGIVEN HIM FOR EXISTING---
HA HA HA HA
BUT NO.
HE GREW ONLY MORE CHEERFUL UNDER MISFORTUNE.
IT WAS Past Endurance.
GET ME CLAVERHOUSE'S MORTGAGE! I WANT TO FORCE A---
HUGO T. BLAZES
MONIES LENT
LEGALITIES BENT

FORECLOSURE
ON THE HOME OF
JOHN CLAVERHOUSE
MUST VACATE
HE HAD LIVED THERE UPWARDS OF TWENTY YEARS, I KNEW---
I STROLLED DOWN TO SEE HOW HE WAS TAKING IT---
NOK
HOHOHOHOHOHO
...THE FUNNIEST TYKE, THAT YOUNGSTER OF MINE! DID YOU EVER HEAR THE LIKE? AS WE WERE PACKING, HE---
IODINE
IODINE
THEATRE.
HOTEL

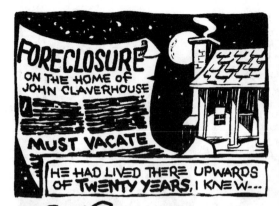

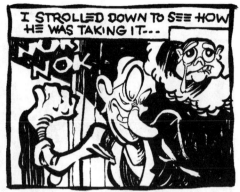

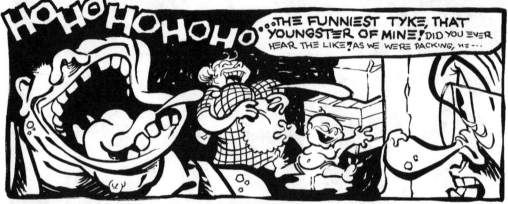

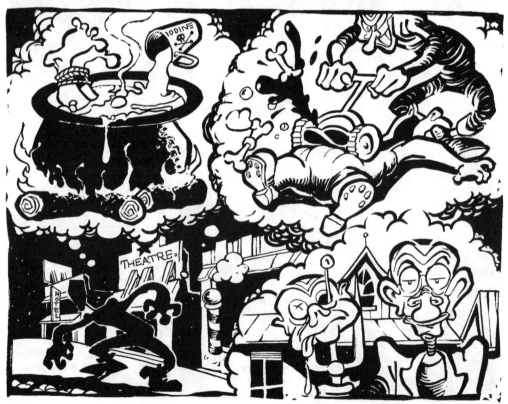

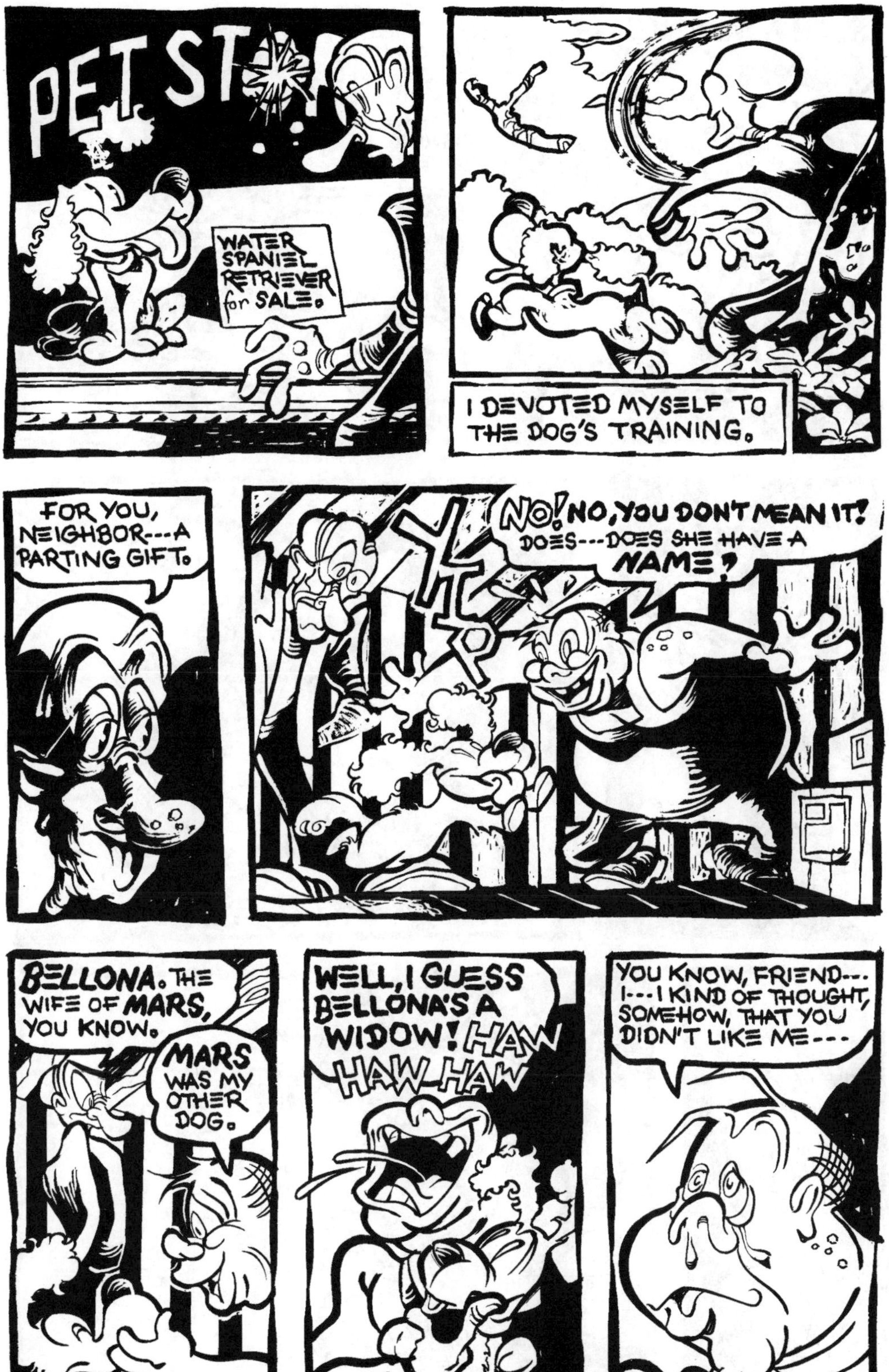
PET ST
WATER SPANIEL RETRIEVER for SALE.
I DEVOTED MYSELF TO THE DOG'S TRAINING.
FOR YOU, NEIGHBOR---A PARTING GIFT.
YIP
NO! NO, YOU DON'T MEAN IT! DOES---DOES SHE HAVE A NAME?
BELLONA. THE WIFE OF MARS, YOU KNOW.
MARS WAS MY OTHER DOG.
WELL, I GUESS BELLONA'S A WIDOW! HAW HAW HAW
YOU KNOW, FRIEND---I---I KIND OF THOUGHT, SOMEHOW, THAT YOU DIDN'T LIKE ME---

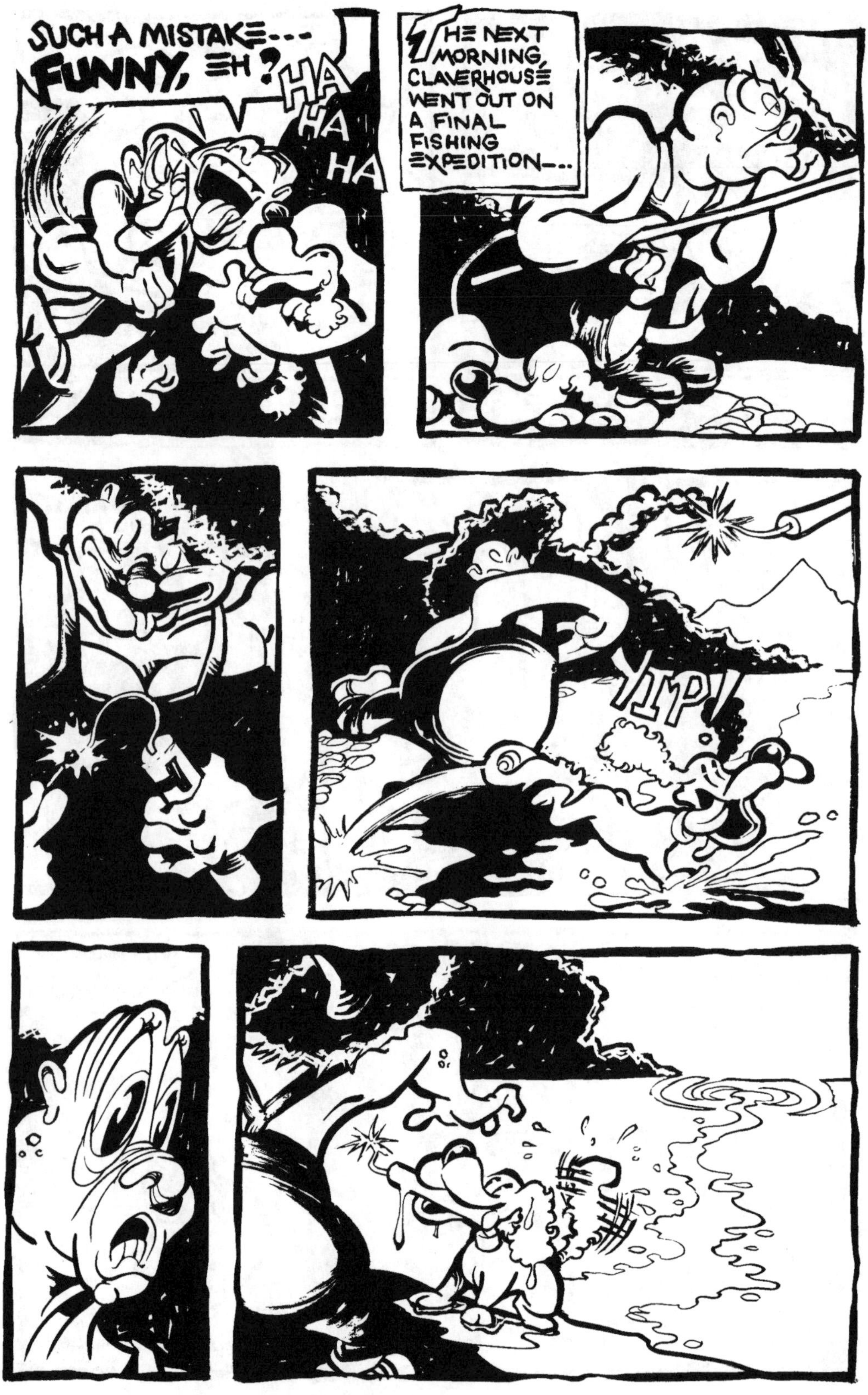
SUCH A MISTAKE...
FUNNY, EH?
HA
HA
HA
THE NEXT MORNING, CLAVERHOUSE WENT OUT ON A FINAL FISHING EXPEDITION...
YIP!

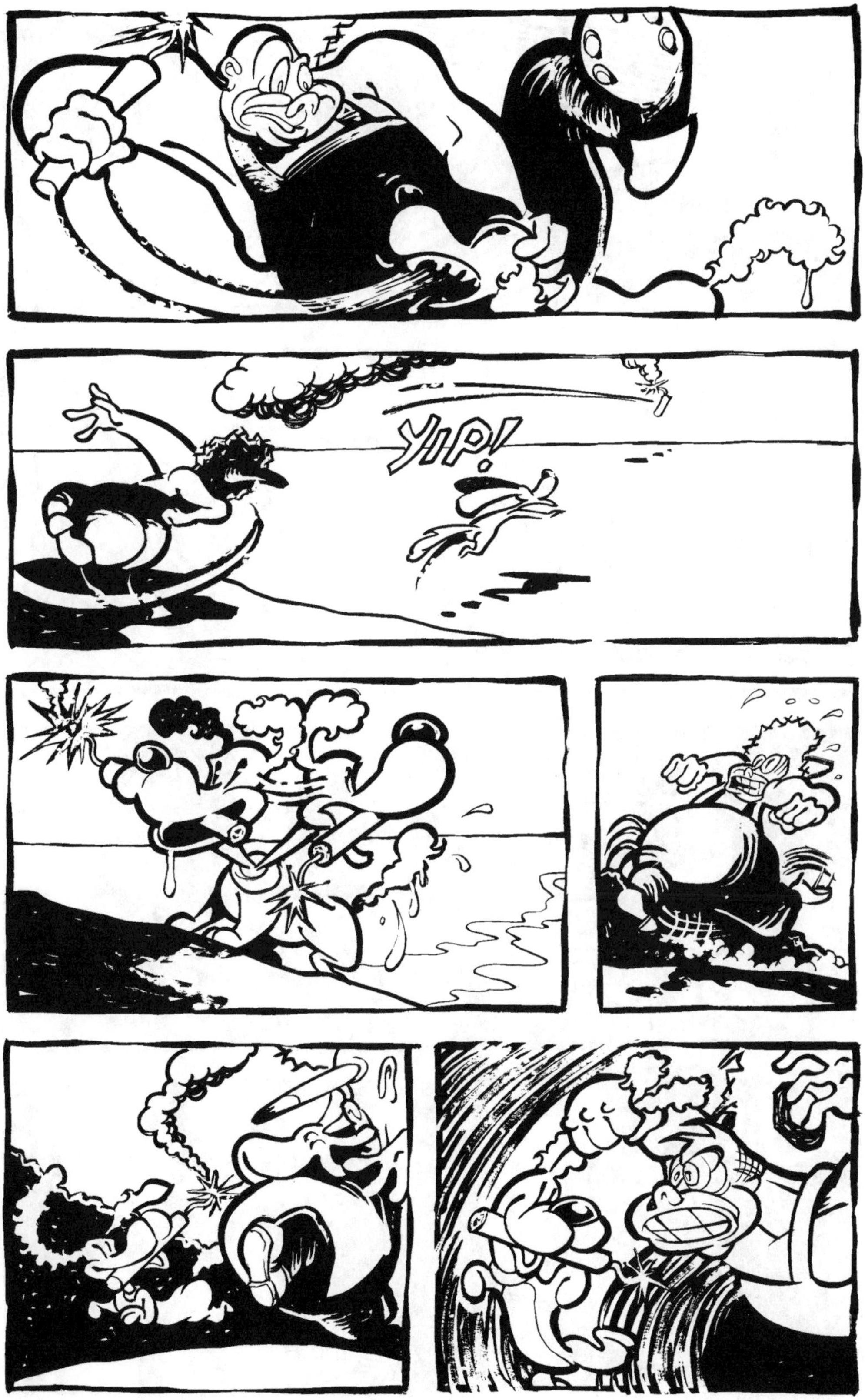
YIP!

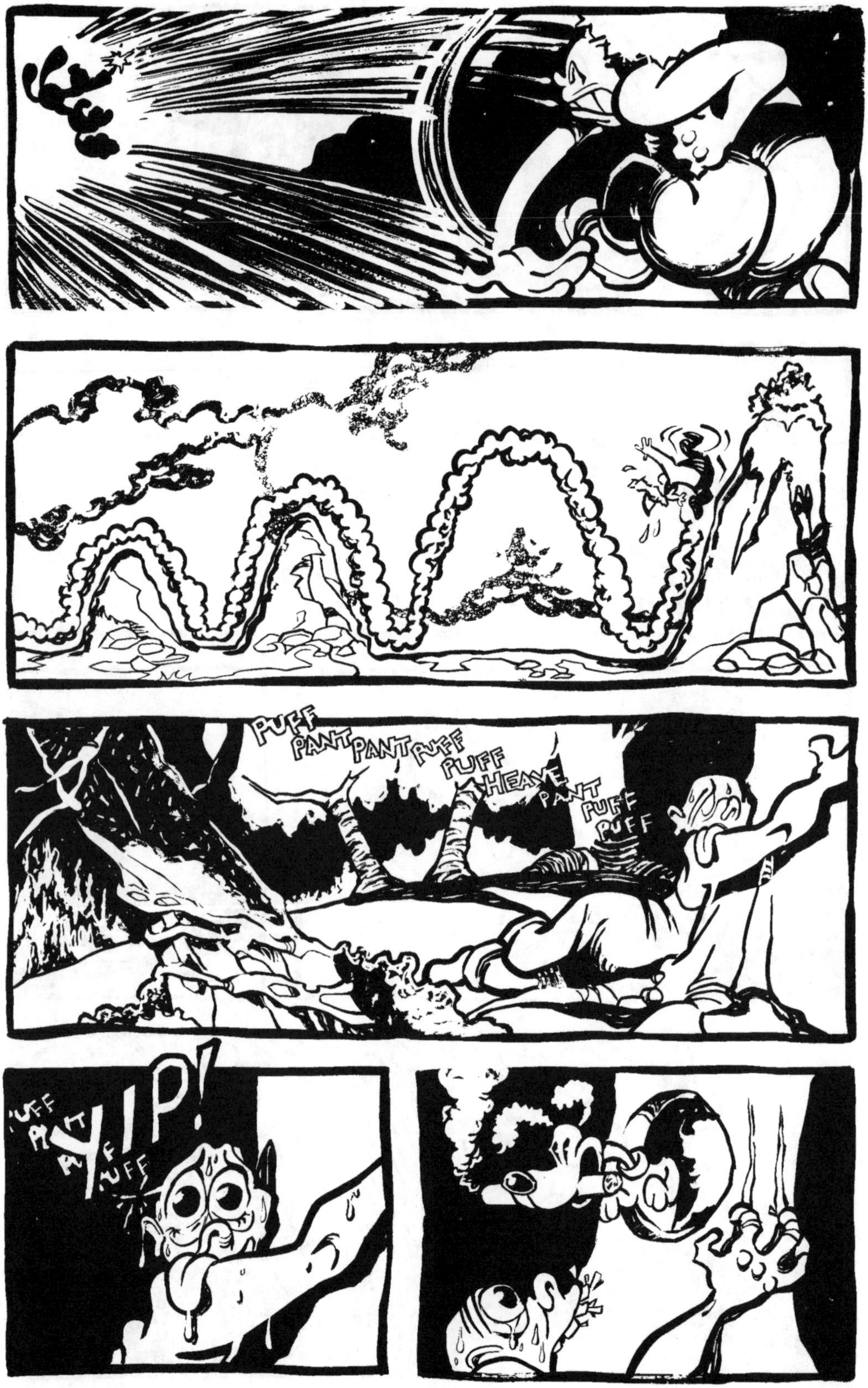
PUFF
PANT PANT PUFF
PUFF
HEAVE
PANT
PUFF
PUFF
YIP!

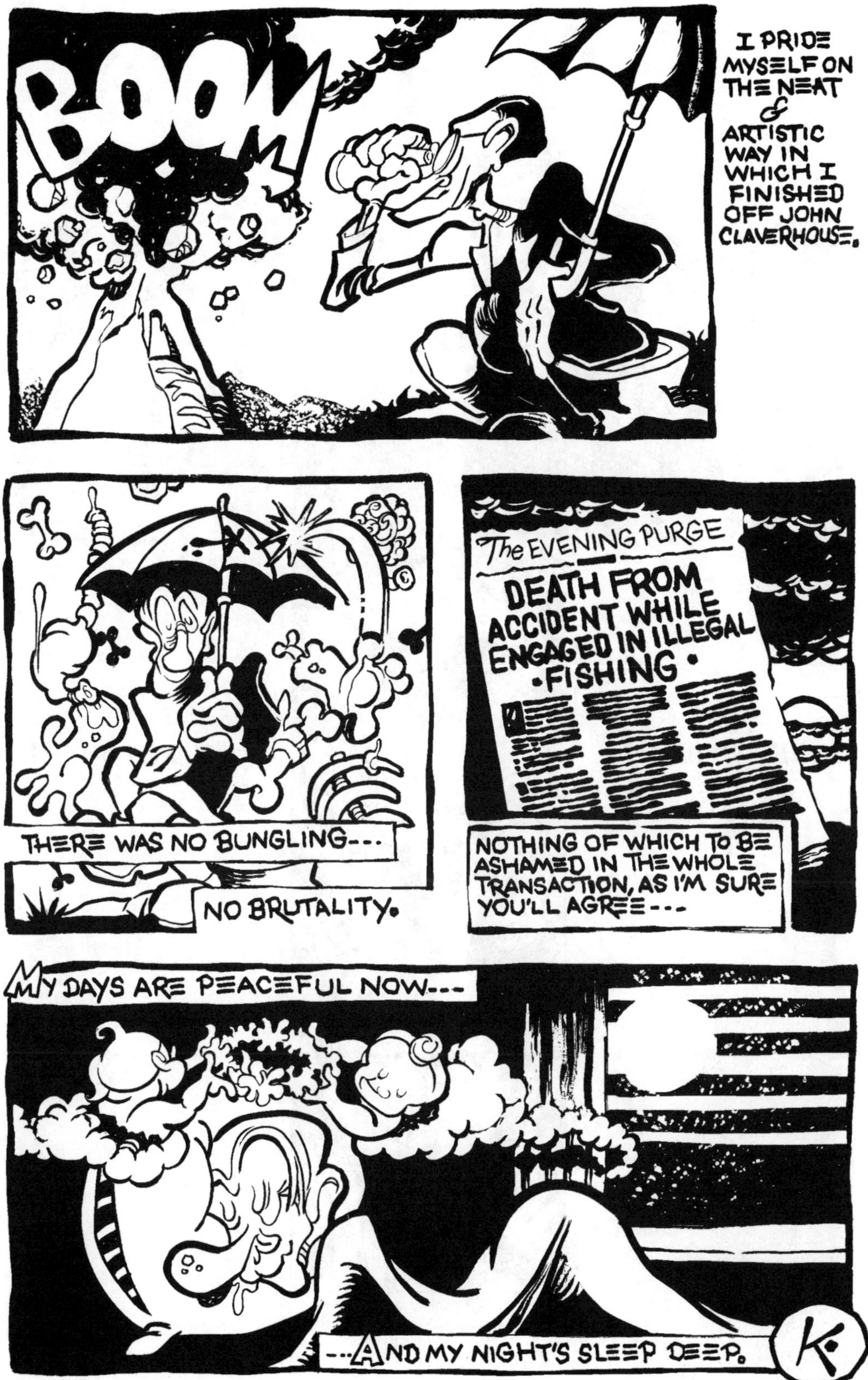
BOOM
I PRIDE MYSELF ON THE NEAT & ARTISTIC WAY IN WHICH I FINISHED OFF JOHN CLAVERHOUSE.
THERE WAS NO BUNGLING---
NO BRUTALITY.
The EVENING PURGE
DEATH FROM ACCIDENT WHILE ENGAGED IN ILLEGAL •FISHING•
NOTHING OF WHICH TO BE ASHAMED IN THE WHOLE TRANSACTION, AS I'M SURE YOU'LL AGREE---
MY DAYS ARE PEACEFUL NOW---
---AND MY NIGHT'S SLEEP DEEP.
K.

A THOUSAND DEATHS

story by
JACK LONDON

adapted & illustrated by
J.B. BONIVERT

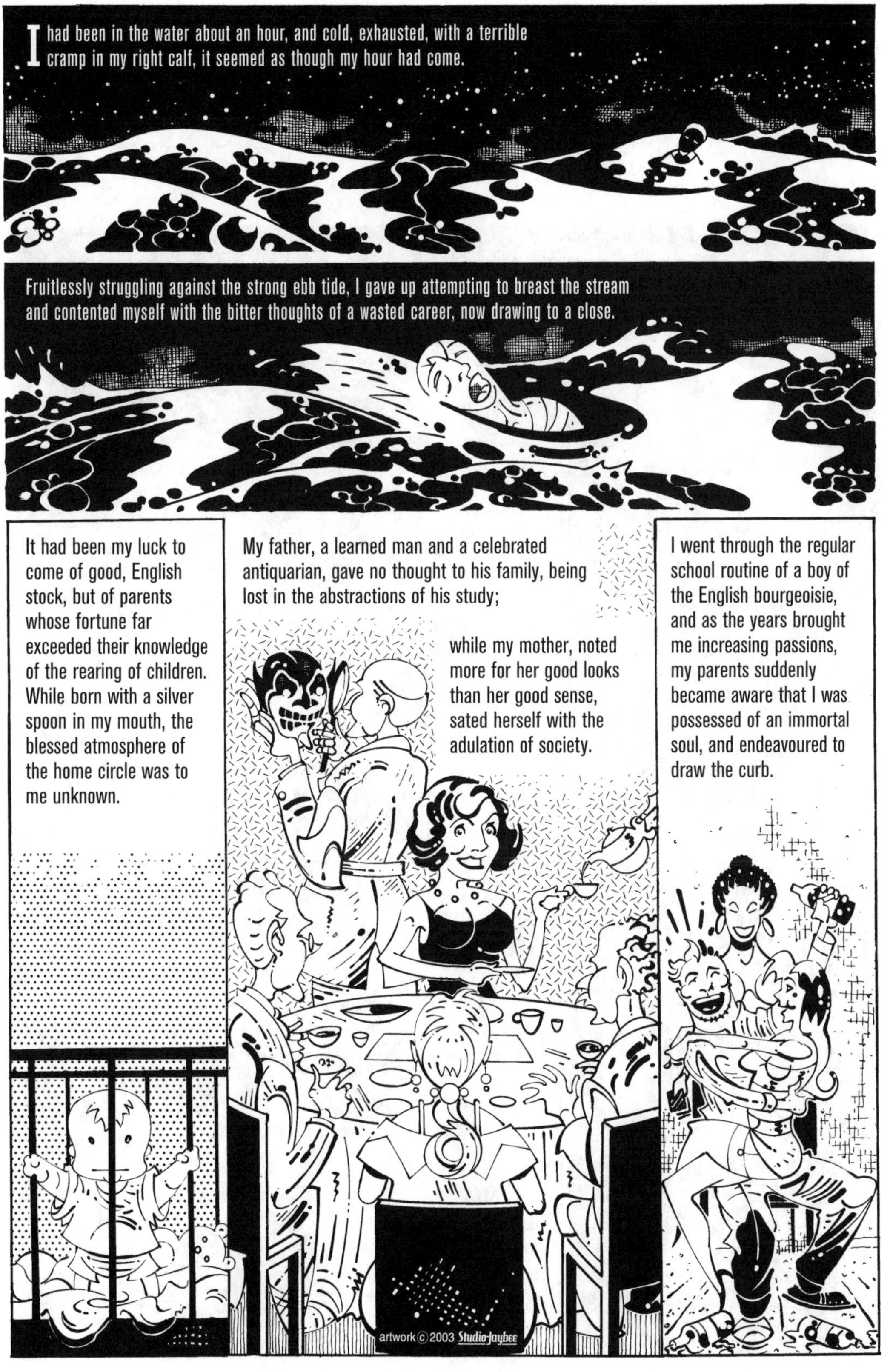
I had been in the water about an hour, and cold, exhausted, with a terrible cramp in my right calf, it seemed as though my hour had come.
Fruitlessly struggling against the strong ebb tide, I gave up attempting to breast the stream and contented myself with the bitter thoughts of a wasted career, now drawing to a close.
It had been my luck to come of good, English stock, but of parents whose fortune far exceeded their knowledge of the rearing of children. While born with a silver spoon in my mouth, the blessed atmosphere of the home circle was to me unknown.
My father, a learned man and a celebrated antiquarian, gave no thought to his family, being lost in the abstractions of his study;
while my mother, noted more for her good looks than her good sense, sated herself with the adulation of society.
I went through the regular school routine of a boy of the English bourgeoisie, and as the years brought me increasing passions, my parents suddenly became aware that I was possessed of an immortal soul, and endeavoured to draw the curb.
artwork © 2003 Studio-Jaybee

But it was too late; I perpetrated the most audacious folly, and was disowned by my people, ostracized by the society I had so long outraged, and with the thousand pounds my father gave me, with the declaration that he would neither see me again nor give me more, I took a passage to Australia.

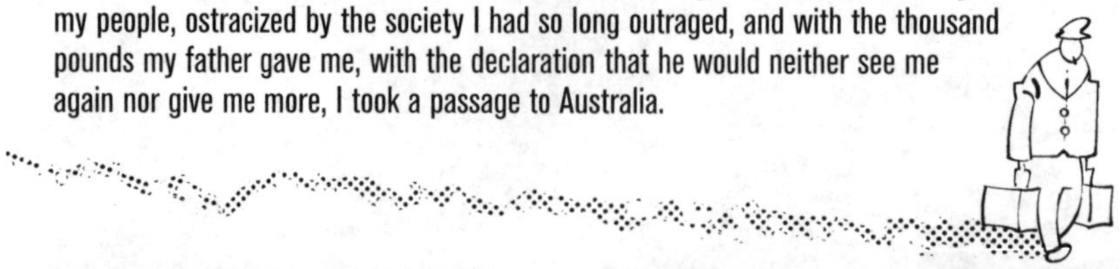

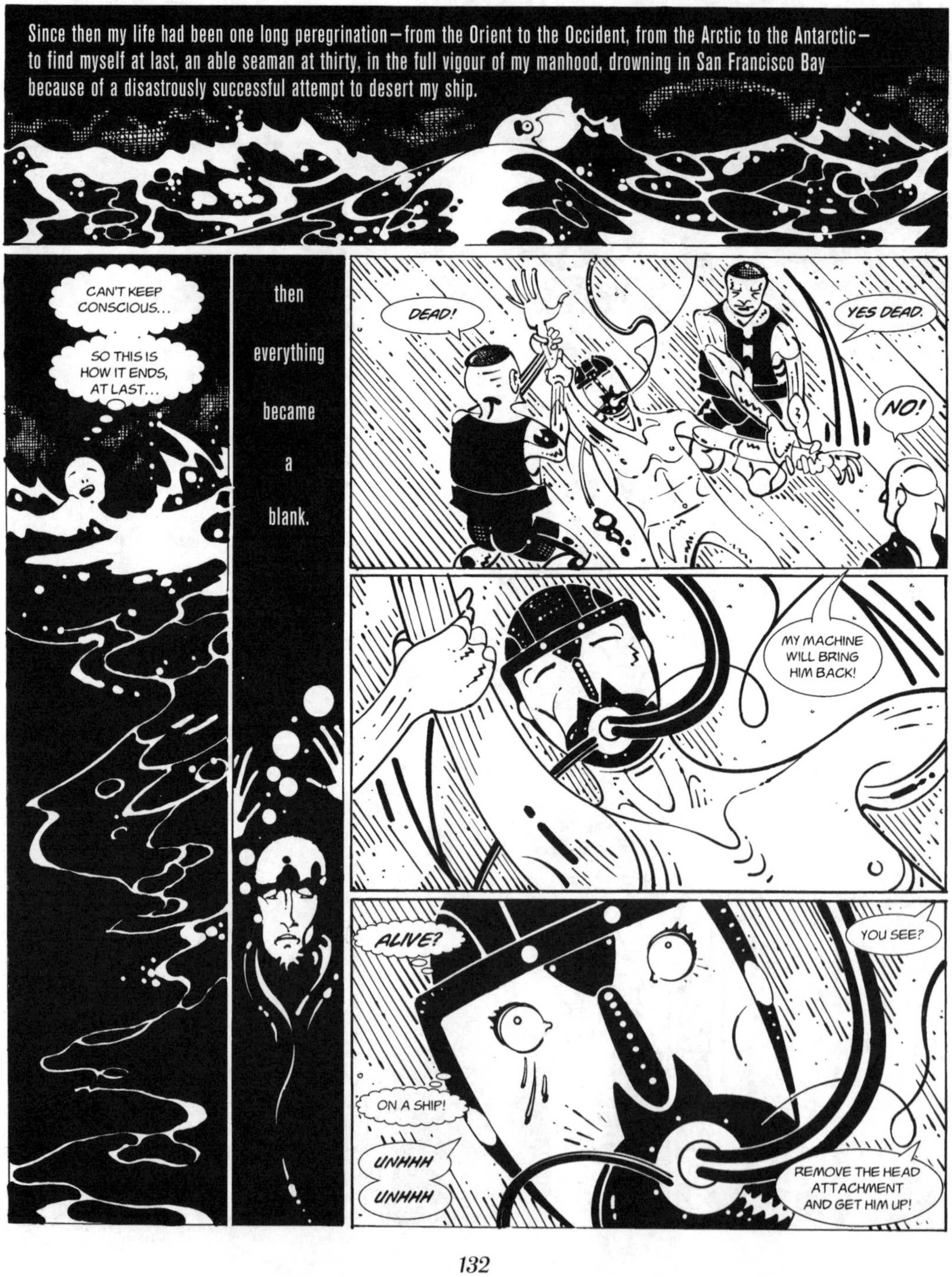
Since then my life had been one long peregrination—from the Orient to the Occident, from the Arctic to the Antarctic—to find myself at last, an able seaman at thirty, in the full vigour of my manhood, drowning in San Francisco Bay because of a disastrously successful attempt to desert my ship.
CAN'T KEEP CONSCIOUS...
SO THIS IS HOW IT ENDS, AT LAST...
then everything became a blank.
DEAD!
YES DEAD.
NO!
MY MACHINE WILL BRING HIM BACK!
ALIVE?
YOU SEE?
ON A SHIP!
UNHHH
UNHHH
REMOVE THE HEAD ATTACHMENT AND GET HIM UP!

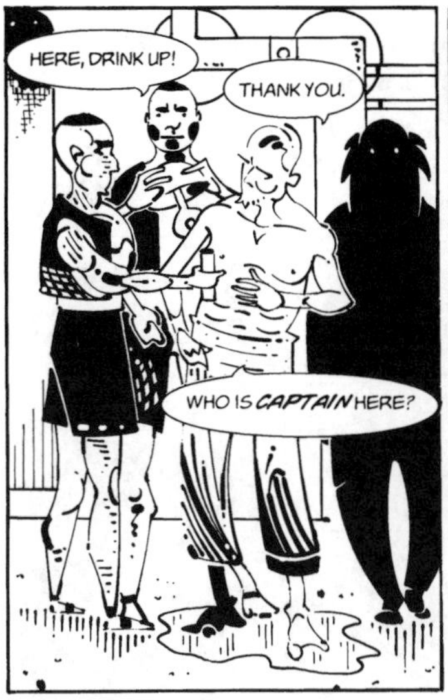
HERE, DRINK UP!
THANK YOU.
WHO IS *CAPTAIN* HERE?

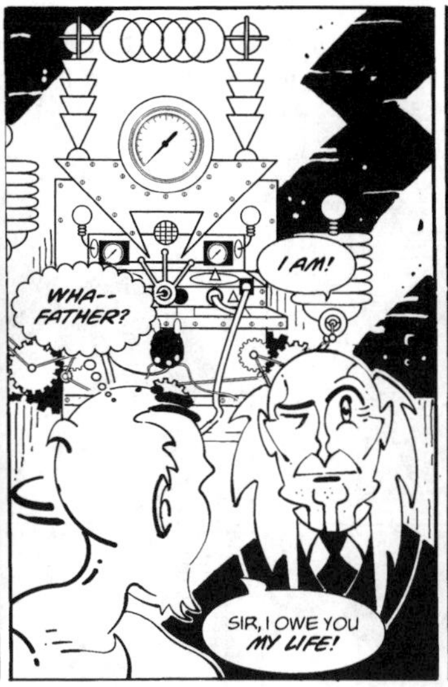
WHA-- FATHER?
I AM!
SIR, I OWE YOU *MY LIFE!*

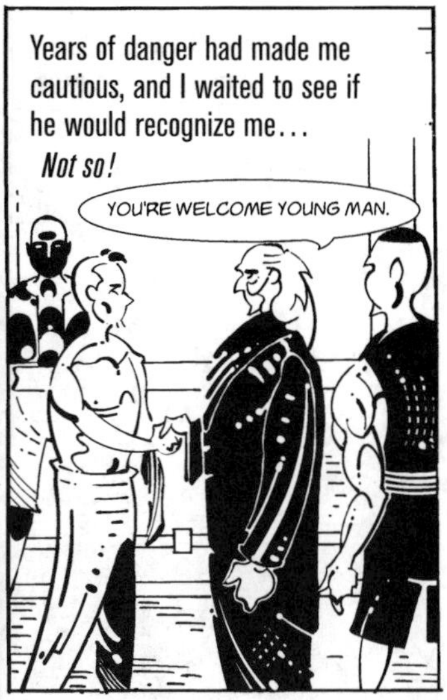
Years of danger had made me cautious, and I waited to see if he would recognize me...
Not so!
YOU'RE WELCOME YOUNG MAN.

Leaving me to the care of his men, he fell to revising the notes he had made on my resuscitation. As I ate the handsome fare served to me, the rattling of blocks and tackles began on deck, and I surmised that we were getting under way.

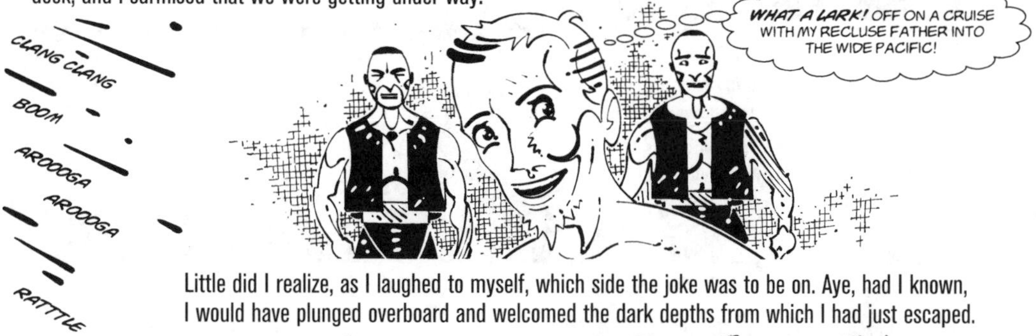
CLANG CLANG
BOOM
AROOOGA
AROOOGA
RATTTLE
WHAT A LARK! OFF ON A CRUISE WITH MY RECLUSE FATHER INTO THE WIDE PACIFIC!

Little did I realize, as I laughed to myself, which side the joke was to be on. Aye, had I known, I would have plunged overboard and welcomed the dark depths from which I had just escaped.

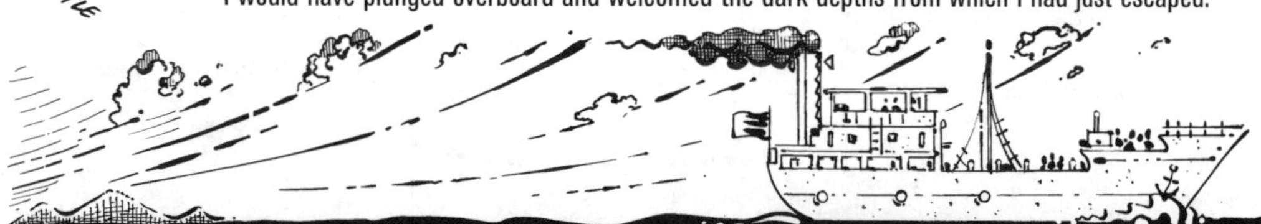

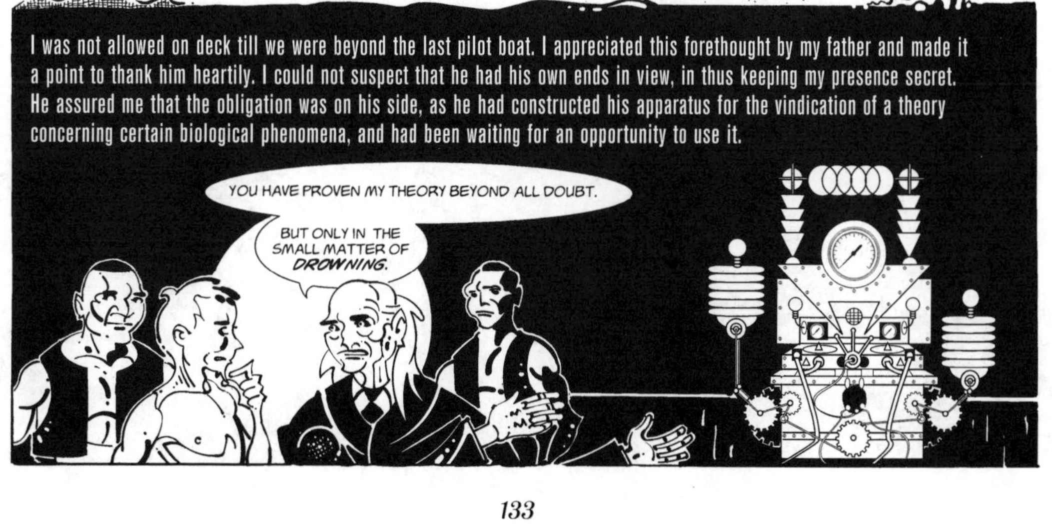
I was not allowed on deck till we were beyond the last pilot boat. I appreciated this forethought by my father and made it a point to thank him heartily. I could not suspect that he had his own ends in view, in thus keeping my presence secret. He assured me that the obligation was on his side, as he had constructed his apparatus for the vindication of a theory concerning certain biological phenomena, and had been waiting for an opportunity to use it.
YOU HAVE PROVEN MY THEORY BEYOND ALL DOUBT.
BUT ONLY IN THE SMALL MATTER OF *DROWNING*.

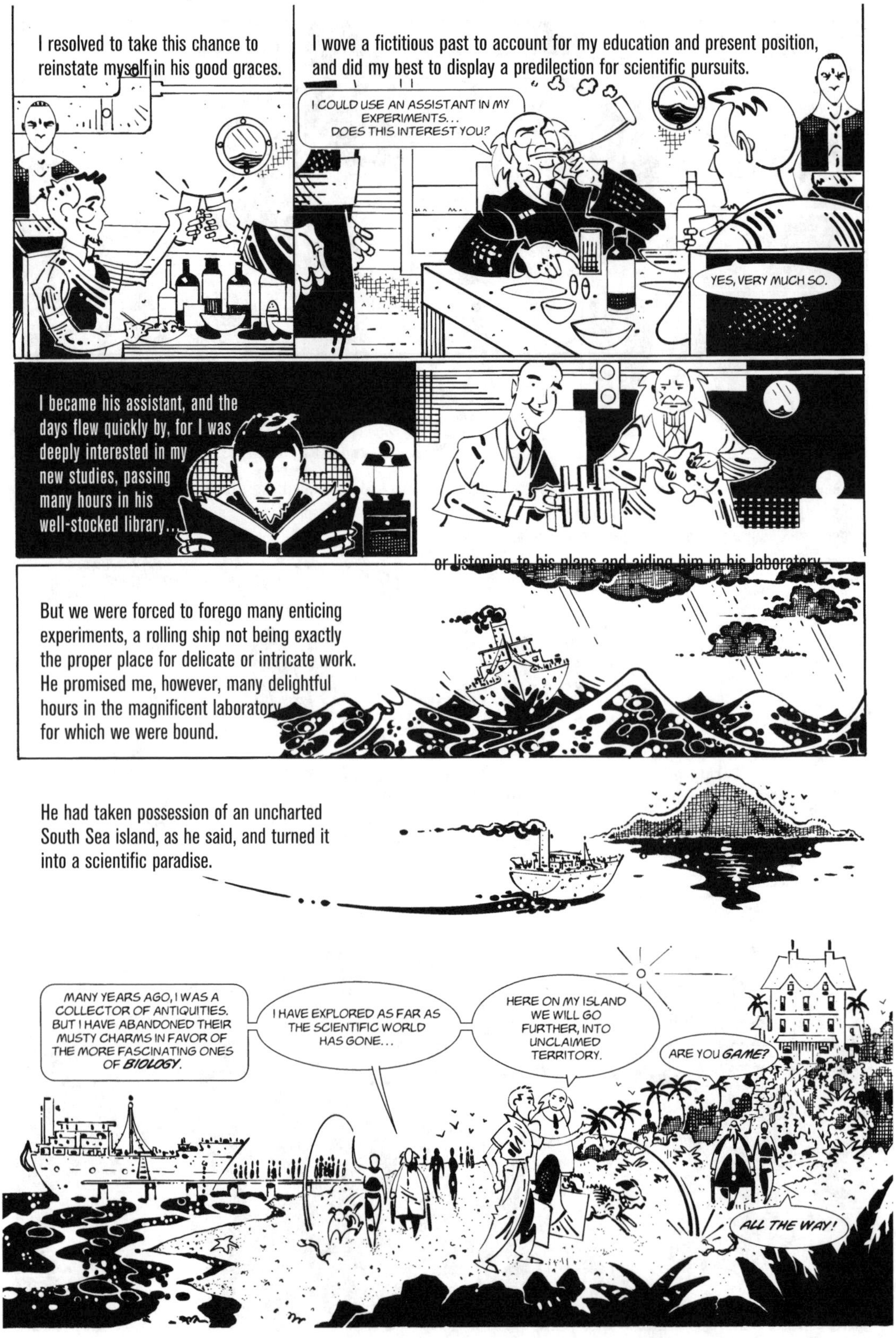
I resolved to take this chance to reinstate myself in his good graces.
I wove a fictitious past to account for my education and present position, and did my best to display a predilection for scientific pursuits.
I COULD USE AN ASSISTANT IN MY EXPERIMENTS... DOES THIS INTEREST YOU?
YES, VERY MUCH SO.
I became his assistant, and the days flew quickly by, for I was deeply interested in my new studies, passing many hours in his well-stocked library...
or listening to his plans and aiding him in his laboratory.
But we were forced to forego many enticing experiments, a rolling ship not being exactly the proper place for delicate or intricate work. He promised me, however, many delightful hours in the magnificent laboratory for which we were bound.
He had taken possession of an uncharted South Sea island, as he said, and turned it into a scientific paradise.
MANY YEARS AGO, I WAS A COLLECTOR OF ANTIQUITIES. BUT I HAVE ABANDONED THEIR MUSTY CHARMS IN FAVOR OF THE MORE FASCINATING ONES OF BIOLOGY.
I HAVE EXPLORED AS FAR AS THE SCIENTIFIC WORLD HAS GONE...
HERE ON MY ISLAND WE WILL GO FURTHER, INTO UNCLAIMED TERRITORY.
ARE YOU GAME?
ALL THE WAY!

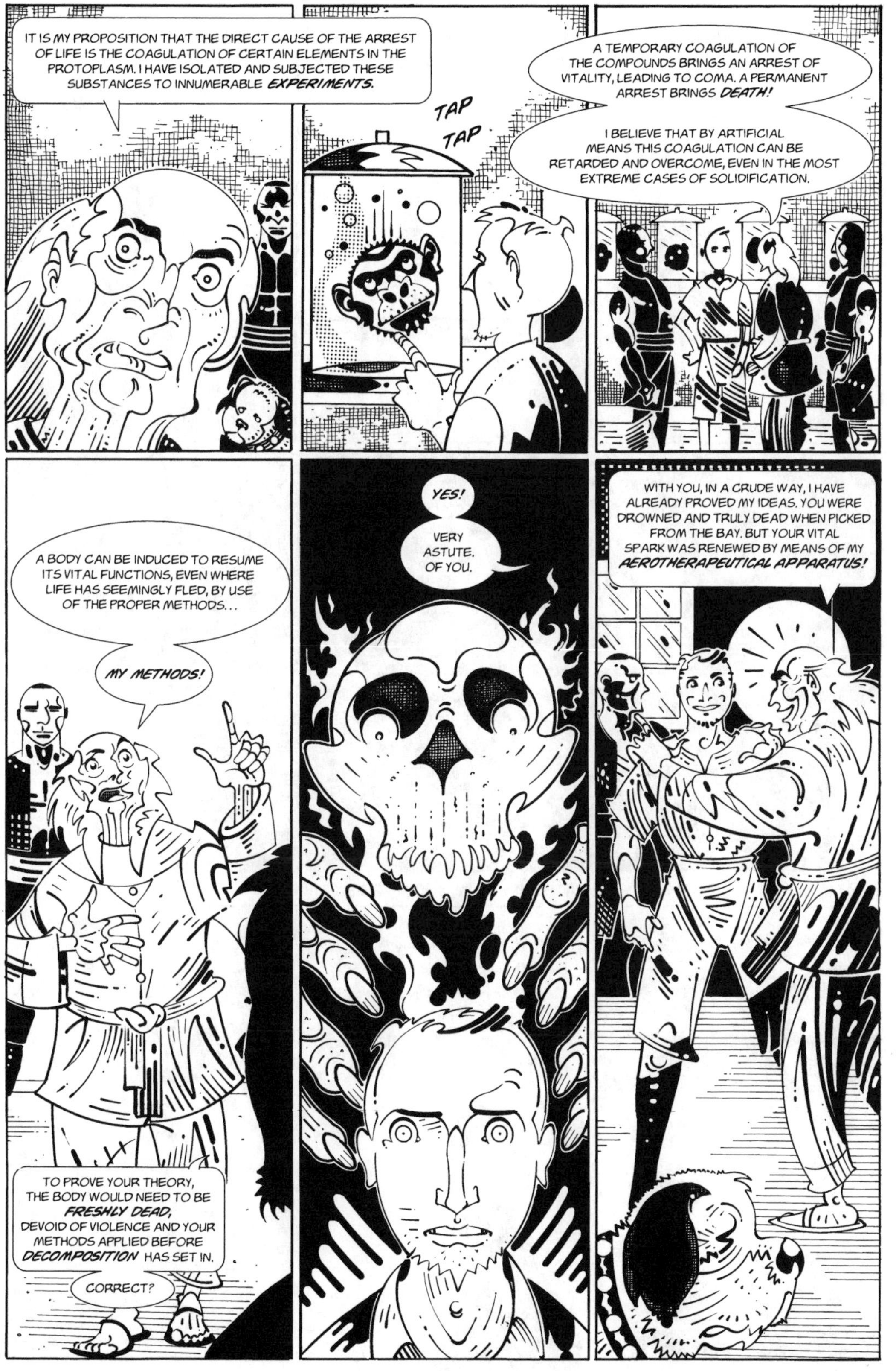
IT IS MY PROPOSITION THAT THE DIRECT CAUSE OF THE ARREST OF LIFE IS THE COAGULATION OF CERTAIN ELEMENTS IN THE PROTOPLASM. I HAVE ISOLATED AND SUBJECTED THESE SUBSTANCES TO INNUMERABLE EXPERIMENTS.
TAP
TAP
A TEMPORARY COAGULATION OF THE COMPOUNDS BRINGS AN ARREST OF VITALITY, LEADING TO COMA. A PERMANENT ARREST BRINGS DEATH!
I BELIEVE THAT BY ARTIFICIAL MEANS THIS COAGULATION CAN BE RETARDED AND OVERCOME, EVEN IN THE MOST EXTREME CASES OF SOLIDIFICATION.
A BODY CAN BE INDUCED TO RESUME ITS VITAL FUNCTIONS, EVEN WHERE LIFE HAS SEEMINGLY FLED, BY USE OF THE PROPER METHODS...
MY METHODS!
TO PROVE YOUR THEORY, THE BODY WOULD NEED TO BE FRESHLY DEAD, DEVOID OF VIOLENCE AND YOUR METHODS APPLIED BEFORE DECOMPOSITION HAS SET IN.
CORRECT?
YES!
VERY ASTUTE. OF YOU.
WITH YOU, IN A CRUDE WAY, I HAVE ALREADY PROVED MY IDEAS. YOU WERE DROWNED AND TRULY DEAD WHEN PICKED FROM THE BAY. BUT YOUR VITAL SPARK WAS RENEWED BY MEANS OF MY AEROTHERAPEUTICAL APPARATUS!

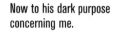

Now to his dark purpose concerning me.
He first showed me how completely I was in his power.
He sent the yacht away for a year.
And retained only his two servants, who were utterly devoted to him.
IN IS OUT
NORMAL/ABNORMAL
AND YOU...
He then made a review of his theory, concluding with the startling announcement...
YOU WILL PROVIDE THE ***BODY***.
ME!? YOU WANT ME TO BE YOUR TEST SUBJECT?
I had weighed my chances in many a desperate venture, and I can swear I am no coward, yet this proposition of journeying back and forth across the borderland of death put the yellow fear upon me.
I'LL NEED SOME TIME TO GET USED TO THE IDEA.
YOU HAVE 24 HOURS.
AND REMEMBER, THERE IS ***NO ESCAPE*** FROM THE ISLAND!

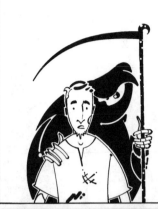

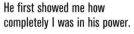

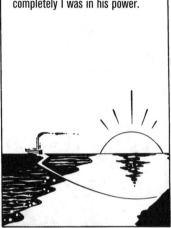

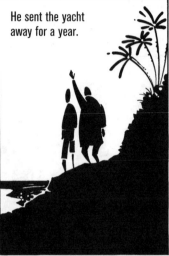

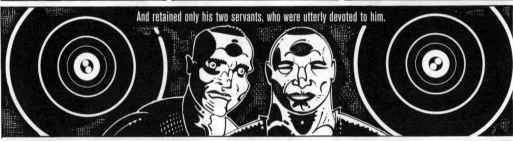

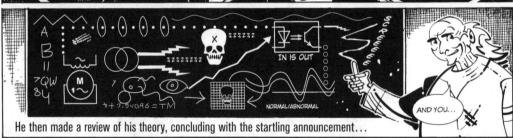

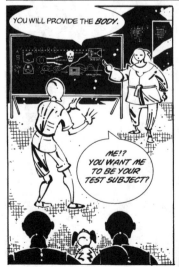

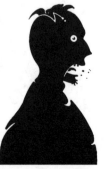

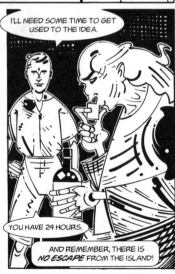

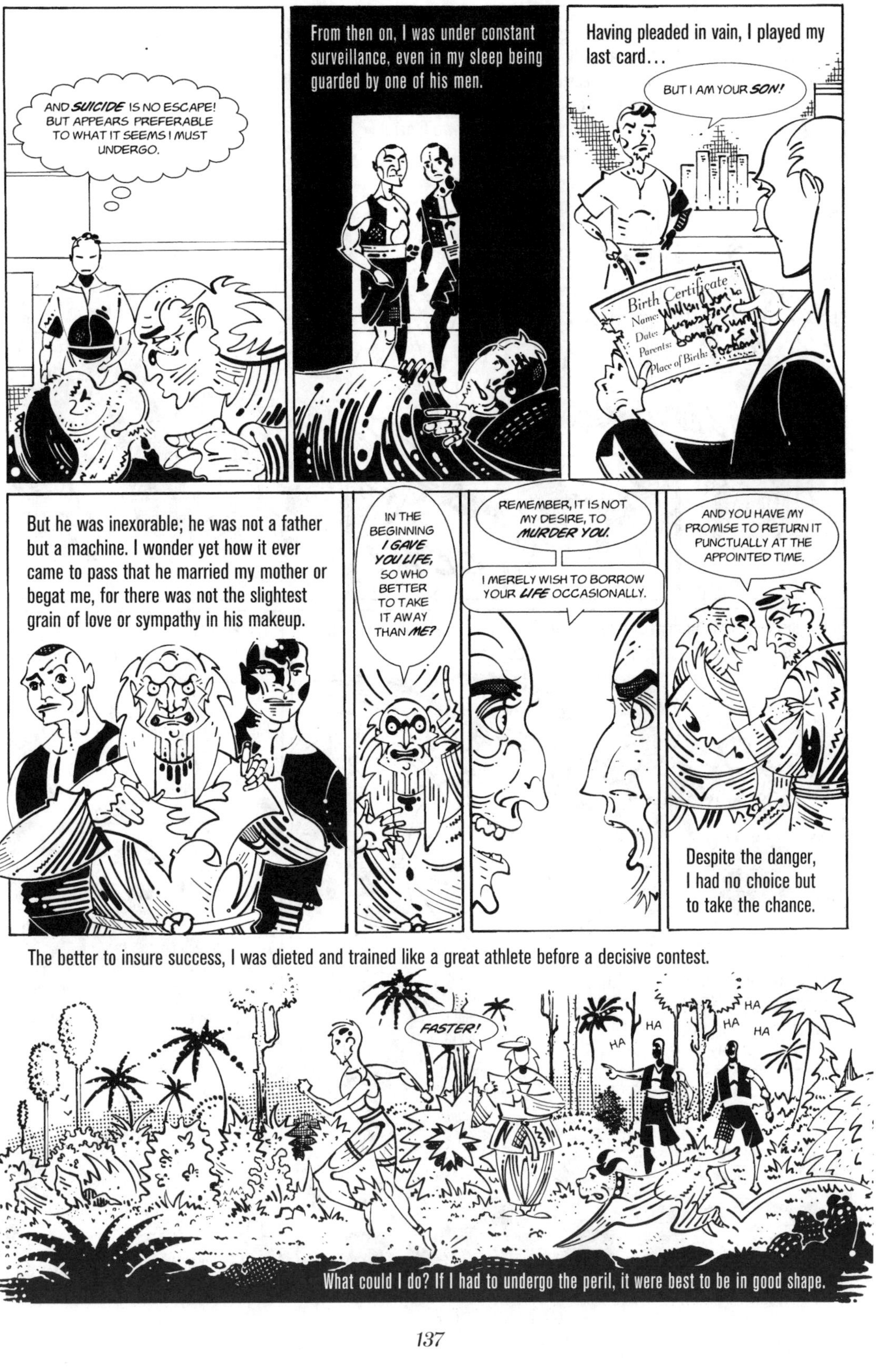
AND SUICIDE IS NO ESCAPE! BUT APPEARS PREFERABLE TO WHAT IT SEEMS I MUST UNDERGO.
From then on, I was under constant surveillance, even in my sleep being guarded by one of his men.
Having pleaded in vain, I played my last card…
BUT I AM YOUR SON!
Birth Certificate
Name:
Date:
Parents:
Place of Birth:
But he was inexorable; he was not a father but a machine. I wonder yet how it ever came to pass that he married my mother or begat me, for there was not the slightest grain of love or sympathy in his makeup.
IN THE BEGINNING I GAVE YOU LIFE, SO WHO BETTER TO TAKE IT AWAY THAN ME?
REMEMBER, IT IS NOT MY DESIRE, TO MURDER YOU.
I MERELY WISH TO BORROW YOUR LIFE OCCASIONALLY.
AND YOU HAVE MY PROMISE TO RETURN IT PUNCTUALLY AT THE APPOINTED TIME.
Despite the danger, I had no choice but to take the chance.
The better to insure success, I was dieted and trained like a great athlete before a decisive contest.
FASTER!
HA HA HA HA HA
What could I do? If I had to undergo the peril, it were best to be in good shape.

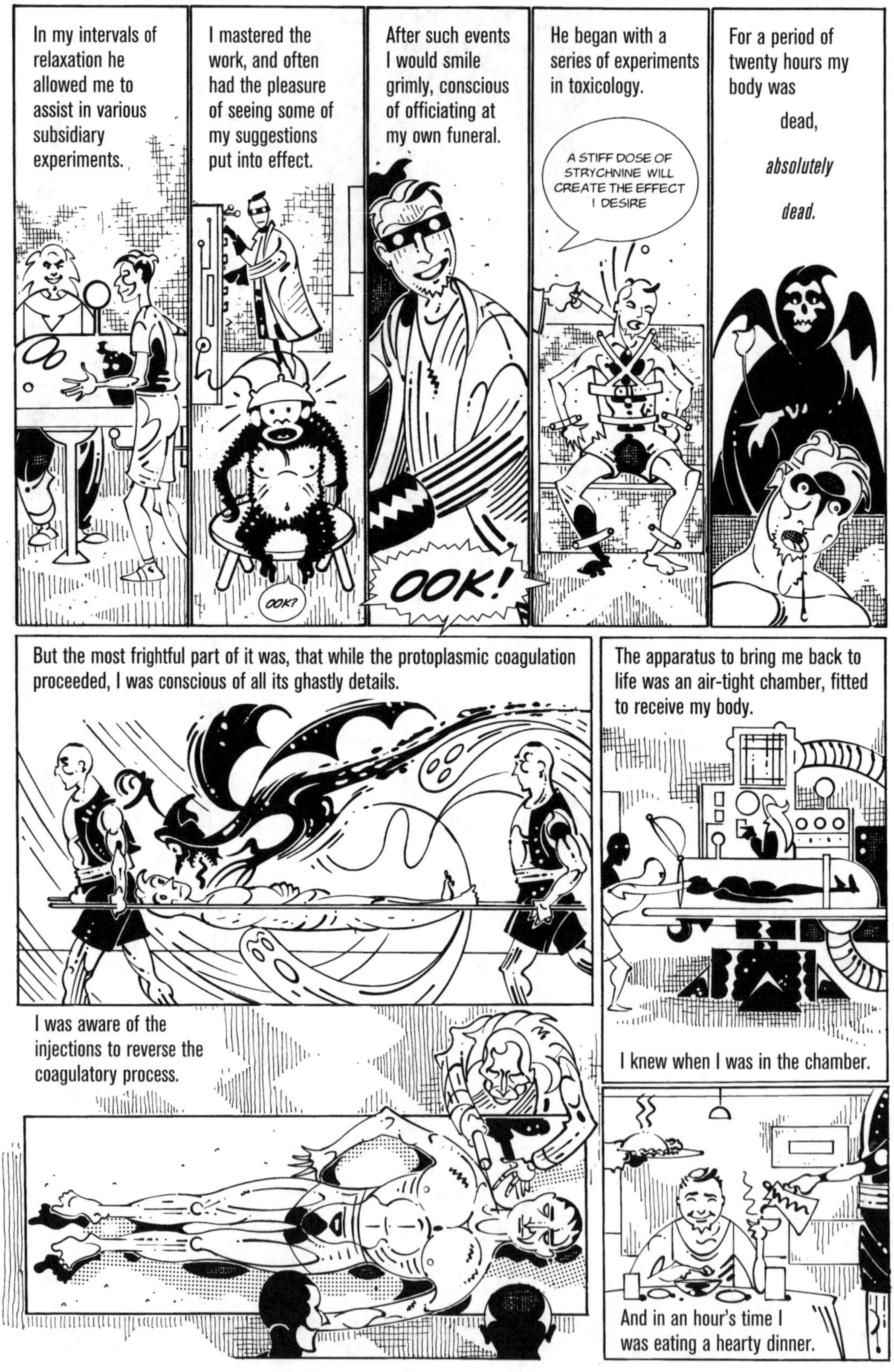
In my intervals of relaxation he allowed me to assist in various subsidiary experiments.
I mastered the work, and often had the pleasure of seeing some of my suggestions put into effect.
OOK?
After such events I would smile grimly, conscious of officiating at my own funeral.
OOK!
He began with a series of experiments in toxicology.
A STIFF DOSE OF STRYCHNINE WILL CREATE THE EFFECT I DESIRE
For a period of twenty hours my body was
dead,
absolutely
dead.
But the most frightful part of it was, that while the protoplasmic coagulation proceeded, I was conscious of all its ghastly details.
The apparatus to bring me back to life was an air-tight chamber, fitted to receive my body.
I was aware of the injections to reverse the coagulatory process.
I knew when I was in the chamber.
And in an hour's time I was eating a hearty dinner.

I attempted escape…

twice…

…to no avail.

In the weeks that followed, I died many times and ways.

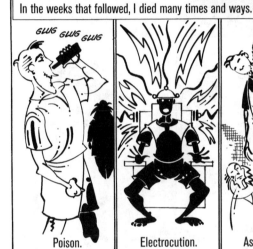

GLUG GLUG GLUG

Poison.

Electrocution.

Asphyxiation.

Drug overdose.

I was
continually dying.

Finally, my father kept me in cold storage for three months, not permitting me to freeze or decay. This was without my knowledge, and I was in a great fright on discovering the lapse of time.

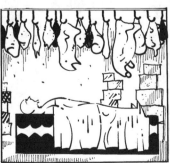

I became afraid of what he might do with me when I lay dead.

During my convalescence I evolved the plan by which I ultimately escaped.

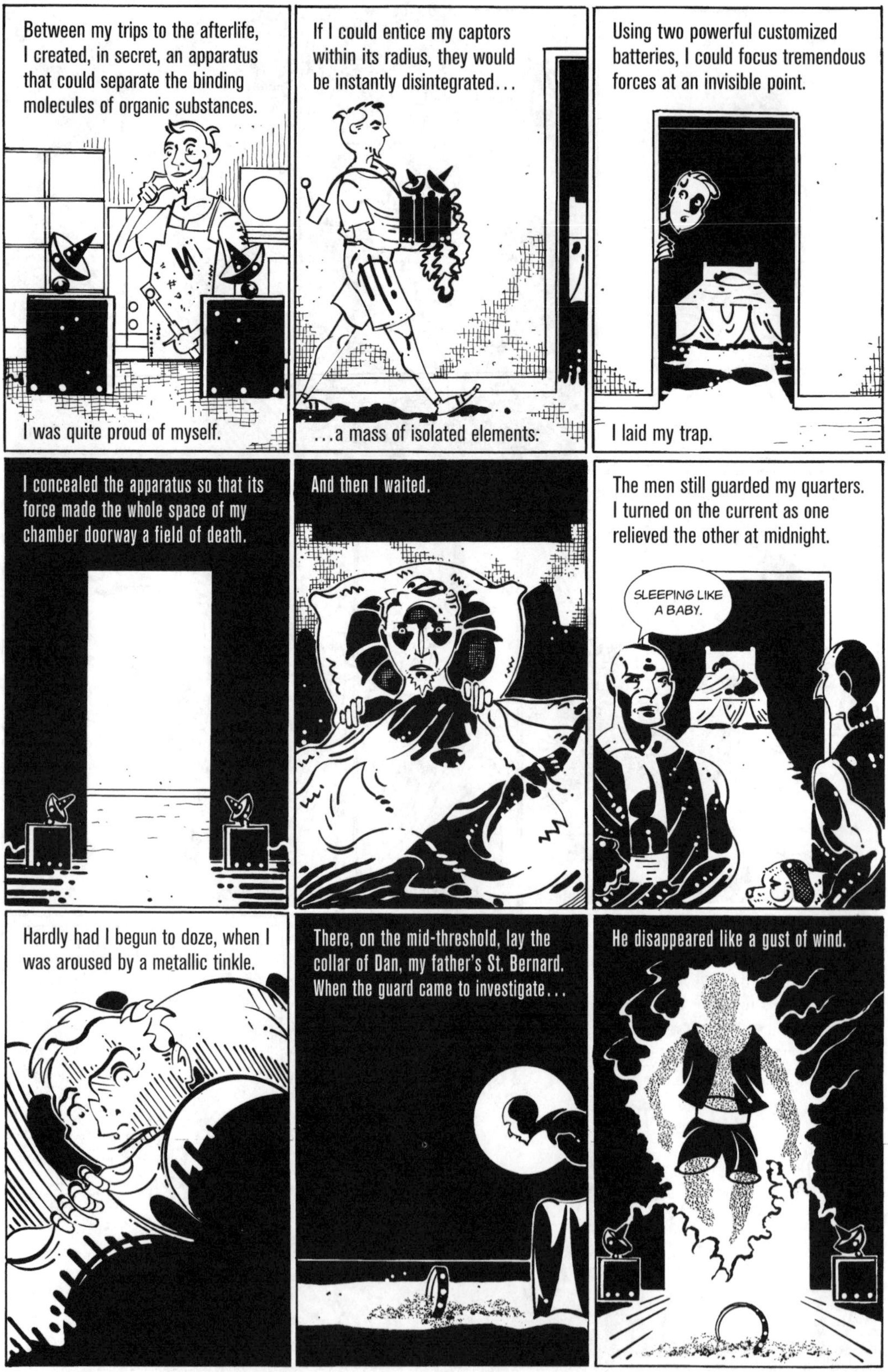
Between my trips to the afterlife, I created, in secret, an apparatus that could separate the binding molecules of organic substances.
I was quite proud of myself.
If I could entice my captors within its radius, they would be instantly disintegrated...
...a mass of isolated elements:
Using two powerful customized batteries, I could focus tremendous forces at an invisible point.
I laid my trap.
I concealed the apparatus so that its force made the whole space of my chamber doorway a field of death.
And then I waited.
The men still guarded my quarters. I turned on the current as one relieved the other at midnight.
SLEEPING LIKE A BABY.
Hardly had I begun to doze, when I was aroused by a metallic tinkle.
There, on the mid-threshold, lay the collar of Dan, my father's St. Bernard. When the guard came to investigate...
He disappeared like a gust of wind.

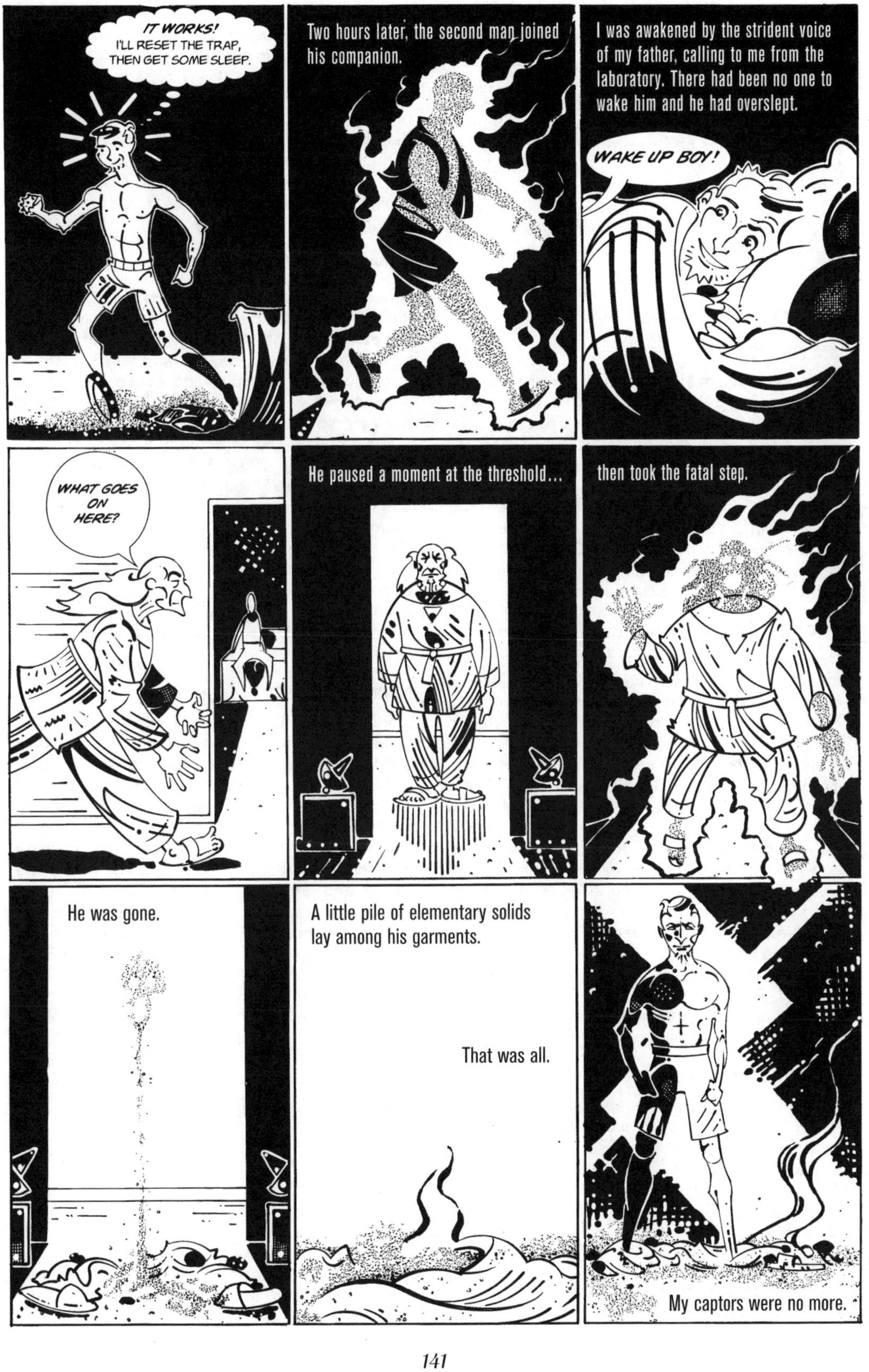
IT WORKS!
I'LL RESET THE TRAP, THEN GET SOME SLEEP.
Two hours later, the second man joined his companion.
I was awakened by the strident voice of my father, calling to me from the laboratory. There had been no one to wake him and he had overslept.
WAKE UP BOY!
WHAT GOES ON HERE?
He paused a moment at the threshold...
then took the fatal step.
He was gone.
A little pile of elementary solids lay among his garments.
That was all.
My captors were no more.

JACK LONDON

As a sailor, petty thief, hobo, prospector, rancher, war correspondent and socialist spokesman, Jack London led a life that was as exciting, inspiring, and tragic as any of his many stories. London was born in San Francisco in 1876, an illegitimate child. His mother and stepfather were never far from poverty, and at the age of 13, Jack left school and began the life of a common laborer. But his appetite for reading allowed him to continue educating himself, and his talent for writing of the experiences of his life at sea, in the Klondike and around the world eventually made him, by the time of his premature death in 1916, the most popular author in America.

JIM NELSON (front cover)

Chicago artist Jim Nelson's work has appeared in fantasy role-playing games, books and magazines. He has been represented in *Spectrum: The Best in Contemporary Fantastic Art* as both an artist and art director. Jim contributes to Wizards of the Coast's popular *Magic: The Gathering* card game and is also involved in projects for White Wolf, *Weekly Reader* and *Riotminds*. More of his art can be seen in *Graphic Classics: H.P. Lovecraft*, *Graphic Classics: H.G. Wells* and at http://www.theispot.com/artist/jnelson.

ROGER LANGRIDGE (pages 1,2)

New Zealand-born artist Roger Langridge is the creator of Fred the Clown, whose online comics appear every Monday at www.hotelfred.com. Fred also shows up in print three times a year in *Fred the Clown* comics. With his brother Andrew, Roger's first comics series was *Zoot!* published in 1988 and recently reissued as *Zoot Suite*. Other titles include *Knuckles, The Malevolent Nun* and *Art d'Ecco*. Roger's work has also appeared in numerous magazines in Britain, the U.S., France and Japan, including *Deadline, Judge Dredd, Heavy Metal, Comic Afternoon, Gross Point* and *Batman: Legends of the Dark Knight*. For *Graphic Classics* he has adapted poems by Edgar Allan Poe and Arthur Conan Doyle, a fable by Robert Louis Stevenson, and a mystery by Rafael Sabatini. Roger now lives in London, where he divides his time between comics, children's books and commercial illustration.

MORT CASTLE (page 2)

A writing teacher and author specializing in the horror genre, Mort Castle has written and edited fourteen books and around 500 short stories and articles. His novels and collections include *Cursed Be the Child, The Strangers, Moon on the Water* and *Nations of the Living, Nations of the Dead*. He has produced an audio CD of one of his stories, *Buckeye Jim in Egypt*, and is the author of the essential reference work for aspiring horror writers, *Writing Horror*. Mort has won numerous writing awards, and he has had several

dozen stories cited in "year's best" compilations in the horror, suspense, fantasy, and literary fields. He has been a writer and editor for several comics publishers, and is a frequent keynote speaker at writing conferences. Mort's comics biographies appear in *Graphic Classics: Ambrose Bierce, Graphic Classics: Robert Louis Stevenson* and *Graphic Classics: Rafael Sabatini*. He created the unique introduction to *Graphic Classics: Bram Stoker*, and co-authored an O. Henry "sequel" in *Graphic Classics: O. Henry*.

ARNOLD ARRE (pages 3, 54)

Arnold Arre worked in several ad agencies in the Philippines before deciding on a career as a freelance artist, saying, "I guess I'm more of a storyteller than an advertiser." Arnold tells his stories through both illustration and comics, as can be seen by the examples on his website at www.arnold-arre.com. He has won awards for his graphic novels *The Mythology Class* (2000) and *Trip to Tagaytay* (2001). His most recent offering is *After Eden*, a 254-page graphic novel. In addition to comics work, Arnold still does commercial design and and has moved into gallery paintings. He had his first solo show, *Mythos*, in 2000, and was also part of the 2001 Filipino American Art Expo Exhibits in San Francisco and New Jersey. Arnold's art also appears in *Graphic Classics: Arthur Conan Doyle* and *Graphic Classics: H.P. Lovecraft*.

MARK A. NELSON (page 4)

Mark Nelson was a professor of art at Northern Illinois University for twenty years. From 1998 to 2004 he was a senior artist at Raven Software, doing conceptual work, painting digital skins and creating textures for computer games. Mark is now the lead instructor of the Animation Department of Madison Area Technical College in Madison, Wisconsin. His comics credits include *Blood and Shadows* for DC, *Aliens* for Dark Horse Comics, and *Feud* for Marvel. He has worked for numerous publishers, and his art is represented in *Spectrum #4, 5, 6, 8, 10* and *From Pencils to Inks: The Art of Mark A. Nelson* (2004 Baron Publishing). Mark's comics and illustrations have appeared in *Graphic Classics: Edgar Allan Poe, Graphic Classics: Arthur Conan Doyle, Graphic Classics: Ambrose Bierce, Graphic Classics: H.P. Lovecraft, Graphic Classics: O. Henry, Horror Classics, Rosebud 18* and *The Best of Rosebud*, all from Eureka Productions.

HUNT EMERSON (page 24)

Hunt Emerson describes himself as "a cartoonist and occasional musician." Others consider him the dean of British comics artists. He has drawn comics since the early 1970s, and has published around 30 books, including *Lady Chatterley's Lover, The Rime of the Ancient Mariner*, and *Casanova's Last Stand*, and his comics have been translated into ten languages. His work also appears in *Graphic Classics: Bram Stoker*, *Graphic Classics: Robert Louis Stevenson*, *Graphic Classics: Rafael Sabatini* and *Adventure Classics*. Hunt says he "likes sleep, beer, and Laurel & Hardy, and dislikes artichokes, both singly and in gangs." You can see more of Hunt's comics at www.largecow.demon.co.uk.

ROD LOTT (page 32)

Based in Oklahoma City, Rod Lott is a freelance writer and graphic designer in advertising and journalism. For twelve years, he has published and edited the more-or-less quarterly magazine *Hitch: The Journal of Pop Culture Absurdity* (www.hitchmagazine.com), and recently started *Bookgasm*, a daily book review and news site at www.bookgasm.com. Rod's humorous essays have been published in several anthologies, including *May Contain Nuts* and *101 Damnations*. He has scripted comics adaptations of stories by Edgar Allan Poe, Clark Ashton Smith, Sax Rohmer, H.G. Wells, O. Henry and Rafael Sabatini for *Graphic Classics*, and is now scripting a comics adaptation of J. Sheridan Le Fanu's erotic vampire tale *Carmilla* for *Gothic Classics*. You can learn more about Rod's work online at www.rodlott.com.

KOSTAS ARONIS (page 32)

In addition to his illustration work, Kostas is an architect in Thessaloniki, Greece and works as a scenographer for the theater, State TV and private channels. He teaches in AKTO, a school of fine arts in Thessaloniki and established the theater group ACHTHOS, to create performances and installations with a comics aesthetic. Kostas organized the first Intervalkanian Comics Festival as part of Cultural Olympiade 2004. His illustrations and comics have been published in books, on CDs, and in magazines and newspapers in Greece. His first personal comics album, *ANTIGONI*, was published in 2005. His book, *Between the Legs – Unbelievable Stories*, was published in 2001, and his second book, *Different in the Internet*, in 2005. His spot illustrations for *To Kill a Man* appeared in the first edition of this book in 2003, and Kostas expanded them to a complete comics adaptation for this edition, his first comics work to appear in the U.S.

ONSMITH JEREMI (page 46)

Onsmith Jeremi (*aka* Jeremy Smith) grew up in a couple of small towns in central Oklahoma, putting in his factory and fast food time while nurturing an interest in small press comics, cartoons, and "zines." He then moved to Chicago, where he started a small press anthology, *Bomb Time for Bonzo*, with fellow artists Ben Chandler and Henry Ng (of the early *Non* anthology). Onsmith's work has appeared in anthologies including *Expo 2002*, *Studygroup 12* and *Proper Gander*, as well as *Graphic Classics: H.P.*

Lovecraft, *Graphic Classics: Bram Stoker* and *Horror Classics*. To see more of his work, visit www.onsmithcomics.com.

TRINA ROBBINS (page 75)

Trina has been writing and drawing comics for more than thirty years, and since 1990 she has become a writer and feminist pop culture herstorian. Aside from her award-winning books on comics from a feminist perspective (*The Great Women Cartoonists* was listed among *Time Magazine*'s top ten comics of 2001), she has written about goddesses and murderesses, and her newest book is *Tender Murderers: Women Who Kill*. Currently, she scripts *GoGirl!*, a teen superheroine comic illustrated by Anne Timmons. Early art by Trina was reprinted in *Graphic Classics: H.P. Lovecraft*, and she is currently scripting an adptation of Jane Austen's *Northanger Abbey* for *Gothic Classics*. Check out her website at www.trinarobbins.com.

ANNE TIMMONS (page 75)

Anne was born in Portland, and has a BFA from Oregon State University. In addition to her collaboration on the Lulu Award-winning *GoGirl!* with Trina Robbins, Anne's work includes the Eisner Award-nominated *Dignifying Science* and the comics version of *Star Trek: Deep Space Nine*. She has also drawn and painted children's books and covers and interior art for magazines including *Comic Book Artist* and *Wired*. She illustrated a poem in *Graphic Classics: Robert Louis Stevenson*, and her art from the anthology *9-11 Artists Respond* is now included in the Library of Congress Collection. Samples of Anne's work can be seen at www.homepage.mac.com/tafrin.

ANTONELLA CAPUTO (page 84)

Antonella was born and raised in Rome, Italy, and now lives in Lancaster, England. She has been an architect, archaeologist, art restorer, photographer, calligrapher, interior designer, theatre designer, actress and theatre director. Her first published work was *Casa Montesi*, a fortnightly comic strip which appeared in the national magazine *Il Giornalino*. She has since written comedies for children and scripts for comics and magazines in the UK, Europe and the US. She works with Nick Miller as the writing half of Team Sputnik, and has also collaborated with other artists in the *Graphic Classics* volumes *Edgar Allan Poe*, *Arthur Conan Doyle*, *H.G. Wells*, *Ambrose Bierce*, *Mark Twain*, *O. Henry*, *Rafael Sabatini*, *Horror Classics* and *Adventure Classics*.

NICK MILLER (page 84, back cover)

Nick was born and raised in the depths of rural England, and now lives in Lancaster, UK with his partner, Antonella Caputo. The son of two artists, he learned to draw at an early age. After leaving art school he worked as a graphic designer before switching to cartooning and illustration full-time in the early '90s. Since then his work has appeared in many comics and magazines in the UK, US and Europe, as well as in comic anthologies, websites and in advertising. His weekly comic strip, *The Really Heavy Greatcoat*, can be seen at www.lancasterukonline.net. He works as part of Team Sputnik with Antonella Caputo, and also independently with other writers including John Freeman, Tony Husband, Mark Rogers and Tim Quinn. Nick's stories have appeared in *Graphic Classics: Arthur Conan Doyle*, *Graphic Classics: H.G. Wells*, *Graphic Classics: Ambrose Bierce*, *Graphic Classics: Mark Twain*, *Horror Classics* and *Adventure Classics*.

PETER KUPER (page 94)

Highly regarded by both fans and his peers, Peter Kuper has been active in the comics community since the early 1970s. In 1979 he co-founded the political comics magazine *World War 3 Illustrated* and remains on its editorial board. He has been an instructor at the School of Visual Arts since 1986 and is also an art director for the political illustration group INX (www.inxart.com). Peter's illustrations and comics appear regularly in *Time*, *The New York Times* and *MAD*. He has written and illustrated many books including *Comics Trips*, a journal of an eight-month trip through Africa and Southeast Asia. Other works include *Mind's Eye*, *Stripped— An Unauthorized Autobiography*, *The System*, a wordless graphic novel, and an adaptation of Kafka's *The Metamorphosis*. Peter's recent book, *SPEECHLESS*, collects his career to date. More of his work can be seen at www.peterkuper.com.

JOHN W. PIERARD (page 100)

John Pierard has had a varied career in illustration. After leaving the bosom of his beloved Syracuse University for New York City, he immediately found work in publications such as *Screw* and *Velvet Touch Magazine*, where he illustrated stories like *Sex Junky*. In a major departure, he then graduated to illustrating children's fiction, including Mel Gilden's *P.S. 13* series, and various projects by noted children's author Bruce Coville. He has worked for Marvel Comics, *Asimov's Magazine* and Greenwich Press and has exhibited his art in New York galleries. John's comics adaptations are also featured in *Graphic Classics: Bram Stoker*, *Graphic Classics: O. Henry* and *Horror Classics*.

SPAIN RODRIGUEZ (page 112)

Manuel "Spain" Rodriguez, born 1940 in Buffalo, New York, first gained fame as one of the founders of the underground comix movement of the 1960s. After drawing comics in New York for the *East Village Other*, he moved to San Francisco where he joined Robert Crumb and other artists on *Zap Comix*. Spain's early years with the Road Vultures Motorcycle Club and his

reportage of the 1968 Democratic Convention in Chicago are chronicled in the comics collection, *My True Story*. Along with autobiographical stories and politically-oriented fiction featuring his best-known character, Trashman, Spain has produced a number of historical comics, and his work can also be seen in the online comic *The Dark Hotel* at www.salon.com, and in *Graphic Classics: Bram Stoker*.

MILTON KNIGHT (page 115)

Milton Knight claims he started drawing, painting and creating his own attempts at comic books and animation at age two. "I've never formed a barrier between fine art and cartooning," says Milt. "Growing up, I treasured Chinese watercolors, Breughel, Charlie Brown and Terrytoons equally." His work has appeared in magazines including *Heavy Metal*, *High Times*, *National Lampoon* and *Nickelodeon Magazine*, and he has illustrated record covers, posters, candy packaging and T-shirts, and occasionally exhibited his paintings. Labor on *Ninja Turtles* comics allowed him to get up a grubstake to move to the West Coast in 1991, where he became an animator and director on *Felix the Cat* cartoons. His comics titles include *Midnite the Rebel Skunk* and *Slug and Ginger*. His adaptation of *The Fool's Love Story* for *Graphic Classics: Rafael Sabatini* features characters from his long-running series *Hugo*. Milt has also contributed to the *Graphic Classics* volumes *H.G. Wells*, *Ambrose Bierce*, *Mark Twain*, *O. Henry*, *Horror Classics* and *Adventure Classics*. Check the latest news at www.miltonknight.net.

J. B. BONIVERT (page 130)

Jeffrey Bonivert is a Bay Area native who has contributed to independent comics as both artist and writer, in such books as *The Funboys*, *Turtle Soup* and *Mister Monster*. His art is also published in *Graphic Classics: Edgar Allan Poe*, *Graphic Classics: Arthur Conan Doyle*, *Graphic Classics: Ambrose Bierce*, *Graphic Classics: Bram Stoker* and *Adventure Classics*, and he was part of the unique four-artist team on *Reanimator* in *Graphic Classics: H.P. Lovecraft*. Jeff's biography of artist Murphy Anderson appears in *Spark Generators*, and *Muscle and Faith*, his Casey Jones / Teenage Mutant Ninja Turtles epic, can be seen online at www.flyingcolorscomics.com.

TOM POMPLUN

The designer, editor and publisher of the *Graphic Classics* series, Tom previously designed and produced *Rosebud*, a journal of poetry, fiction and illustration, from 1993 to 2003. He is now working on a revised edition of *Graphic Classics: H.P. Lovecraft*, scheduled for release in January 2007, and *Gothic Classics*, a multi-author collection including adaptations of Ann Radcliffe, Le Fanu and Jane Austen. You can find previews, sample art, and much more at www.graphicclassics.com.